A COPYRIGHT GUIDE FOR AUTHORS

Kent Press
• *Stamford, CT* •

Other Titles of Interest from Kent Press

A COPYRIGHT GUIDE FOR AUTHORS

Robert E. Lee

Publisher's Cataloging in Publication
(Prepared by Quality Books Inc.)

Lee, Robert E., 1935-
    A copyright guide for authors / Robert E. Lee.
    p. cm.
    ISBN 0-9627106-7-9 (hc)
    ISBN 0-9627106-8-7 (pbk)

    1. Copyright--United States. 2. Copyright, International. I.
Title.

KF2995.L44 1995   346.7304'82
                                QBI95-20521

Dedication

In loving memory of my parents, Vera Dell Lee and Robert E. Lee, Sr.

Acknowledgment

My special thanks to Larry Abelman (Abelman, Frayne & Schwab, New York) for reading the manuscript, helping determine the scope of the work, and looking up last minute case citations, but mostly for encouraging me to proceed.

Disclaimer

This publication is designed to provide general information about the subject matter covered. Neither the publisher nor the author are engaged in rendering legal advice to purchasers. The facts in every case are different and the law is always changing. If legal advice is required, the services of a competent attorney should be sought. All examples are hypothetical, and any coincidences of names, or situations with those of real people or companies are unintentional. The governmental material included in the Appendices is in the public domain and no copyright claim is made thereto.

About the Author

Robert E. Lee has thirty-five years of intellectual property law experience. During that time, he has negotiated more than 2,000 intellectual property agreements in over thirty-five countries. Mr. Lee's areas of expertise include copyrights, trademarks, patents, trade secrets, technology protection and licensing, copyright and trademark licensing, franchising, software agreements, research agreements, joint ventures and export control compliance and licensing.

Mr. Lee is registered to practice before the U.S. Patent and Trademark office. He presently works for a major multi-national corporation where he has worldwide responsibility for trademarks and copyrights for the parent company and its subsidiaries and affiliates.

Mr. Lee has a J.D. Degree from Baylor University, an M.A. from Rice University, and a B.S. from the University of Texas at Austin. He is a member of the State Bar of Texas, where he scored the highest grade on the bar examination. He is a trustee of the Citizens' Scholarship Foundation of America, Inc. and is a trademark and copyright advisor to the Community Redevelopment Agency of the City of Los Angeles. Mr. Lee has been a member of the Licensing Executives Society (LES) for over twenty years. Mr. Lee resides in Plano, Texas.

Table of Contents

Preface

Authors usually think of copyrights in terms of notice, publication, deposit, and registration — the so-called traditional cornerstones of copyright. The fact is, *none of these elements are contemporary requirements of copyright*. Forget what you think you know about the old law and focus on the new rules of copyright. The Copyright Act of 1976 and the Berne Convention Implementation Act of 1988 set a new course for U.S. copyrights.

This work provides a commentary on the current law as it affects authors of creative works. The term "author" herein is used in the Constitutional sense to encompass all creators of copyrighted works. This book has application to novelists, playwrights, poets, biographers, journalists, historians, educators, artists, designers, musicians, composers, performers, choreographers, photographers, architects, engineers and computer programmers.

Each chapter of this book is independent, so that one can start with any subject which is appealing. An overview at the beginning of each chapter shows the subject matter covered, and each chapter is divided into sections with headings highlighted. The highlighted boxes serve as "easy access" information for the reader; they are helpful hints or definitions that are especially important to the author. A number of "scenarios" are also interspersed throughout the book, which serve to illustrate common problems that authors face, and offer solutions. Key cases are discussed. Cross references at the end of each chapter suggest other chapters on related topics which the reader may want to review.

An overview of copyright law and subject matter is given in Chapter One. Chapter Two shows the evolution of copyright from its origin in Great Britain until the present. The remaining chapters cover topics of special interest to the author. Chapters on wills and inheritance and publication are included.

Case citations are in Appendix A. Copyright forms are located in Appendices B through P. Countries with which the U.S. has international copyright relations are listed in Appendix Q. Appendix R includes a circular on copyright basics and information about contacting the Copyright Office. Appendix S is a reprint of the GATT copyright regulations.

The Copyright Act

"The Copyright Act" or "The Act" has reference to the Copyright Law of the United States as contained in Title 17 of the U.S. code. All Section references herein, unless otherwise specified, are to The Copyright Act, as amended. Copies of the Act are available from the Government Printing Office. Government Bookstores are found in some major cities. The Act can be ordered as Circular 92 from the Copyright Office through the Superintendent of Documents. Information about the Copyright Act and other Circulars can be obtained by writing the Copyright Office, Library of Congress, Washington, D.C. 20558. Orders can be placed by phoning (202) 707-9100.

The reader is encouraged to obtain a copy of The Act. While many of the Sections of The Act have been included herein, the Act is too long to totally incorporate, and some of the Sections were skipped entirely. Also, having a copy of the Act and updating it regularly will allow the author to stay on top of any law changes.

Chapter One:

INTRODUCTION AND SUBJECT MATTER

1.1 OVERVIEW

Copyrights are automatic. Any original work of authorship is copyrighted *immediately upon* its creation, so long as it is fixed in a tangible medium. Although the Copyright Act lists the types of works available for protection, this list is not exhaustive. The types of works listed in the Copyright Act are examples of the works which are afforded protection and not intended to limit the Act's scope of protection.

Publication is *not* a prerequisite for copyright protection. Both published and unpublished works are copyrighted. Copyright notice, registration and deposit are no longer conditions of copyright, although deposit of published works is mandatory. Copyright notice and registration are optional.

Copyright results *as a matter of law* when an original work of authorship is fixed in a tangible medium from which it can be perceived or recorded.[1] If a work is original, meets certain minimal standards and can be perceived, even briefly, it is copyrighted.

THE MEANING OF COPYRIGHT

The name "copyright" was coined from the words "copy" and "right," to indicate that the author has the right to make copies. The copyright or the copyrighter (one who obtains a copyright) is to be distinguished from the term "copywriter," meaning one who writes advertising copy.

---

[1] §102(a) of The Copyright Act

Most of us produce copyrighted works everyday; we just don't realize it. We acquire our first copyrights as children when we scribble with crayons on paper or form designs in a sandbox. When you write a letter, prepare a report, draw a picture or take a photograph, copyrights are created. Typically, we die owning tens of thousands of copyrights.

Since a work is born copyrighted, there are no prerequisites for acquiring a copyright. There is no need to register, publish or embellish it with a copyright notice. Also, while *copies of published works* are required to be deposited, the copyrights are unaffected if deposit is not made.

Copyright belongs to the author of the work. A copyright vests the author with certain exclusive rights. Some rights apply to all works and others are limited to certain works. By definition, copyrights last fifty years after the death of an author. Works made for hire and other special types of copyrights have terms the shorter of seventy-five years from publication or one-hundred years from creation. Once formed, copyrights are durable — there are no maintenance requirements.

In modern society, where the public has access to numerous works and technology provides ready means for copying, copyrights are essential. Our intellectual infrastructure depends upon copyright law as one of its creative and balancing forces.

1.2   A WORLD WITHOUT COPYRIGHTS

It was one thing not to have copyrights in the medieval world — before printing proliferated. However, modern life couldn't exist without copyrights. Since all control would be lost when a copy of a work was transferred, the author would have to have a contract with each and every recipient of the work. These contracts would have to include provisions for non-copying, adaptation and sales restrictions. However, even then, if the party violated the agreement, the author would be totally at risk, since he or she would have no recourse against third parties. Would a system based on contracts work in our fast-paced society? It is not very likely. Creativity would be thwarted and the supply of works would dwindle.

1.3 SUBJECT MATTER OF COPYRIGHTS

The 1976 Copyright Act adopted an open-ended approach to subject matter. As noted earlier, subject matter listings in the Act are exemplary rather than limiting. This is in contrast to the 1909 Copyright Act, where only specifically listed works could be copyrighted.

Eight categories of works protected by copyright are listed in the 1976 Copyright Act.[2] They are as follows: (1) literary works; (2) musical works, including words; (3) dramatic works, including music; (4) pantomimes and choreographic works; (5) pictorial, graphic, and sculptural works; (6) motion pictures and other audiovisual works; (7) sound recordings; and (8) architectural works.[3] A work can fit under one or more, or none, of the above categories and be copyrighted.

EXCLUSIONS FROM COPYRIGHT

Some works are excluded from copyright. U.S. Government works are not subject to copyright protection. Also, copyright protection does not extend to any idea, procedure, process, system, method of operation, concept, principle or discovery. Additionally excluded from copyright protection are titles and short phrases.

1.4 CATEGORY DEFINITIONS

The variety and scope of works protected by copyright are illustrated by the following definitions:[4]

"Literary works" are defined as:

Works, other than audiovisual works, expressed in words, numbers, or other verbal or numerical symbols or indicia, regardless of the nature of the material objects, such as books, periodicals, manuscripts, phonorecords, film, tapes, disks, or cards, in which they are embodied.

---

[2] ibid.

[3] The eighth category, architectural works, was added in 1990. (See discussion of "Architectural Rights" in Chapter Two)

[4] §101

"Motion pictures" are defined as:

Audiovisual works consisting of a series of related images which, when shown in succession, impart an impression of motion, together with accompanying sounds, if any.

"Audiovisual works" are defined as:

Works that consist of a series of related images which are intrinsically intended to be shown by the use of machines or devices such as projectors, viewers, or electronic equipment, together with accompanying sound, if any, regardless of the material objects, such as films or tapes, in which the works are embodied.

"Pictorial, graphic, and sculptural works" include:

Two-dimensional and three-dimensional works of fine, graphic and applied art, photographs, prints and art reproductions, maps, globes, charts, diagrams, models and technical drawings, including architectural plans.

"Sound recordings" are:

Works which result from the fixation of a series of musical, spoken, or other sounds, but not including the sounds accompanying a motion picture or other audiovisual work, regardless of the nature of the material objects, such as disks, tapes or other phonorecords, in which they are embodied.

An "architectural work" is defined as:

The design of a building as embodied in any medium of expression, including a building, architectural plans or drawings. This work includes the overall form as well as the arrangement and composition of spaces and elements in the design, but does not include individual design elements.

Computer programs are recognized as copyrightable subject matter. However, this was not always the case. Originally, no greater rights were given to them than existed under the 1909 Act. Then, in 1980, following a report of a special commission (CONTU), computer programs were accorded the same treatment as any other literary works.

EXAMPLES OF COPYRIGHTED WORKS

There is a wide variance in subject matter of copyrighted works. The following is a listing of some works which are considered to be copyrighted:
Novels, Short Stories, Nonfictional Books, Biographies, Text Books, Poetry, Periodicals, Dramatic Works, Catalogs, Cartoons, Comic Strips, Directories, Magazines, Newspapers, Lectures, Sermons, Addresses, Reviews, Bulletins, Newscasts, Sport Broadcasts, Scientific Treatises, Greeting Cards, Book Jackets, Records, CD and Tape Jackets, Letters, Reports, Memoranda, Databases, Computer Programs, Maps, Photographs, Globes, Charts, Paintings, Sculptures, Drawings, Lithographs, Etchings, Advertisements, Posters, Wallpaper, Jewelry, Jewelry Boxes, Fabrics, Lamps, Prints and Labels, Music, Lyrics, Musical Arrangements, Operas, Pantomimes, Choreographic Works, Motion Pictures, Toys, Games, Dolls, Christmas and Easter Decorations, Bookends, Lamps, Piggy Banks, Music Boxes, Candle Sticks, Ash Trays, Decorative Plates, Floor Tiles, Models, Floats, Jigsaw Puzzles, Architectural Drawings, and now Semiconductor Chips and Buildings.

1.4.1 Compilations and Derivative Works

The subject matter of copyrights includes compilations and derivative works.[5] Copyrights can result where pre-existing works are compiled or transformed to form an original work of authorship.

A "compilation" is defined as:[6]

A work formed by the collection and assembly of pre-existing materials or of data that are selected, coordinated or arranged in such a way that the resulting work as a whole constitutes an original work of authorship.

---

[5] §103(a).
[6] §101

A "derivative work" is defined as:[7]

A work based upon one or more pre-existing works, such as a translation, musical arrangement, dramatization, fictionalization, motion picture version, sound recording, art reproduction, abridgment, condensation, or any other form in which the work may be recast, transformed or adapted.

Compilations include "collective works," where a number of separate works are assembled into a collective whole. An example of a collective work is a periodical. The copyright to a compilation or derivative work does not cover any pre-existing material used without permission.[8] Also, the copyright only extends to the material contributed by the author and is independent of the copyright in the pre-existing material.[9]

1.4.2 Works of Visual Art

Works of visual art are unique, since their authors have rights of attribution and integrity. Authors of other works do not have similar rights. (See "Rights of Copyrights" following herein and "Moral Rights" in Chapter Five.)

A "work of visual art" is defined as:[10]

(1) a painting, drawing, print, sculpture, existing in a single copy, or in a limited edition of 200 or fewer that are signed and consecutively numbered by the author, or, in case of a sculpture, in multiple cast, carved or fabricated sculptures of 200 copies or fewer that are consecutively numbered by the author and bear the signature or other identifying mark of the author, or
(2) a still photographic image produced for exhibition purposes only, existing in a single copy that is signed by the author, or in a limited edition of 200 or fewer that are signed and consecutively numbered by the author.

---

[7] ibid.
[8] §103(a)
[9] §103(b)
[10] §101

1.5 ORIGINALITY

To be copyrighted, a work must be an *original work of authorship.*[11] Fortunately, originality as determined by copyright law is nothing akin to novelty in patent law. To be original, a work does not have to be original to all the world, it only has to be original to the author. This makes a big difference. If an author prepares a work using a modicum of creativity, without copying from another source, the work is original. It is irrelevant that the work may be similar to an existing work which was unknown to the author. The copyright results on the creation of a work, and no particular intent is required.

ORIGINALITY: A STATE OF MIND

Copyrights, unlike patents, can be recycled. If an author produces a work which is similar to a pre-existing work, which was unknown to the author, that work is original with the author and is copyrightable. Others cannot copy it without the author's consent. However, others may be able to copy the pre-existing version, if it is unprotected.

Example: If you had spent your life in a remote forest, and without knowledge of Charles Dickens' novel, "A Tale of Two Cities," had produced a similar work, even though in the eyes of people who are familiar with Dickens you would draw a lot of laughs, the work would be original with you. Therefore, you own a copyright in that work.

Originality may result where the author adapts a pre-existing work to form a derivative work or compiles pre-existing works into a collective work. Adapting or transposing a work to a different form, or assembling and arranging the components to form a collective work, provides the requisite originality. Originality has also been found under a "sweat of the brow" theory, where a compilation was based principally on public data or facts which the author compiled or collected.

---

[11] §102

1.6 TANGIBLE FORM

Another requirement of copyright is tangible form or fixation. You can tell an original story to a thousand people, but unless it is put in a tangible form, it is not copyrightable. As mentioned before, to be copyrighted, a work must be "fixed" in a tangible medium from which it can be perceived, reproduced or otherwise communicated. [12]

FIXATION: THE NEW TOUCHSTONE

Copyrights result by operation of law upon creation of a work in a tangible form. Original works of authorship are copyrighted upon fixation. Intent on the part of the author is irrelevant to the process. Even if the author does not want a copyright, a copyright occurs when the work is produced because the law says it is. It is similar to the granting of U.S. citizenship to anyone who is born in the U.S.

Fixation requires that a work be embodied in a "copy" or "phonorecord," as these are the only two categories that the law recognizes. [13] If a work is not contained in a copy or phonorecord, it is precluded from copyright.

"Copies" are defined as: [14]

Material objects, other than phonorecords, in which a work is fixed by any method now or later developed, and from which it can be perceived, reproduced or otherwise communicated, either directly or with the aid of a machine or device.

"Phonorecords" are defined as: [15]

Material objects in which sounds, other than those accompanying a motion picture or other audiovisual work, are fixed by any means now known or later developed, and from which

---

[12] ibid.
[13] §101 "Fixed"
[14] §101
[15] ibid.

the sounds can be perceived, reproduced or otherwise communicated, either directly or with the aid of a machine or device.

The law allows considerable flexibility in regard to methods of fixation. Any method now or later developed is satisfactory, if the work can be "perceived, reproduced, or otherwise communicated for a period of more than transitory duration." [16] This has resulted in copyright protection for such temporal works as icing designs on cakes.

1.7 PUBLICATION

Under the 1909 Act, publication, i.e., making the work available to the public on an unrestricted basis, was a condition of copyright. Upon publication with notice of copyright, a work lost its common law copyright protection and was protected by federal statutory copyright.

Under the 1976 Act, creation replaced publication. This has resulted in both *unpublished* and *published* works being copyrighted, so that now private business and personal writings are protected. This change in the law was a major step in expanding the scope of federal copyright protection as there are many more unpublished works than published works.

Susan's Diary

Susan keeps a diary in which she records all her secrets. The diary was started in 1973 and was continued until 1983. She never published the diary nor disclosed it to anyone. Susan became a public figure. Her brother found the diary and threatened to sell it to "Hard Copy."

Susan seeks an injunction against publication based on her copyright rights. Because the law changed in 1978, a copyright is attached to her writings automatically. The portion of the diary written before 1978 is protected by copyright as well, under a provision covering works which were unpublished when the new law took effect.

---

[16] §101 "Fixed"

1.8 RIGHTS OF COPYRIGHT

The significance of copyright depends on scope of the exclusive rights given the copyright owner.[17] Under the 1976 Copyright Act, five exclusive rights of copyright are granted. Three are applicable to all works, while two are limited to certain types of works.[18]

The rights to reproduce the copyrighted work, to prepare derivative works and to distribute copies or phonorecords are applicable to all works of all kinds and types. Limited to particular types of works are the rights to publicly perform and to publicly display. (The works listed for these two rights vary slightly.) Also, under a 1990 revision of the Copyright Act, rights of attribution and integrity are given authors of certain works of visual art.[19] (See "Works of Visual Art" earlier in this Chapter and "The Visual Artists Rights Act of 1990" in Chapter Two.)

1.9 NOTICE OF COPYRIGHT

Notice of Copyright was one of the requirements of copyright under the 1909 Act. Each publication had to include a copyright notice, or the work was not copyrighted.[20] However, the Berne Convention Implementation Act of 1988 removed copyright notice as a requirement of copyright for published works. Now, use of a notice is optional, and the absence of a notice is no longer indicative of, nor affects, the work's copyright status.

1.10 DEPOSIT

Deposit is usually made in conjunction with registration. Under the 1909 Act, deposit of copies of the "best edition" of a work was required as a condition of copyright registration. While deposit of copies or phonorecords of *published* works is still mandatory, deposit is no longer a prerequisite of copyright.[21] The

---

[17] §106
[18] See Chapter Five for a more detailed discussion.
[19] §106A
[20] At least this was the rule before GATT. See Chapter Seven.
[21] §407(a)

only penalty for non-deposit is a small monetary fine.[22] However, since the copyright is unaffected, this usually has minimal consequence.[23]

1.11 REGISTRATION

Under the 1909 Act, registration was required. An author did not own a copyright until he or she received a certificate of registration from the Copyright Office. However, since under the 1976 Act, copyrights result upon fixation, registration is no longer a precondition of copyright, and a work can be registered, or not.

However, it is still necessary to register Berne Convention works first published in the U.S. before an infringement suit can be brought, or an action on the author's rights of attribution and integrity can be maintained.[24] In contrast, Berne Convention works first published abroad are not similarly restricted.[25] Also, failure to register can result in being unable to recover statutory damages and attorney fees in an infringement suit. Therefore, the bias is still on registration.

1.12 CROSS REFERENCES

Chapter Two provides an historical review of copyrights. Ownership is discussed in Chapter Three, and copyright transfers are covered in Chapter Four. Chapter Ten covers registration. Appendix R contains a circular on copyright basics published by the Copyright Office.

---

[22] §407(d)

[23] The Copyright Office neither has the time nor incentive to collect non-deposit fees. Its concern is with disposing of books on deposit.

[24] §411(a)

[25] This is one of several examples, which will be noted, where U.S. authors are disadvantaged relative to foreign authors under the Copyright Act.

Chapter Two:

EVOLUTION OF COPYRIGHTS

2.1 OVERVIEW

Copyrights originated in Great Britain. The concept of copyright protection was brought to America in pre-Revolutionary times and was later embodied in the U.S. Constitution.

The 1909 Copyright Act, an early but significant piece of U.S. copyright legislation, required that a work be published with notice of copyright, registered and deposited in order to receive protection. Under the 1909 Act, copyrights had an initial term of twenty-eight years and were renewable for twenty-eight years thereafter.

The Copyright Act of 1909 was eventually replaced by the Copyright Act of 1976. Under the 1976 Act, works were copyrighted on *creation*; published and unpublished works were copyrighted; registration was permissive and lack of a copyright notice was curable. Copyright terms ran for the life of the author plus fifty years, except that certain works had a fixed term of a minimum of seventy-five years.

The Berne Convention Implementation Act of 1988 followed, and this Act removed notice as a condition of copyright. As a result of this Act, recordal of title is no longer a condition of suing. While copyright registration is still required to bring suit, the requirement was modified to be consistent with the Berne Convention.

In 1990, the Visual Rights Artists Act ("VARA") granted moral rights to authors of certain works of visual art, and the Architectural Works Rights Protection Act protected the designs of certain buildings.

Legislation was passed in 1992 concerning renewals, criminal liability and fair use of unpublished works. In 1993 and 1994, U.S. adherence to NAFTA and GATT brought about more changes to the copyright laws. Their effects are discussed below.

What follows in this chapter is a more detailed discussion of the history of copyrights from the early beginnings of English copyright laws to the recent global treaties that have affected U.S. protection policy.

2.2 EARLY ENGLISH STATUTES AND LAWS

Copyrights, like gin and tonic, derived from the British. Early English law recognized that an author had rights to a manuscript based on principles of "natural justice." The person who prepared a work owned it on the premise that one should enjoy the fruits of one's labor.[1]

Because reproductions were made by hand, there was little concern about copying, and copyright laws neither existed or were needed. However, technology eventually leapt ahead. With the invention of moveable type in the fifteenth century, both publishing and copying proliferated. Authors and publishers alike found themselves without recourse when illicit copies were made. Since the Church and government of England often disapproved of what was being published, in 1556, the Stationers' Company was chartered by Royal Decree. As a result of this charter, all printing had to be contracted through the Company's members, giving the government a monopoly over printing.

2.2.1 The Statute of Anne

The first written law recognizing the rights of authors was the Statute of Anne, passed by British Parliament in 1710. Upon registration and deposit with official libraries, authors were given an exclusive right to print their books for fourteen years. If the author was living at the end of the term, the copyright term could be renewed for another fourteen years.

Many provisions of the Statute of Anne were later reiterated in U.S. law. The English statute laid the foundation for such concepts as registration, deposit and renewal. Even the twenty-eight year copyright term, which was part of U.S. law for many years, derived from the Statute of Anne.

---

[1] It has been reported that American Indians may have had rights similar to copyrights to protect teepee designs from being copied.

What is significant about the Statute of Anne is that it served as the basis for copyright law worldwide. It is not very often that a statute addresses concepts so fundamental that much of the rest of the world emulates it. However, the Statute of Anne is a case in point. As a consequence of this statute, almost every country in the world now has some form of copyright law.

2.3 THE CONSTITUTION

Following the American Revolution, many states passed pre-Constitutional copyright statutes based on British law. However, as commerce developed, it became apparent that a uniform system of copyright *among all states* was needed. When the Constitution was drafted, a basis for copyright and patent legislation was included. Although neither copyrights nor patents are expressly named in the Constitution, the rights of authors and inventors to their writings and discoveries are clearly protected.[2]

**U.S. CONSTITUTIONAL PROVISION
REGARDING ORIGINAL WORKS**

Article I, Section 8, Clause 8, reads as follows:

To Promote the Progress of Science and the Useful Arts, by Securing for Limited Times to Authors and Inventors the Exclusive Right to their Respective Writings and Discoveries.

2.4 THE COPYRIGHT ACT OF 1909
AND EARLY U.S. LAW

The first U.S. copyright legislation was enacted in 1790.[3] Numerous amendments and several new acts have occurred over

---

[2] "Authors" and "inventors" are specifically mentioned in the Constitution and designated to have certain rights. Trademark legislation, by contrast, is based on the Commence clause.

[3] The Act had a fourteen year initial term and a like renewal term. Title to the work had to be recorded with the district court where the author lived, the recordal had to be published, and a copy of the work deposited with the Secretary of State.

the years, and new copyright legislation continues to be introduced in each session of Congress. One of the most significant acts of legislation occurred in 1909, when the copyright law was rewritten to be in step with the twentieth century. This Act survived essentially intact until 1976. Because it was in force for so long, the 1909 Act is still ingrained in peoples' minds.

Under the 1909 Act, a dual system of statutory and common law copyright protection existed. Unpublished works were protected at common law and under various state copyright statutes. When a work was published, the common law protection ceased and the work was protected, if proper steps were taken, under federal statutory copyright. To qualify for federal copyright, works had to be writings and fit particular subject matter categories. (See Chapter 5, Section 5.1) Copyright was obtained by publication with notice of copyright, registration and deposit.

PUBLICATION DRIVEN

The 1909 Copyright Act was "publication driven." It was publication, i.e., making the work available to the public, that resulted in the copyright. If a work was published with notice of copyright and an application correctly filed with deposit copies, a copyright registration issued. However, if proper procedures were not followed, the copyright could be lost, any unpublished works were not protected.

Copyrights were unitary and indivisible under the 1909 Act. There was only one copyright per work, belonging to one party. The statutory term of copyright was twenty-eight years, based on the date of publication or registration. If renewed, the copyright could extend for another twenty-eight year term, for a total of fifty-six years.

The formalized structure of the 1909 Act was contrary to the copyright concepts followed by most countries, which prescribed a non-conditional approach. Most of those countries which followed a less structured copyright law became members of the Berne Convention. The Berne Convention was the clear-cut choice of copyright conscious countries, although the U.S. seemingly had forgone that avenue long ago. In order for the U.S. to establish a common copyright link with other countries, the

Universal Copyright Convention (UCC) was formed. In practice, however, it proved cumbersome and many countries did not join. Consequently, a campaign of attrition to modify the U.S. law was begun.

2.5 THE COPYRIGHT ACT OF 1976

Seldom has legislation so totally revamped existing law as the Copyright Act of 1976.[4] The 1976 Act, which took effect January 1, 1978, had only three requirements of copyright, where there had previously been five. Of the three, one requirement was new. Additionally, there was a long list of major changes affecting almost every area of the law.

THE TRIUMVIRATE OF COPYRIGHT

The "triumvirate of copyright" under the 1976 Act became: (1) originality, (2) fixation and (3) notice of copyright. With the passage of the 1976 Copyright Act, copyrights resulted upon fixation, i.e., upon creation of a work in a form where it can be perceived or reproduced. It is fixation, not publication, which is the catalyst of copyright. Other essential components are: originality and, for published works, notice of copyright.
The 1976 Act removed publication, registration and deposit as requirements of copyright; they became only window dressings. Notice of copyright survived being cut, but not for long as Berne loomed on the horizon.

Key changes brought about by the 1976 Act included the following.
   • The requirement that a work be published in order to be copyrighted was repealed. This resulted in copyright protection for both published and unpublished works, which was one of the Berne Convention requirements.
   • Copyright protection was no longer dependent upon registration. This removed another condition which was objection-

---

[4] General Revision of the Copyright Law, Pub. L. 94-553, 90 Stat. 2541, October 19, 1976.

able under Berne. However, registration remained a condition for bringing a copyright infringement suit.

- Failure to deposit only resulted in a monetary penalty and no longer affected the validity of the copyright, removing another condition of copyright.
- The term of copyright was changed from twenty-eight years from the date of publication to life of the author plus fifty years, which satisfied another Berne requirement. An alternative term for certain works was defined as the shorter of one-hundred years from creation or seventy-five years from publication.
- Rights of copyright were made divisible and subject to multiple ownership. Previously, copyrights were unitary and singularly owned.
- Copyright protection was expanded to cover "original works of authorship" consistent with language in the Constitution.
- The categories of copyright works in the statute were made exemplary and non-restrictive rather than specific and limiting.
- The scope of copyrights was broadened by granting copyrights for derivative works and compilations.
- A right of public display was granted for the first time for certain works.
- The scope of protection for performances was broadened by removing the "for-profit" requirement.
- A right of termination of grants was introduced to allow authors to selectively terminate licenses and assignments.
- Copyright renewals were to be phased out. Works formed after January 1, 1978 could no longer be renewed.
- The requirement that publications in English be *initially* published in the U.S. or Canada was to be phased out.

Any of the above changes unitarily would have been significant. Collectively, they resulted in a revamping of the U.S. copyright law that was unprecedented.

2.5.1 Shortcomings of the 1976 Act

All of the changes made in the 1976 Act notwithstanding, the U.S. was having difficulties eliminating all conditions of copyright and completely complying with the Berne Convention requirements. Certain traditional procedures had been adhered to over a number of years, and it was difficult to get a consensus to change. In the end, it was get what you could and return to do battle another day.

REQUIREMENTS OF BERNE

Member countries of the Berne Convention were obligated to (1) eliminate conditions for copyright protection, (2) provide protection for both published and unpublished works, (3) establish a copyright term based on the life of the author plus fifty years, (4) give authors of member states the same protection as their own citizens, and (5) provide authors with protection for moral rights and architectural works.

The following issues were left hanging which prevented the U.S. from joining Berne.

• Notice of copyright was still a requirement of copyright for published works. Although the consequences for failing to include a notice had been lessened, notice nevertheless remained a condition of copyright.

• Registration of the copyright was a condition of bringing a copyright infringement suit and, therefore, another condition of copyright.

• Assignments of copyrights had to be recorded with the Copyright Office before the assignee could bring infringement actions.

• Moral rights implied under U.S. law were questionable. While some considered that the U.S. already sufficiently complied with Berne standards, others held that additional legislation was necessary.

• U.S. copyrights did not adequately protect architectural works. While architectural drawings were protected, three-dimensional structures had never been part of U.S. law.

2.6 THE BERNE CONVENTION IMPLEMENTATION ACT

The Berne Convention Implementation Act was signed into law on November 1, 1988, and became effective March 1, 1989.[5] This continued the transformation of the copyright law begun by the 1976 Copyright Act. The Act followed a "minimalist" approach, in that as few changes in the copyright law as possible were made to achieve Berne compatibility. The key change that resulted in Berne compatibility was making notice of copyright *optional* for published works.

Eliminating copyright registration as a condition for bringing suit was done with smoke and mirrors. Registration remained a requirement of bringing suit for works of U.S. origin, but was optional for works where a foreign country was the country of origin. Apparently this one-sided solution was sufficient to satisfy the Convention requirements.

The requirement that title be recorded with the Copyright Office as a condition of bringing copyright suit was stricken. To maintain a suit, the plaintiff need only establish ownership of the right of copyright involved in the action. Recordal of title with the Copyright Office is unnecessary.

New Ground Rules

Sam wants to protect a short story before sending it to a publisher and consults with an intellectual property attorney. Sam wants to copyright the work and wants to know if a copyright needs to be on the manuscript.

The attorney advises Sam that the story was automatically copyrighted when it was formed and says that use of a copyright notice is optional. The attorney says that using a notice merely prevents an infringer from claiming to be an innocent infringer.

Sam asks about registering the work. The attorney explains that registration is a condition for bringing suit and is not a requirement of copyright. Registration is suggested, if it appears that the work will have market value, since it is inexpensive and this will enable Sam to recover statutory damages and attorney fees.

---

[5] Pub. L. 100-568, 102 Stat. 2853.

2.7 THE VISUAL ARTISTS RIGHTS ACT OF 1990

The Visual Artists Rights Act ("VARA") was part of the Judicial Improvements Act of 1990.[6] VARA granted rights of attribution and integrity to authors of certain works of visual art.[7] Instead of granting moral rights to all authors, the focus was on artists, and even then, the scope of applicable works was limited. (See "Moral Rights" in Chapter Five for a discussion of the rights of attribution and integrity.)

2.8 ARCHITECTURAL WORKS COPYRIGHT PROTECTION ACT

The Judicial Improvements Act of 1990 created a new category of copyrightable subject matter for architectural works.[8] The design of a building as embodied "in any medium of expression, including a building, architectural plans, or drawings" is protected. This covers "the overall form, as well as the arrangement and composition of spaces and elements in the design."

2.9 THE COPYRIGHT RENEWAL ACT

The Copyright Renewal Act was signed into law on June 26, 1992.[9] This law extended the copyright terms of works first published between January 1, 1964 and December 31, 1977.[10] The following sentence was added to Section 107: "The fact that a work is unpublished shall not of itself bar a finding of fair use if such finding is made upon consideration of all of the above factors." What this means is that the same fair use standards are applied to both unpublished and published works, overruling a line of cases (see Chapter Six) that had found fair use inapplicable to unpublished works.

---

[6] Pub. L. 101-650, 104 Stat. 5089, 5128, Dec. 1, 1990.
[7] A "work of visual art" is restricted to "a painting, drawing, print, sculpture, or still photographic image existing in a single copy or in a signed and numbered limited edition of 200 or fewer copies or casts." §101
[8] Pub. L. 101-650, 104 Stat. 5089, 5133, Dec. 1, 1990.
[9] Pub. L. 102-307, 106 Stat. 264, June 26, 1992.
[10] Pub. L. 102-492, 106 Stat. 3145.

2.10 CRIMINAL LIABILITY ACT

Legislation was signed into law on October 28, 1992, establishing enhanced criminal sanctions for infringements of copyrighted works.[11] The result was the implementation of criminal sanctions, including possible felony charges, for reproduction and distribution of all types of works. (See "Criminal Sanctions" in Chapter Twelve.)

2.11 NORTH AMERICAN FREE TRADE AGREEMENT IMPLEMENTATION ACT ("NAFTA")

NAFTA is intended to provide effective protection of intellectual property (copyrights, trademarks, patents, trade secrets, etc.). From a copyright perspective, few substantive changes were made when this treaty was signed, since the U.S. acted to preserve its existing copyright structure and avoided committing to moral rights or removing formalities.

Films belonging to another party which were in the public domain due to non-compliance with U.S. formalities have had their copyrights resurrected. However, this Section has lost importance, since a more comprehensive renewal provision in GATT applied to all types of works.

2.12 GENERAL AGREEMENT ON TARIFFS AND TRADE ("GATT")

GATT made several sweeping changes in U.S. copyright law.[12] Under GATT, copyrights are restored to foreign copyright owners for all works throughout the world that had fallen into the public domain in the U.S. because of non-compliance with formalities. For example, if under the 1909 Copyright Act the copyright notice was left off a published work, whether by accident, mistake or otherwise, the copyright would have been forfeited, and the work would have gone into the public domain. Under GATT, such works, if owned by citizens of a country in the World Trade Organization ("WTO"), will be restored for the

---

[11] Pub. L. 102-561, 106 Stat. 4263, Oct. 28, 1992.

[12] GATT was signed into law on Dec. 8, 1994. Pub. L. 103-465, 1994.

remainder of what their term would have been, assuming proper warning notice is given, if an infringement suit is to be brought.[13] (See Chapter Seven.)

Additionally, GATT reversed the law which precluded the rental of computer programs, and made the unauthorized fixation and trafficking of sound recordings and music videos actionable. Significant aftershocks of these changes are expected to rumble throughout the copyright world for some time. (See Appendix S for a copy of GATT Regulations pertaining to copyrights.

PROPOSED LEGISLATION

The Senate has passed legislation granting performance rights to sound recordings. This would provide an exclusive right to perform a copyrighted sound recording publicly by means of a digital audio transmission. Currently, the U.S. is the only western nation not to recognize performance rights in sound recordings.

2.13 CROSS REFERENCES

The subject matter and basic provisions of copyright are covered in Chapter One. Ownership of copyrights is discussed in Chapter Three. The rights of copyright and limitations thereon are discussed in Chapters Five and Six, respectively.

---

[13] This is another example where one thing is done abroad to conform to treaty obligations, and the opposite, to the detriment of U.S. authors, is done at home.)

Chapter Three:

COPYRIGHT OWNERSHIP

3.1 OVERVIEW

Copyrights are intangible personal property represented by works embodied or "fixed" in material objects. Copyright ownership initially vests in the author or authors of the work and is independent of the ownership of the material object.[1] This chapter will discuss ownership issues relative to copyright, including situations where joint ownership or works made for hire may arise. In a work made for hire, the employer, or the commissioning party for whom the work was prepared, is the author.[2] This a convenient fiction to explain why title is not in the creator, as it is in other instances.

The divisibility of copyrights and what this means in terms of granting exclusive and non-exclusive rights in a work is discussed. Anyone who owns one or more exclusive rights in a work has all the rights of a copyright owner. Title to copyrights and exclusive licenses can only be transferred by written instruments, while non-exclusive licenses can be written or oral.

Any copyrighted work has to have a physical embodiment. However, a copyright and the material object in which it is fixed are separate and distinct.[3] The copyright is an *intangible* property right that can not be seen or gripped, and the material object is *tangible* property that you can pick up and hold.

Fixation in a copy or phonorecord is necessary to create a copyright, but once formed, the copyright exists independently. Rights to the copyright and the copy or phonorecord can be sold or disposed of separately. The transfer of ownership of the object or the copyright does not convey property rights to the other.[4]

---

[1] §201(a)

[2] §201(b)

[3] §202 of the Copyright Act.

[4] ibid.

3.2 WORKS MADE FOR HIRE

Works made for hire result under two types of circumstances.[5] They are formed when works are prepared by employees acting within the scope of employment, or they are created by contractors preparing commissioned works. If the work was prepared within the scope of employment, the work belongs to the employer. If the work is prepared outside the employment, it belongs to the employee.

WORK MADE FOR HIRE CATEGORIES

To qualify as "a work made for hire," the work must be for use as:

a contribution to a collective work, as a part of a motion picture or audiovisual work, as a translation, as a supplemental work, as a compilation, as an instructional text, as a test, as answer material for a test, or as an atlas.

A "supplemental work," as used above, is defined as:

a work prepared for publication as a secondary adjunct to a work by another author for the purpose of introducing, concluding, illustrating, explaining, revising, commenting on, or assisting in the use of the other work. Examples include forewords, afterwards, pictorial illustrations, maps, charts, tables, editorial notes, etc.

Unless audiovisual productions or supplemental works are involved, odds are the copyright to a commissioned work will belong to the contractor or commissioning party.
NO BENDING OF THE RULES IS POSSIBLE HERE: THESE LISTINGS ARE ABSOLUTES AND RECITAL LANGUAGE DOES NOT WORK.

The transfer of copyrights from employees to employers is by operation of law. As the employer is deemed the author of

---

[5] A "work made for hire," §101

any works produced by employees,[6] there is no need for the employee to have signed an agreement. There is no intermediate state, as with patents, where the employer is awarded a non-exclusive license as a shop right where the work was done on the employer's time or using the employer's materials.

The major factors concerning copyright ownership by employers are determining (1) whether an employer-employee relationship exists and (2) whether the work in question was prepared within the scope of employment. Determining whether a work was prepared in the scope of employment is fact-driven. The facts of each case have to be looked at and weighed independently.

3.2.1 Determining Employment

In *The Community For Creative Non-Violence v. Reid*, 109 S.Ct. 2166 (1989), *aff'd. and remanding* 846 F.2d 1485 (D.C. Cir. 1988), the Supreme Court explained the tests for determining if a party is an employee or an independent contractor.

The Community For Creative Non-Violence (CCNV), a non-profit group, had commissioned Reid to create a statue. Reid donated his time and received his expenses. After the statue was finished, each party claimed the copyright as a means to control the exhibition of the work. The CCNV sued Reid for a declaration that the copyright belonged to the CCNV as a work made for hire.

The District Court found for the CCNV, since the CCNV was the motivating factor for the work's creation. The Circuit Court reversed, holding that the statue was not prepared by an employee and did not qualify as a specially ordered and commissioned work because it did not fall under one of the nine enumerated categories.

In delivering the opinion for the Supreme Court, Justice Thurgood Marshall said that the issue was whether the statue was a work prepared by an employee within the scope of his or her employment. Marshall noted that nothing in the 1976 Copyright Act indicated that Congress used the words "employee"

---

[6] Since the transfer is by operation of law, the copyright is transferred to the employer automatically. There is no need for any special confirming assignment to be signed.

and "employment" to describe anything other than the conventional master-servant relationship under the general common law of agency.

The Court found that Reid worked as an independent contractor. He was a skilled sculptor who supplied his own tools and worked in his own studio. Reid was only hired for a short period of time, and CCNV did not have the right to assign other work to him. He had absolute freedom to decide when and how long to work and was paid a flat fee dependent on completion. Reid had total discretion in hiring and paying assistants. The CCNV did not provide any employee benefits or payroll and social security taxes and was not in the business of sculpturing.[7]

To qualify a *contracted* work as a work made for hire poses another order of difficulties. Not only must an independent contractor relationship be established following the tests prescribed in *The Community For Creative Non-Violence*, but the potential subject matter of the work is also restricted.[8] Furthermore, there must be a *written agreement* confirming that the work was prepared as a work made for hire.[9]

The commissioning party may have paid to have a work prepared, and the work may have been delivered, but that does not transfer title to the copyright. Unless the ownership of the copyright has been assigned *in writing* to the commissioning party, or qualifies as a work made for hire, which also requires a *written* agreement, the copyright belongs to the contractor.

---

[7] The Supreme Court remanded the case to the district court to consider whether the parties were joint authors. After extensive negotiations the parties reached an agreement whereby (1) the CCNV was the exclusive owner of the statue, (2) Reid was the owner of copyright for three-dimensional reproductions, and (3) they were to have joint ownership of two-dimensional reproductions. The parties returned to court because they could not agree on how to utilize their rights. The court ordered the statue to be delivered to Reid's designee so that a mold could be made to form the three-dimensional works. Within a specified time after preparing the mold, Reid was to return the statue.

[8] A "work made for hire," §101

[9] ibid.

The Photographer

Carmel Popcorn, an up-and-coming rock group, hired a photographer to prepare publicity shots of the group for use on posters. The photographs were delivered and paid for, but no assignment of copyright was made.

After Carmel Popcorn became famous, use of the photographs was expanded to T-shirts, sweaters, mugs, umbrellas and other merchandising articles. The photographer demanded a share of the royalties.

Because there was no written assignment of copyright, the photographer is the copyright owner and potentially has a valid claim. For the posters, it could be argued that Carmel Popcorn had an implied license. However, because the photographs were used on products not originally contemplated, this argument becomes tenuous.

MORAL: Deal with copyright ownership up front. If the issue cannot be promptly resolved, find another party to do the work.

3.3 JOINT OWNERSHIP

The authors of a joint work are co-owners of the copyright in the work. Each co-owner can exercise all of the rights of copyright. However, any co-owner which licenses a third party must account to the other co-owners.[10] A "joint work" is defined as:[11] "A work prepared by two or more authors with the intention that their contributions be merged into inseparable or independent parts of a unitary work."

Therefore, producing a joint work takes more than just working together. Custom and intent are major factors as well. For example, an editor, peer reviewer or proofreader may make a number of substantial changes which are incorporated into a work, but this does not mean that they are co-authors.

Intent to co-author requires a meeting of the minds (agreement) by the parties, and because of their well-understood roles,

---

[10] This is opposite the rule for jointly owned patents. In the case of patents, there is no accounting unless there is an agreement to do so. The copyright rule seems fairer.

[11] §101

editors, peer reviewers and proofreaders are not normally co-authors. The use of a ghostwriter, however, is more borderline, and the uncertainty of the situation is increased. Sometimes there is co-authorship, and sometimes there is not.

Ghostwriters

Sharon Pretty, a star actress in a hit movie, is asked to write a novel by a publisher who thinks that there will be a significant market for her work. A ghostwriter (who is an employee of the publisher) is assigned to assist her. After the book is written with the help of this ghostwriter, the publisher and Sharon have a falling out, and she threatens to have the book published elsewhere. The publisher, however, claims joint ownership because of the contribution by the ghostwriter.

While the trend is to recognize ghostwriters as co-authors, authorship is determined by intent. If the parties intended that their works be merged into a unitary work, they are co-authors. If the intent was not mutual, the work is not jointly owned.

So long as Ms. Pretty considered the ghostwriter an assistant, there was no intent for co-authorship. The fact that the ghostwriter or publisher may have considered otherwise is irrelevant.

Even if the requisite intent for co-authorship exists, the co-authorship may fail if the parties do not make sufficient contributions. The contributions do not need to be equal, but each should be substantial.[12]

3.4 DERIVATIVE WORKS

Derivative works are modifications or transformations of existing works. The "author" starts with an existing work and transforms it into something different. It is the changes that the author makes which result in the derivative copyright.

---

[12] Probably the best way to handle this is to define in an agreement what the respective authors are to do.

A "derivative work" is defined as:[13]

A work based upon one or more pre-existing works, such as a translation, musical arrangement, dramatization, fictionalization, motion picture version, sound recording, art reproduction, abridgment, condensation or any other form in which work may be recast, transformed or adapted; or a work consisting of editorial revisions, annotations, elaborations or other modifications which, as a whole, represent an original work of authorship.

To form a derivative work, the author must have the *consent* of the owner of the original work.[14] Failure to obtain consent will not only void the copyright in the derivative work, but may infringe the original owner's copyright.[15] The copyright to derivative works is independent of the copyright to the original work. The latter extends only to the newly contributed material and has no effect on the scope, duration, ownership or subsistence of copyright in the pre-existing material.[16]

The Translation

Assume that a novel written by Party A is translated from English to French by Party B. If the translation was prepared with the permission of A, it qualifies as a derivative work. (If consent was not obtained, the resulting work is not copyrighted.)

Assuming consent was given, and that B has a copyright to the translation, but not to the original work, if Party C infringed B's work, B would have a cause of action under the derivative copyright, while A would have a cause of action under the original version. If Party C copied Party A's work, only Party A would have a cause of action.

---

[13] §101

[14] §103(a)

[15] When obtaining rights to derivative works, it is important to determine the status of underlying works. If proper consents were not obtained, the party has nothing to license.

[16] §103(b)

3.5 COLLECTIVE WORKS

A "collective work" is defined as:[17] "A work, such as a periodical issue, anthology, or encyclopedia, in which a number of contributions, constituting separate and independent works in themselves, are assembled into a collective whole."

The copyright of the contributions to a collective work is distinct from the copyright in the collective work as a whole. To copyright a collective work, the author must obtain consents from the respective individual copyright owners to use their contributions.[18] Absent consent, use is improper, and there is no copyright to the resulting work.

The author of a collective work is assumed to have only acquired the right to distribute and reproduce the contributions as part of the collective work.[19] Unless specifically granted, no rights exist to independently utilize one of the separate contributions.

3.6 DIVISIBILITY OF COPYRIGHTS

Until January 1, 1978, copyrights were unitary and indivisible. There was a single owner of the copyright, and any other parties having an interest in the copyright were considered licensees. Now, rather than unitary copyright ownership, the law follows a divisibility concept where any of the exclusive rights of copyright, including subdivisions thereof, can be owned separately.[20] For instance, one party owns the movie rights, another party owns hardback publication rights, a third owns paperback rights, etc.

3.7 OWNERSHIP BY OPERATION OF LAW

We have already seen where employers acquire copyrights to works prepared by employees as a matter of law when the work is created as a condition of employment. Joint ownership of copyrights can also result by operation of law under state laws in community property situations.

---

[17] §101
[18] §103(a)
[19] §201(c)
[20] §201(d)(2)

For example, an author's spouse may have an interest in royalties relating to works made by the author during marriage. In some states, such as Texas and Idaho, where income on personal property is considered community property, royalties may have to be shared for individually owned works that were published before marriage. Even in non-community property states, there is a growing tendency for the courts on dissolution of a relationship to divide property by equitable distribution. (See Chapter Fourteen, "Community Property Rights.")

3.8 CROSS REFERENCES

Chapter Four covers transfers of copyrights rights. Chapter Nine deals with termination of grants. Chapter Fourteen discusses transfers by wills and inheritance.

Chapter Four:

COPYRIGHT TRANSFERS

4.1 OVERVIEW

Transfers of copyright ownership are made by assignments and exclusive licenses. Any transfer of copyright ownership rights must be accompanied by a *written agreement* signed by the owner of the rights to be conveyed. Written copyright agreements *may* be recorded with the Copyright Office. Recordal is necessary to perfect security interests in a copyrighted work.

In this chapter, involuntary transfers and the copyright owner's rights as transferor and transferee in bankruptcy matters are covered. The right of agents to transfer copyrights on behalf of the authors they represent is also discussed.

Ownership of a copyright is transferred by means of conveyances, or by operation of law.[1] Transfers of copyright ownership interests require a written instrument of conveyance. Assignments are transfers of title where the party divests himself or herself of all rights, titles and interests. Exclusive or non-exclusive licenses are grants of rights that do not qualify as assignments. In an exclusive license, the licensor or copyright owner is unable to license the same rights to other parties. Party A agrees to license Party B and no one else. A non-exclusive license is basically an agreement or covenant not to sue. Party A gives Party B consent to use certain rights of copyright, and so long as the Party B operates within the conditions of the consent, Party A is estopped to sue Party B. Party A still reserves the right to grant licenses to the same rights to others.

Suppose that you sell an original picture or other artistic work that you had prepared for your own amusement to another party. He shakes your hand and walks away. Who owns the copyright? Ownership of the material object and ownership of the associ-

---

[1] §201(d)(1)

ated copyright are different property rights and must be dealt with independently. A material object can be sold by handing it over, or by transferring title in a contract of sale.

The copyright is *intangible* property. It is only a legal invention and can not be embodied separate from the work it represents. When the picture is removed, the copyright stays behind, unless it has been expressly assigned to the purchaser in a written agreement. Even if there was a contract of sale, there most likely was not an assignment of the copyright. Using the same example, if you assigned the copyright to the picture to your Aunt in writing, she owns the copyright, but the purchaser still owns the picture. Therefore, ownership of the copyright and material object can be in the same party or different parties, and the total transaction must be dealt with to keep from splitting the rights in an unintended manner.

4.2 TRANSFERS OF OWNERSHIP

A "transfer of copyright ownership" is defined as:[2] "An assignment, mortgage, exclusive license or any other conveyance, alienation or hypothecation of a copyright or of any of the exclusive rights comprised in a copyright, whether or not it is limited in time or space, but not including a non-exclusive license." Transfers of copyright ownership include assignments, exclusive licenses and all types of conveyances, including pledges and mortgages. One would not normally think of mortgages as being transfers of ownership interests, but they are included within the definition. Non-exclusive licenses were expressly excluded from this definition,[3] because if an author gives consent to one party while retaining the right to use the work or license it to others, there has not been a transfer of ownership interests.

Copyright ownership rights can be transferred in whole or in part and limited by time and territory. This means that an author can grant any part of his or her rights of copyright and can territorially restrict the granted rights, or limit them to a specific period of time. Party A can license Party B for five years East of the Mississippi, and Party C for ten years West of the Mississippi.

---

[2] §101

[3] ibid.

The owner of any *exclusive* right is entitled to all the protection and remedies accorded a copyright owner.[4] This means that an exclusive licensee can sue and recover damages when his or her rights are violated in the same way as the original copyright owner. This is one reason why many publishers no longer insist on acquiring copyright title from the author.

4.2.1 Written Agreement and Signature

A transfer of copyright ownership, other than by operation of law, must be *in writing* in a conveyance signed by the owner of the rights conveyed, or by that party's authorized agent.[5] Therefore, all exclusive licenses, liens or assignments have to be in writing and signed by the owner of the interest being transferred.

Prior to January 1, 1978, handling copyright conveyances did not present much of a problem. For any work, there was only one copyright and one owner, so keeping track of rights was easy. Now, however, copyrights are divisible, and for any work there can be any number of copyright owners. That makes recordal with the Copyright Office even more important.

4.2.2 Acknowledgment

A certificate of acknowledgment from the grantor is prima facie evidence of the execution of the transfer.[6] Assignments and exclusive licenses should be acknowledged to take advantage of this presumption.

To acknowledge an agreement, the grantor appears before a notary, or other officer authorized to administer oaths and states under penalty of perjury that he or she executed the agreement for the purposes stated therein.

---

[4] §201(d)(2)
[5] §204(a)
[6] §204(b)

ACKNOWLEDGMENT FORM

A typical acknowledgment form is as follows:

State of _____
County of _____

Before me, (Notary Public's name), as notary public, on this day appeared _____ , known to me the person whose name is subscribed to the foregoing instrument and acknowledged to me that he/she executed the same for the purposes and consideration therein expressed.

Given under my hand and seal of office this ___ day of _____ 199__.

_____
Notary Public
(Seal)

4.3 RECORDATION

Any transfer of copyright ownership, or other document pertaining to copyright, may be recorded in the Copyright Office.[7] For recordal, it is necessary that the document have the actual signature of the person who executed it, or be accompanied by a certification that it is a true copy of the original signed document.[8]

4.3.1 Document Cover Sheet

A standard Document Cover Sheet must be submitted with each document for recordation with the Copyright Office. A copy

---

[7] §205(a)

[8] A recordal fee of $20 is currently required for the first title, and $10, for each additional title. After recordal, the document that is submitted is returned with a certificate of recordation. The fees are due to be adjusted.

of this form is found in Appendix P. The Form asks for information about the parties named in the document and the document being recorded. Titles and registration numbers to all works listed in the document must be included. The fee for recordation is based on the number of titles listed.

An affirmation that the information is true and correct, and a certification, if a photocopy of the original document is submitted, are required.

Two copies of the Document Cover Sheet, the original document being recorded, or photocopy thereof, and proper fee should be mailed to the following address:

> Documents Unit
> Cataloging Division
> Copyright Office
> Library of Congress
> Washington, D.C. 20559

4.3.2 Constructive Notice

Recordation gives constructive notice of the facts stated in a document, if the document refers to the copyright by registration number, or otherwise identifies the work so it can be found by a reasonable search.[9] This statutory notice provision is useful to keep third parties from claiming good faith in subsequent conflicting transfers. In addition to recordation of the document, for there to be constructive notice, the work must be registered with the Copyright Office.[10]

If there is a dispute between two conflicting transfers, the one executed first prevails if it is recorded in a manner which gives constructive notice. The transfer should be recorded within one month of its execution (two months if executed outside the U.S.), or before the second transfer is executed.[11] However, the later transfer may prevail if recorded first, and if in good faith and for valuable consideration, or on the basis of a binding promise to pay royalties and without notice of the earlier transfer.[12]

---

[9] §205(c)

[10] §205(c)

[11] §205(d)

[12] ibid.

The Double Dealer

Suppose that Charles gives NEW Publishers an exclusive license to publish a short story. The exclusive license is commemorated by a written agreement, but is not recorded with the Copyright Office.
The publication is delayed, so Charles sells title to the short story to Sundown Studio which, in publishing the short story, acted in good faith and had no notice of the prior license. Sundown agrees to pay Charles future royalties and promptly acts to record its title to the copyright.
Since NEW had not recorded, Sundown's rights prevail, and all NEW has is a cause of action against Charles.

A seeming quirk of the law is that a non-exclusive license, *whether recorded or not*, will prevail over a subsequent transfer, if the license is *in writing* and signed by the owner or the owner's agent.[13] Most likely this is because a non-exclusive license is only a covenant not to sue, and a substantial grant of rights can still be made. There is no provision which deals with priorities between two non-exclusive licenses, since a copyright owner can grant as many non-exclusive licenses as he or she chooses, and the existing licenses are in no position to complain.

4.3.3 Security Interests

Security interests in copyrights are perfected by recordal, the same as other transfers of title. The copyright recordal statute provides the exclusive means for recording a security interest and preempts the recordal provisions of the Uniform Commercial Code.[14]

4.4 INVOLUNTARY TRANSFERS

A provision of the Copyright Act precludes *involuntary* transfers.[15] It holds that if the owner had not previously voluntarily

---

[13] §205(e)
[14] *National Peregrine Inc. v. Capital Federal Savings and Loan Association of Denver*, 16 USPQ 2d 1017 (D. Cal. 1990), CV-90-1083A4
[15] §201(e)

transferred the rights, no action can be taken by any governmental body to seize or appropriate any rights of ownership of any individual copyright owner. This provision was purportedly put in to protect against foreign governments trying to seize copyrights belonging to their citizens and has nothing to do with any actions by the U.S. Government.[16]

4.5 BANKRUPTCY

Bankruptcy can affect the author in several ways. The author can take bankruptcy after entering into a copyright transfer agreement and may want to undo it. The publisher's business can fail after contracting to publish the author's book and the author may want to terminate the agreement.

Whether the agreement between the author and the publisher will be honored or canceled depends on whether the agreement is "executory." If executory, i.e., performances are still required on *both* sides, the bankruptcy trustee has the option of canceling the agreement if it would be in the interests of the estate.

The choice of whether to terminate lies with the bankrupt party, not the other side. If there is a clause in the agreement giving a right to terminate upon bankruptcy, it will be given no effect. Many lawyers, however, still routinely include a bankruptcy clause in their boilerplate agreements.

Legislation passed in 1988 protects a licensee's right to use intellectual property in certain situations.[17] A non-debtor licensee has the right to continue a *non-exclusive* "intellectual property" license, if rejected by the trustee in bankruptcy, under the same terms and conditions as existed before the bankruptcy.[18]

---

[16] This interpretation has been muddled since an amendment was made to §201(e) excluding Title 11 (bankruptcy, voluntary and involuntary) from the effects of the provision. If this section had no application to actions by the U.S. Government, why did Congress deem it necessary to expressly exclude bankruptcy?

[17] Title 11, Bankruptcy Code, § 101 & 365. This provision became effective on Oct. 18, 1988.

[18] "Intellectual property" is defined to include works of authorship, including *copyrights*.

If a *non-exclusive* contract is executory and is rejected by the bankruptcy court, it can be maintained by the copyright owner. No rights to maintain exclusive licenses are given. Therefore, when receiving a license from a party who is in financial trouble, it may be preferable to take a non-exclusive license rather than an exclusive license. This way, you would know that the license will continue, while if you took an exclusive license, you might lose it.

4.6 TRANSFERS BY AGENTS

Transfers of ownership can be made by an author's agent.[19] Presumably this federal right overrides state agency law. If the author has worked with the agent before and trusts him or her unconditionally, this is fine. Otherwise, this provision may be inviting danger. There is no requirement for a written agreement between the copyright owner and the agent. If the agent is known to represent the copyright owner, he or she may have apparent authority to bind the copyright owner to an exclusive license or assignment. Copyright owners need to be careful however; when rights to the owner's works have been assigned to a third party without any payment to the owner, there is little that can be done.[20]

An interesting aspect of this statute is that it is only applicable to "transfers of ownership," which, by definition, excludes *non-exclusive* licenses. This means that while an agent can make assignments and grant exclusive licenses, the agent's authority to grant non-exclusive licenses is not as clear. Also undetermined is to what extent state law is applicable.

4.7 CROSS REFERENCES

See Chapter One for an introduction to copyrights and Chapter Three regarding ownership. Chapter Nine deals with termination of transfers and Chapter Fourteen discusses testamentary rights.

---

[19] §204(a)

[20] Since there is no requirement under the Copyright Act that the agency agreement be in writing, this is left to state agency law, which may or may not be codified.

Chapter Five:

EXCLUSIVE RIGHTS

5.1 OVERVIEW

The 1976 Copyright Act granted the copyright owner certain exclusive rights of copyright.[1] These rights are (1) the right to reproduce the work, (2) the right to prepare derivative works, (3) the right to distribute the work, (4) the right to perform publicly and (5) right to display publicly. The rights to reproduce, to prepare derivative works and to distribute are applicable to all works. Rights of public performance and public display are limited to certain types of works.[2] By contrast, the 1909 Act granted a number of narrowly defined rights dealing with designated works. The 1976 Act offers much more flexibility in both pursuing infringers, and in protecting new works.

Under the Visual Artists Rights Act of 1990, rights of attribution and integrity (the so-called "moral rights") were additionally granted. While other exclusive copyright rights are transferable and can be owned separately by different parties and subdivided, the rights of attribution and integrity are personal to the individual author and nonassignable. Additionally, the rights of attribution and integrity are restricted to certain works of visual art.[3]

The rights of a copyright owner frequently overlap, and several rights may be infringed by the same action.[4] For example,

---

[1] §106 of the Copyright Act.

[2] The works covered by the rights of performance and display, while similar, are not identical. The particular works covered by each right will be detailed later in this Chapter.

[3] A "work of visual art," §101. This is defined in Chapter One under "Works of Visual Art."

[4] The plaintiff normally will allege alternative counts of infringement so as to assert all possible claims.

43

when a derivative work is prepared, the rights of reproduction and distribution may be violated, as well as the right to prepare derivative works. This chapter will discuss, in detail, the various exclusive rights of a copyright holder.

RIGHTS UNDER THE 1909 ACT

The rights of copyright under the 1909 Act were as follows:

"The right to print, reprint, publish, copy and vend the copyrighted work."

"The right to translate the copyrighted work into other languages or dialects, or to make any other version thereof, if it be a literary work."

"To dramatize if it be a non-dramatic work."

"To convert it into a novel or other dramatic work if it be a novel."

"To arrange or adapt it if it is a musical work."

"To complete, execute, and finish it if it be a model or design for a work of art."

"To deliver, authorize the delivery of, read or present the copyrighted work in public for profit ...; to make or procure the making of any transcription or record ...; and to play or perform it in public for profit ...."

"To perform or represent the copyrighted work publicly if it be a drama."

"If it not be a dramatic work and not be reproduced in copies for sale, to vend any manuscript or any record whatsoever thereof."

"To perform the copyrighted work publicly for profit if it be a musical composition."

5.2 RIGHT OF REPRODUCTION

The first and most basic right of copyright is the right of reproduction:[5] "To reproduce the copyrighted work in copies or phonorecords." This is what we think of first in connection with copyrights — the right to control copying or duplication of a

---

[5] 106(1)

work. The owner of copyright has the exclusive right to make and to authorize the making of copies or phonorecords embodying the work. "Reproduction" is generally understood to be the duplication or simulation in whole, or in any substantial part, of a work. Therefore, making a copy of a work by drawing it would be a violation even without actual photocopying. In the case of sound recordings, the *actual* sounds fixed in the copyrighted work must be recaptured for there to be a reproduction.[6] If there is a totally independent fixation of sounds, there is no copyright infringement.

For the right of reproduction to be violated, copies or phonorecords have to be produced, i.e., a tangible embodiment of the infringing work must result. Thus, the public reading of a copyrighted poem is not an actionable reproduction.[7]

"Copies" are defined as: "material objects, other than phonorecords, in which a work is fixed."[8] "Phonorecords" are: "material objects in which sounds, other than a motion picture or other audiovisual work, are fixed."[9]

A work is "fixed" when: "its embodiment in a copy or phonorecord, by or under the authority of the author, is sufficiently permanent or stable to permit it to be perceived, reproduced, or otherwise communicated for more than a transitory period of time."[10]

The right of reproduction for pictorial, graphic and sculptural works includes "the exclusive right to reproduce the work on or in any kind of article."[11] However, in relation to *useful* articles, the copyright owner does not have the right to restrict the making, distribution or display of pictures of such works.[12] There-

---

[6] 114(b)

[7] If the work is recited publicly, the right of performance may be infringed even though the right of reproduction is not.

[8] "Copies," §101

[9] "Phonorecords," §101

[10] "fixed," §101

[11] §113(a)

[12] If a work reproduced in a useful article is offered for sale, the copyright does not include "the right to prevent the making, distribution or display of pictures or photographs of such articles ... in connection with advertisements, distribution or display ... or in news reports." §113(c).

fore, the copyright to pictorial and graphic works is protected, whatever the object the work is formed on, whether it be a parasol or the head of a pin. But if the article the work is reproduced on is useful, the copyright owner can not prevent others from photographing it and distributing or displaying the photograph.

5.3 RIGHT TO FORM DERIVATIVE WORKS

The second exclusive right is the right to:[13] "prepare derivative works based upon the copyrighted work." A "derivative work" is defined as:[14] "a work based upon one or more pre-existing works, such as a translation, musical arrangement, dramatization, fictionalization, motion picture version, sound recording, art reproduction abridgment, condensation or any other form in which a work may be recast, transformed or adapted." The right to prepare derivative works is the right to transform a copyrighted work into another form. Therefore, for there to be a derivative work, a previous work has to exist which the derivative work is based on.

Another aspect of derivative works that cannot be overly emphasized is that *consent* from the copyright owner of the original work is required.[15] If there is no consent, there is no copyright. Consent, therefore, is a condition precedent to the derivative work.[16]

The copyright to the derivative work only extends to the *new material* which is added by the author and does not grant any exclusive rights in the preexisting material.[17] The derivative work copyright is totally independent of, and has no effect on, the original copyright.

---

[13] §106(2)

[14] §101

[15] §103(a) — This says that copyright protection does not extend to any pre-existing copyrighted material which is used unlawfully.

[16] It has been stated that copyrights are automatic if the work is original and there is fixation. An exception to this rule is derivative works. Because of the consent factor, copyrighting is not automatic, but rather is conditioned upon obtaining the consent.

[17] §103(b)

5.4 RIGHT OF DISTRIBUTION

The third exclusive right is the right of public distribution, which allows the owner of copyright:[18] "to distribute copies or phonorecords of copyrighted work to the public by sale or other transfer of ownership, or by rental, lease or lending." In other words, the author is allowed to control publication and marketing of the work. "Distribution" is not defined, but "publication" is defined as:[19] "the distribution of copies or phonorecords of a work to the public by sale or other transfer of ownership, or by rental, lease or lending."

Offering to distribute copies or phonorecords to a group of persons for purposes of further distribution, public performance or public display constitutes publication.[20] However, public performance or public display does not constitute publication, since copies or phonorecords are not distributed.[21]

Under the "first sales doctrine," a copyright owner's rights of distribution cease in respect to any particular copy or phonorecord that has been sold under the owner's authority.[22] This permits book stores to sell books, libraries to loan books and video rental stores to rent video cassettes.

The right of first sale has had its ups and downs. It was overwritten by the Record Rentals Act of 1984 to preclude the rental and lease of sound recordings, and by the Computer Software Rental Act of 1990 to prohibit the rental of computer software. Under GATT, the copyright law will be amended, effective January 1, 1996, by deleting the exemption for the rental of computers from the "first sale" rule. As a result, it is expected that computer software rental businesses will start popping up.

5.5 RIGHT OF PUBLIC PERFORMANCE

The fourth exclusive right of copyright is that of public performance.[23] This right is limited to certain classes of works,

---

[18] §106(3)
[19] §101
[20] ibid.
[21] ibid.
[22] §109(a)
[23] §106(4)

namely: literary, musical, dramatic, choreographic and pantomimes and motion picture and other audiovisual works.

To "perform" a work is defined as:[24]

> To recite, render, play, dance, or act it, either directly or by means of any device or process, or in the case of a motion picture or other audio visual work, to show its images in any sequence; or
> (1) to perform it at a place open to the public or at any place where a substantial number of persons outside a normal circle of a family and its social acquaintances are gathered; or
> (2) to transmit or otherwise communicate a performance to a place specified by clause (1) ... whether the members of the public ... receive it in the same place or separate places and at the same time or different times.

Under the 1909 Act, public performances had to be "for profit" for the copyright owner's rights to be infringed. However, under the 1976 Act, the for-profit requirement has been removed. Now, a performance is public if given before a substantial number of people outside the home environment, or at a place open to the public.[25]

Performances of certain works in certain situations are excused, e.g., classroom teaching, places of worship, nonprofit veteran and fraternal organizations, etc., or, alternatively, are subject to compulsory licenses (see Chapter Six). Also, the owner of a copy of an electronic audiovisual game, intended for use in coin-operated equipment, can perform the work without authority of the copyright owner.[26]

---

[24] §101

[25] In *Columbia Pictures v. Aveco*, 945 F.2d 500, 505 (2nd Cir. 1991), a "public place" was characterized as a place open to the public. It was said that "a telephone booth, a taxi cab, and even a pay toilet are commonly regarded as open to the public, even though they are usually occupied by only one person." In this case, exhibition of a motion picture in a small private screening room in a videocassette rental store was held to be a public performance.

[26] §109(e). This overturned a previous court decision that video games played in public arcades are publicly performed.

5.6 RIGHT OF PUBLIC DISPLAY

The fifth exclusive right of copyright is the right of public display.[27] This right is applicable to literary, musical, dramatic, choreographic and pantomimes, pictorial, graphic and sculptural works, including individual images of a motion picture, or other audiovisual work.[28]

To "display" a work is: "to show a copy of it, either directly or by means of a film, slide, television image or other device or process, or, in the case of a motion picture or other audiovisual work, to show individual images nonsequentially."

"Publicly" has the same meaning as it had for "publication," namely, display at a place open to the public, or at any place where a substantial number of persons are gathered other than one's family or close social acquaintances.

However, there is an important distinction between the right of public display and the right of public performance. The right of display is subject to the first sale doctrine while the right of performance is not. Works which have been legally bought can be displayed by the purchaser, but cannot be publicly performed.

The Timid Romance Writer

Sandra, a writer, spent all her spare hours cranking out romance novels. None of her works were ever published. Her thrill came from imagining herself as the heroine in her books. Sandra always sent copies of her manuscripts to Aunt Ruth, who lived in the house where Sandra was born. These manuscripts usually included Sandra's handwritten notes making fun of her plotting and characters. On Sandra's death, her estate published her works and they became best sellers. Aunt Ruth opened her house to the public and displayed the manuscripts. The estate, being the owner of the copyright, objected because it thought that the annotations would be detrimental to book sales.

---

[27] §106(5)

[28] Performances cover motion pictures and other audiovisual works, as well as literary, pantomimes, and pictorial, graphic, and sculptural works. Displays cover pictorial, graphic, and sculptural works, individual images of a motion picture or other audiovisual work. The definitions overlap but are dissimilar.

In this case, the estate is out of luck. Aunt Ruth, being the owner of the manuscripts, is entitled to display them to the public. However, if Aunt Ruth wanted to publish the manuscripts, she would be restricted from doing so.

5.7 MORAL RIGHTS

The Visual Artists Rights Act of 1990 added a sixth right of copyright. The concept of moral rights (or "droit moral") protects the author's reputation and guards against a work being altered against the author's wishes. Under the 1990 Act, artists of certain visual works have a right of attribution to claim or disclaim authorship and a right of integrity to prevent destruction, distortion, mutilation or other modification of their works.[29]

EXCLUSIONS TO WORKS OF VISUAL ART

Certain works which have visual aspects do not qualify as works of visual art and are not protected by the assertion of moral rights. Exclusions under Section 101 are:

(1) any poster, map, globe, chart, technical drawing, diagram, model, applied art, motion picture or other audiovisual work, book, magazine, newspaper, periodical, database, electronic information service, electronic publication or similar publication;

(2) any merchandising item or advertising, promotional, descriptive, covering or packaging material or container;

(3) any work made for hire; or

(4) any work not subject to copyright protection.

Moral rights are personal to the artist and only apply during the artists' lifetime, as opposed to the other rights which are transferable, or which cover the full copyright term.[30] Not only can't moral rights be transferred by the artist, but neither are they inheritable.

---

[29] §106A. See Chapter One, "Works of Visual Art."

[30] This legislation, however, does not limit or preempt any state legislation that gives rights that survive the death of the artists.

It may seem a great victory that moral rights have finally been granted in the U.S. However, what came out of the legislative hopper was little more than a tidbit. Foreign countries have moral rights which are more inclusive and apply to any author who prepares a copyrighted work. Also, some countries have moral rights that pass to the author's family, as well as additional types of moral rights.[31]

5.8 PARTIES OWNING RIGHTS

The rights of reproduction and distribution and the rights to prepare derivative works, to publicly perform and to publicly display may be subdivided, transferred and owned separately.[32] The owner of any exclusive right, or any undivided interest therein, has all of the rights of a copyright owner. The rights of integrity and attribution are limited (personal) to the author and do not pass when the copyright or copy of the work is assigned.[33] However, the rights are waivable.

5.9 UNAUTHORIZED FIXATION OF SOUNDS AND IMAGES

GATT provides sanctions against those who fix sounds or sounds and images of live musical performances, or transmit or otherwise communicate the sounds and images of a live musical performance, or distribute, or offer to sell, rent, or offer to traffic in any bootleg copy or phonorecord. (See Appendix S.) These federal bootlegging rights, which will be effective January 1, 1996, are long overdue. They will have the same sanctions as those imposed upon violators of other rights of copyright. In addition, special criminal penalties will apply. However, the federal rights do not preempt state law remedies.

---

[31] For example, *the Droit de Suite* concept, which is followed in some countries, gives the author the right to participate in the proceeds realized from resales of a work.

[32] §201(d)(2)

[33] §106A(e)(2)

5.10 CROSS REFERENCES

The types of works which are subject to copyright are discussed in Chapter One. Moral rights are discussed further in Chapter Two. Ownership is covered in Chapter Three. See Chapter Six for limitations to the exclusive rights. See Appendix R for a summation of copyright rights.

Chapter Six:

LIMITATIONS ON RIGHTS

6.1 OVERVIEW

The author's exclusive rights of copyright are subject to various exceptions. Fair use, library reproduction and rights accorded owners of material objects reduce the scope of the author's rights. Exemptions for certain public performances and displays and for compulsory licensing further restrict the author's rights. The 1976 Copyright Act gave the author broad exclusive rights of copyright (see Chapter Five). However, the government played the game of grant and take away, and various exclusions were made which eroded the granted rights.

One of the exclusions is fair use, which was codified in the 1976 Act. "Fair use" is a justifying expression to explain why, in certain situations, the rights of copyright accorded the author are overridden by the rights of the public. Another exclusion introduced in the 1976 Act was the right of reproduction for libraries. The library photocopying privilege is separate from fair use and was intended to enable libraries to service their clients, on the belief that normal fair use rights would be too restrictive.

Another statutory exclusion relates to persons who have legitimately acquired tangible embodiments of a work. The owner of a copy or phonorecord has rights, notwithstanding the rights of the copyright holder. Other provisions in the Copyright Act exempt certain performances and displays from being infringements. In other situations, compulsory licenses are granted giving certain performance rights upon reporting and paying royalties.

Apart from fair use, which is not defined other than in a guideline manner, the exemptions are as detailed and complex as the copyright grants were general and simple. When an exemption is defined, one has to deal with particulars. Determining whether an exemption is applicable is a difficult, technical exercise and generally not without an element of risk.

6.2 FAIR USE

Early in the development of U.S. copyright law, it became apparent to legislators that there should not be strict enforcement in certain situations. If harm to the author was minimal and the violation was for a legitimate purpose, non-infringement was frequently found by the courts. From this cradle of justice, fair use was born. By the time the 1976 Act was legislated, fair use had become so firmly entrenched that it was codified:[1] "Notwithstanding the provisions of Section 106, the fair use of a copyrighted work, including such use by reproduction in copies or phonorecords for purposes such as criticism, comment, news report, teaching (including making multiple copies for classroom use), scholarship or research, is not an infringement of copyright."

The statute lists *four factors* that are to be considered in determining fair use:[2]

(1) the purpose and character of the use, including whether such use is of a commercial nature or is for a non-profit educational purpose;
(2) the nature of the copyrighted work;
(3) the amount and substantiality of the portion used in relation to the copyrighted work as a whole; and
(4) the effect of the use upon the potential market for or value of the copyrighted work.

The courts have treated the effect on the marketplace as the most significant factor, although all of the factors are usually covered in the decisions. However, it became apparent that the courts frequently looked outside these factors and were reluctant to find fair use where the work was unpublished. This non-statutory element proved to be an overriding consideration in several important cases.

---

[1] §107 of the Copyright Act.
[2] ibid.

6.2.1 Cases Involving Unpublished Works

The following cases illustrate how courts have dealt with the issue of fair use with respect to unpublished works.

1. *Harper & Row Publishers, Inc. v. Nation Enterprises*, 471 U.S. 539 (1985). President Gerald Ford had granted Harper & Row the exclusive right to publish his memoirs. When the book was nearly complete, Harper & Row granted *Time* the exclusive right to run pre-publication excerpts. *The Nation* magazine, having obtained a copy of the manuscript, published an article paraphrasing selected portions.

When *Time* declined to publish the excerpts, Harper & Row brought suit against *The Nation* for copyright infringement. The district court found infringement, but the circuit court found that Ford's memoirs largely disclosed public domain facts and that the fair use doctrine thus insulated *The Nation* from liability.

The Supreme Court reversed the circuit court, concluding that the copying was not fair use, since the right of the author to control the first publication outweighed fair use considerations. It was considered that an author gives an implied consent for fair use upon releasing a work to the public, and since the plaintiff's work was unpublished, fair use was negated.

In considering the "effect of the copying on the market," the Court found that the plaintiff's ability to market the first serialization rights was damaged. Relative to "the amount and substantiality," it was determined that the heart of the manuscript was taken. In considering the "nature of the work," it was found that the most expressive parts were copied, rather than material merely necessary to disseminate facts. For "the character and purpose of use," the Court noted that the publication was commercial rather than non-profit.

2. *Salinger v. Random House*, 811 F.2d 90 (2nd Cir. 1987), *cert. denied* 108 S.Ct. 213 (1987). J.D. Salinger sought to enjoin the distribution of an unauthorized biography of himself by Ian Hamilton that included quotations from a series of unpublished letters Salinger had written.

Under threat of suit, Hamilton revised the book so that it contained no more than ten percent of any one letter and, in most cases, no more than ten words from any one letter. The key issue was whether the defendant, Hamilton, could maintain a fair use defense, considering the pronouncements about unpublished works in *Harper & Row*. In finding for the publisher, Random House, on the fair use issue, the Court held that, while fair use should be applied sparingly in the case of unpublished works, there was no absolute bar to its application. In utilizing the statutory tests of fair use, the Court found that the amount of material taken was minimal and insubstantial and that the effect on the market for the letters was not diminished and may, in fact, have been enhanced.

3. *New Era Publishers International v. Henry Holt & Co.*, 884 F.2d 659 (2nd Cir. 1989), *cert. denied*, 110 S.Ct. 1168 (1990). Plaintiff New Era brought action against publisher Holt to prevent publication of a unauthorized critical biography of L. Ron Hubbard, the founder of the Church of Scientology. After dismissing the claim for fair use because expressions from unpublished letters had been copied, the district court found infringement of New Era's copyrights.

However, for various reasons, including the fact that the overall use was small, the trial court declined to issue a permanent injunction. On appeal, the Second Circuit confirmed the decision denying the fair use, reasoning that while the purpose of use weighed in favor of Holt, the three remaining fair use factors all weighed in favor of New Era. The fact that the material was unpublished appeared to have had substantial influence on precluding fair use.

A rehearing was denied, and, in addition to the majority opinion denying fair use, there were concurring and dissenting opinions. The dissent argued that the Court had not taken the position that copying a small amount of unpublished material to report facts accurately can never be fair use. The concurring opinion attacked the dissent.

6.2.2 Unpublished Works Fair Use Act

Congress passed the "Unpublished Work Fair Use Act" which became law on October 24, 1992. This added the following sentence to Section 107: "The fact that a work is not published shall not itself bar a finding of fair use if such finding is made upon consideration of all of the above factors." This means that the four tests described in Section 107 above are determinative, irrespective of whether a work is published or unpublished.[3] No longer can it be argued that fair use is inapplicable to unpublished works.

6.2.3 Published Works: The *Texaco* Case

A landmark case on fair use concerning the reproduction of published works is the *Texaco* case. *In American Geophysical Union, et. al. v. Texaco Inc.,* 37 F.3d 881 (2d Cir. 1994), a group of publishers sued Texaco for unauthorized copying of technical journals by employees. Texaco argued fair use. The Court found for the plaintiffs. Discounting Texaco's argument that the copying was done for the personal use of its employees, Judge Leval stated that "the copying was in fact being done to assist Texaco in its pursuit of scientific research that is done to bring it into competitive commercial advantage."

It was found that the purpose of the use was to supersede the original work. Further, it was found that the articles were routinely copied before they were read and that this was done for commercial purposes. Because the works being copied were factual rather than fictional, Texaco was favored in regard to the nature of the works. However, it was found that the amount and substance of the portions used were critical and that Texaco's use had a negative effect on marketing rights, since it reduced the number of subscriptions. This decision was appealed and various amicus curiae briefs were filed. In October 1994, a decision was handed down affirming the lower court. Fair use was dismissed, because of the predominantly archival rather than research purpose of the copying.

Texaco filed a Petition for Rehearing and a Petition for Certiorari to the Supreme Court. A settlement was reached pending determination of the Petition of Certiorari whereby Texaco agreed to acquire a license from the Copyright Clearance Center. Therefore, a decision stands that photocopying by an individual scientist employed by a for-profit corporation of scientific articles from periodicals is an infringement of copyright.

---

[3] This is a good example of how the legislative-judicial system should work. Congress passes a law. The courts interpret the law in a manner that was unintended. Congress amends the law to set things right.

6.3 LIBRARY REPRODUCTION

An exemption introduced in the 1976 Act was for "library reproductions." This exemption allows reproduction and distribution by libraries of copies and phonorecords:[4]

> It is not an infringement of copyright for a library or archives, or any of its employees acting within the scope of their employment, to reproduce no more than one copy or phonorecord of a work, or to distribute such copy or phonorecord if —
> (1) the reproduction or distribution is made without any purpose of direct or indirect commercial advantage;
> (2) the collections of the library or archives are
> (i) open to the public, or
> (ii) available not only to researchers affiliated with the library or archives or with the institution of which it is a part, but also to other persons doing research in a specialized field; and
> (3) the production or distribution of the work includes a notice of copyright.

Unpublished, damaged and lost works can be replaced by a library as follows:

> The rights of reproduction and distribution apply to a copy or phonorecord of an unpublished work currently in the collections of the library or archives duplicated solely for purposes of preservation and security or for deposit for research use in a another library open to the public.[5]
> The right of reproduction applies to a copy or phonorecord of a published work duplicated for the purpose of replacing a copy or phonorecord that is damaged, deteriorating, lost or stolen, if an unused replacement copy can not be obtained at a fair price.[6]

A library has rights to provide copies of articles or entire works for another library as follows:

> The rights of reproduction and distribution apply to a copy made from the collections of the library or archives at the request of a user or another library of no more than one article

---

[4] §108(a)

[5] §108(b)

[6] §108(c). "Fair price" is not defined.

or other contribution to a copyrighted collection or periodic issue, or to a copy or phonorecord of a small part of any other work.[7]

The rights of reproduction and distribution apply to an entire work, or substantial part of it, made from the collections of the library or archives where the request is made by a user or another library, if the library or archives has first determined, based on a reasonable investigation, that a copy or phonorecord of the work can not be obtained at a fair price.[8]

LIBRARY PHOTOCOPYING AND THE CCC

When the 1976 Act was passed, library photocopying was a major issue. Now, the subject is hardly ever mentioned. Some say it is because the system is working. Others consider it a failure. No one will argue that the law is complex and difficult.

One reason for the demise of library photocopying was the formation of the Copyright Clearance Center ("CCC"). The CCC offers licenses to universities and corporations to copy articles and chapters from designated journals and books.

Initially, the CCC required transactional reporting. However, now there is an option of paid-up annual licenses. Using a database that was compiled from sample audits of participating companies, the CCC is able to forecast how much copying is done by a given company.

Because of the victory by publishers in the Texaco suit, the CCC can expect a big boost in activity as fence sitters join. What the CCC now needs to do is to authorize electronic communications.

The rights of reproduction and distribution extend only to the *isolated and unrelated* reproduction and distribution of a *single* copy or phonorecord of the same material on separate occasions.[9] Copies or phonorecords resulting from the related or concerted reproduction of multiple copies intended for aggregate use by one or more individuals or members of a group, do not qualify

[7] §108(d)
[8] §108(e)
[9] §108(g)

for the exemption.[10] Additionally, certain types of works are excluded from the exemption. The rights of reproduction and distribution do not apply to a musical work, a pictorial, graphic, or sculptural work, or to a motion picture or other audiovisual work.[11]

EXEMPTIONS FOR COMPUTER PROGRAMS

In order to be used, computer programs need to be loaded (copied) into the hard drive of the computer, or backup copies need to be made for safety reasons, where the programs are run on diskette.

The Copyright Act was amended in 1980 to deal with these matters. Section 117 provides that a copy or adaptation created as an essential step in utilizing a computer program in conjunction with a machine is not copyright infringement. Also, Section 117 authorizes making a copy or adaptation of a computer program for archival purposes.

6.4 OWNERSHIP RIGHTS IN MATERIAL OBJECTS

Ownership of a copyright is distinct from the material object in which the work is embodied.[12] If a party acquires ownership of a lawfully made copy or phonorecord of a work, under the "first sale" doctrine, the party can sell, loan or display the copy of a work without the copyright owner's permission.[13]

However, the right of an owner of a copy or phonorecord to sell, lease or display single images does not apply where possession was acquired *without transfer of ownership*.[14] Therefore, a party can only rely on the first sale doctrine when the copy or phonorecord was acquired by sale or exclusive license.

Further, the copyright owner can prohibit the rental, lending or lease of sound recordings for commercial advantage.[15] The

---

[10] ibid.
[11] §108(h)
[12] §202
[13] §109(a) and 109(c)
[14] §109(d)
[15] §109(b)

copyright owners of computer software had a similar right through 1995, but it has been terminated by GATT.

6.5 EXEMPTION OF CERTAIN PERFORMANCES AND DISPLAYS

The Copyright Act exempts various types of performances and displays from infringement.[16] Many of these exemptions came about when the for-profit element, previously required for performances, was removed from the 1976 Act.

Thus, rather than allowing a blanket exemption for non-profit performances, only particular not-for-profit situations were exempted. At the same time, the burden of proof was shifted from the plaintiff to show a for-profit motive, to the defendant to prove that a not-for-profit exemption applied.

• Teachers and pupils may perform or display a work during the course of *face-to-face* teaching activities in classrooms or similar places devoted to instruction in *non-profit* educational institutions, if lawfully made copies were used.[17]

• Non-dramatic literary or musical works which are performed or displayed by or in the course of a *transmission* are exempted.[18] The transmission must be (1) a regular part of the systematic instructional activities of a government body or a non-profit educational institution and (2) primarily for reception in classrooms, by handicapped persons who are unable to attend class, or by officers or employees of governmental bodies.

• Non-dramatic literary works, musical works or dramatic-musical works of a religious nature, may be performed or any kind of work can be displayed in the course of services at *places of worship*.[19] This authorizes public reading and congregational or choir singing in churches.

• Non-dramatic *non-profit* performances, other than in transmissions, of literary works or musical works are exempted.[20] This

---

[16] §110

[17] 110(1). This exemption does not afford reproduction rights. Reproduction is controlled by fair use.

[18] §110(2)

[19] §110(3). The place of worship limitation would exclude broadcasts to the public at large.

[20] §110(4)

exemption does not apply if there is any direct or indirect commercial advantage, or if there is a payment to the performers, promoters or organizers. This authorizes public reading in libraries and benefit performances of music.[21]

• The public reception of the transmission on a *single* receiving apparatus of the kind commonly used in private homes is not an infringement, unless there is a *direct charge* or the transmission is further transmitted to the public.[22]

• Transmissions of non-dramatic literary works by a governmental body or other designated entity for the blind or handicapped people who cannot hear the sounds are exempted.[23]

• Dramatic literary works published at least ten years previously in the course of a transmission for the blind or other handicapped persons are exempted.[24] This does not apply to more than one performance of the same work by the same performers or of the same work under the auspices of the same organization.

• Non-dramatical literary or musical works can be performed in a social function which is organized and promoted by a non-profit veteran or fraternal organization, where the proceeds are used *exclusively* for *charitable purposes*.[25]

6.6   GROUP LICENSING PROGRAMS

Since exemptions are primarily non-profit based, they cannot be granted for everyone. To fulfill some of the most common requests, in several instances, copyright owners have helped establish clearinghouses to grant licenses to the public.

---

[21] So that copyright owners will not be forced to have their works performed for fund-raising activities which they do not favor, §110(4)(A) provides where a notice of objection can be served at least seven days before the performance.

[22] It is on this basis that musical works can be performed by a record shop to promote the sales of phonorecords.

[23] §110(8)

[24] §110(10)

[25] ibid.

LICENSING CLEARINGHOUSES

Some groups of copyright owners have authorized specialized clearinghouses to license copyright users. One example is the Copyright Clearance Center ("CCC"), which interfaces with publishers to grant photocopying licenses to subscribing companies. Another example is the Motion Picture Licensing Corporation ("MPLC") that offers performance licenses from the movie studios to show movies. And of course, there are the traditional music performance clearinghouses, the American Society of Composers, Authors, and Publishers ("ASCAP") and Broadcast Music, Inc. ("BMI").

This is not a free ride, like with exemptions, since royalties are charged. Clearinghouses are hard to set up and typically have high administration fees. Also, these licensing groups usually do not have all the rights they need, since many of the copyright holders do not participate.

6.7 COMPULSORY LICENSING

A compulsory license gives a party the right to do something that would otherwise infringe the copyright owner's exclusive rights. The license is considered compulsory because the copyright owner's consent is not required. Compulsory licenses differ from exemptions in that *royalties* are prescribed. Compulsory licenses are found relating to music and to broadcasting.

There are licenses of the following types: a mechanical license to record musical works; a juke box license; a non-commercial broadcasting license; a cable retransmission license; a satellite transmission license and a license for the sale of digital recording equipment.

A mechanical license to record non-dramatic musical works applies once a phonorecord of music has been distributed to the public under authority of the copyright owner in the U.S.[26] This allows any interested party to make and distribute a new original sound recording of the music.

---

[26] §115

A license for coin-operated phonorecord players is available in establishments where no direct or indirect admission is charged upon filing an application with the Copyright Office.[27] However, a basis for a consensual license has been established under the Berne Convention Implementation Act.[28]

A license for non-commercial broadcasters allows performance and display in the course of an educational transmission of published non-dramatic musical works.[29] Royalties are paid in an amount specified by the Copyright Royalty Tribunal.

A license allows performances and displays in the course of secondary transmissions to the public.[30] Cable systems can make secondary transmissions to the public of primary transmissions by federally licensed broadcast stations.

A compulsory license relating to satellite transmissions was established under the Satellite Home Viewers Act of 1988, which became effective January 1, 1989, on a trial basis. The Home Audio Taping and Digital Audio Recording Royalties Act of 1992 allows the public to buy digital recording equipment. A royalty is collected on the sale of the recording equipment by the manufacturers.

6.8 CROSS REFERENCES

Chapter Five on exclusive rights and Chapter Twelve on copyright litigation are pertinent to the topics discussed in this chapter.

---

[27] §116
[28] §116A
[29] §118
[30] §119

Chapter Seven:

COPYRIGHT NOTICES

7.1 OVERVIEW

Historically, a copyright notice was one of the requirements of copyright under U.S. law. Placing a notice of copyright on a work indicated to the public that a copyright was being sought. Under the 1909 Copyright Act, to be copyrighted, a work had to be published with a copyright notice, deposited and registered. Copyright notice was a condition precedent for copyright, and publication without a copyright notice placed the work in the public domain.

This was a harsh environment for copyright owners, since the inadvertent distribution of a work without notice of copyright could result in a loss of copyright.[1] The 1976 Act made the notice requirement less onerous by reducing the consequences of making a mistake with the notice. However, it was not until the Berne Convention Implementation Act in 1988, that copyright notice was unequivocally removed as a condition of copyright. Now copyright notices are optional, and non-use of a notice will not forfeit the copyright.

---

[1] *Academy of Motion Picture Arts and Sciences v. Creative House Promotion Inc.*, 728 F.Supp. 1442 (C.D. Cal. 1989), 944 F.2d 1446 (9th Cir. 1991). The Academy of Motion Pictures Arts and Sciences sued a manufacturer of statuettes that resembled the Oscar awards for copyright infringement. The defendant asserted that the copyright was invalid because a copyright notice had been left off some of the statuettes that had been awarded. The district court found for the defendant. On appeal, the 9th Circuit found that the distribution was limited meaning that a copyright notice was not required even though millions of people saw the presentations. In this case, equities prevailed, but the lower court's decision could easily have gone the other way.

Foreign works which had lost their U.S. copyrights because of failure to use a proper notice form have had new life breathed into them. GATT will amend current U.S. copyright law to restore abandoned copyrights for works owned by citizens of FTO countries that have fallen into the public domain for failure to comply with notice or other formalities of the 1909 Act. (See Appendix S.)

THEY'RE BACK!

When the 1909 Copyright Act required that published works contain a prescribed copyright notice, this was considered to be an absolute requirement and if the proper form of notice was not used, the works would go into the public domain and remain there.

Who would have imagined that some seventy years after the 1909 Act had been phased out, all the old copyrights belonging to foreign parties which had lapsed under it would be revived, and their ghosts would come back to haunt us.

The term of copyright for a restored work will be the remainder of the term that the restored work would have had if it had not entered the public domain. To preserve a right to enforce the copyrights, the copyright owners must file a notice of intent to enforce a restored copyright at the Copyright Office within twenty-four months of restoration and serve notice on the alleged infringer.

Although a copyright notice is no longer a condition of copyright, a number of rules relating to copyright notices still apply, depending on when a work was published. Notice may be gone, but its embodiments linger on.

7.2 NOTICE UNDER THE 1976 ACT

Under the 1976 Act, lack of a copyright notice for works published *before* March 1, 1989, was curable in certain situations:[2]

---

[2] These provisions are inapplicable to works published on or after March 1, 1989, since that is when the Berne Convention Implementation Act became effective.

- A copyright notice could be omitted from a small number of the copies or phonorecords distributed to the public, without invalidating the copyright.[3]
- The absence of a copyright notice was excused if (1) the work was registered within *five* years after it was published and (2) a reasonable effort had to be made to add a copyright notice to copies and phonorecords that had been publicly distributed in the U.S.[4]
- Lack of copyright notice had no effect if it was omitted in violation of an agreement in writing, which conditioned public distribution upon its use.[5]

Other provisions in the 1976 Act allowed for elements of a copyright notice to be defective without the copyright to the work being voided:[6]

- If the party named in the copyright notice of a work distributed to the public was not the copyright owner, validity of the copyright was unaffected.[7]
- If the year stated in the copyright notice was *earlier* than when publication first occurred, validity of the copyright was unaffected. However, in this instance, the term of the copyright was computed from the date in the notice.[8]
- Innocent infringers were absolved from any actual or statutory damages if a notice was omitted from works published under authority of the copyright owner.[9] Therefore, if the author had a clause in a publishing contract requiring notice to be used and the publisher failed in its duty, the copyright would not be forfeited.

---

[3] §405(a)(1)

[4] §405(a)(2)

[5] §405(a)(3)

[6] These are now restricted to works published between January 1, 1978 and March 1, 1989.

[7] §406(a). This provision is what allowed an author to authorize a publisher use its name on a copyright notice.

[8] §406(b). The copyright term is normally so long that taking off a year or two at the end is inconsequential.

[9] §405(b). This is now limited to works published prior to March 1, 1989.

7.3 NOTICE UNDER THE 1988 ACT

The Berne Convention Implementation Act resulted in copyright notice being optional. Therefore, one should assume that works which published on or after March 1, 1989 — the effective date of the Act — are copyrighted, even if a copyright notice does not appear.

Use of a copyright notice on *visually perceptible* copies is governed by Section 401(a):

> Whenever a work protected under this title is published in the United States or elsewhere by authority of the copyright owner, a notice of copyright as provided by this section may be placed on publicly distributed copies from which the work can be visually perceived, either directly or with the aid of a machine, i.e., or device.[10]

Section 402(a) governs notice on sound recordings:

> Whenever a sound recording protected under this title is published in the United States or elsewhere under authority of the copyright owner, a notice of copyright as provided by this section may be placed on publicly distributed phonorecords of the sound recording.[11]

"Publication" is defined as:[12] "The distribution of copies or phonorecords of a work to the public by sale or other transfer of ownership, or by rental, lease or lending." Even though lack of a copyright notice no longer affects validity, use of a notice is advantageous since it precludes a claim of innocent infringement by the defendant in mitigation of damages.[13]

---

[10] "Copies" are the material objects in which the work is fixed and from which it can be perceived, reproduced, or otherwise communicated, either with or without the aid of a machine. §101.

[11] "Phonorecords" are material objects in which sounds, other than accompanying a motion picture or other audiovisual work, are fixed by any method now known or later developed, and from which the sounds can be perceived, reproduced, or otherwise communicated, either directly, or with the aid of any machine or device. §101.

[12] ibid.

[13] §401(d)

If a notice of copyright in the form and position specified by this section appears on the published copy or copies to which a defendant in a copyright infringement suit had access, then no weight shall be given to such a defendant's interposition of a defense based on innocent infringement in mitigation of actual or statutory damages.[14]

Another reason for using a copyright notice is to qualify a work under the Universal Copyright and the Pan American Conventions.[15] (Berne is of no concern since it has no form of notice.) Finally, a copyright notice alerts people who may not know the law to the fact that a work is copyrighted.

7.4 VISUALLY PERCEPTIBLE COPIES

The form of notice for visually perceptible copies is prescribed as:[16]

(1) the symbol © (the letter C in a circle), or the word "Copyright," or the abbreviation "Copr."; and
(2) the year of first publication of the work; and
(3) the name of the owner of the copyright in the work, or an abbreviation by which the name can be recognized, or a generally known alternative designation of the owner.

Although several forms of notice are provided, the one most commonly used was the "Circle C" form since it was effective under the Universal Copyright Convention. This copyright symbol provided U.S. and foreign protection, and the habit has carried over even though coverage under Berne is automatic on fixation of the work. For some works, e.g., computer programs, the "Circle C" form of notice cannot be generated. For this reason, you sometimes see a "C" in parenthesis, i.e., "(C)," on computer software. While the U.S. Copyright Office has accepted this usage,[17] it still is not good practice.

---

[14] A similar provision to the above in respect to innocent infringement of phonorecords is found in Section 402(d).

[15] To qualify under the UCC, a particular form of notice must be used. To qualify under the Pan American Convention, only a general claim of copyright need be made.

[16] §401(b).

[17] Compendium of Copyright Practice

7.5 SOUND RECORDINGS

"Sound recordings" are defined as:[18] "Works that result from the fixation of a series of musical, spoken or other sounds, but not including the sounds accompanying a motion picture or other audiovisual work." The copyright notice for sound recordings embodied in phonorecords consists of the following three elements:[19]

(1) (the letter P in a circle — the Circle P); and
(2) the year of first publication of the sound recording;
(3) the name of the owner of copyright in the sound recording.

Normally, all three elements of a notice should appear together. However, the name of the copyright owner can be omitted if the owner is the producer of the sound recording and the producer's name appears on the label or container.[20]

On CD and cassette labels or containers, both the Circle C and Circle P forms of copyright notice may appear. The Circle P relates to the sound recording, while the Circle C protects the words and music and any accompanying written material or artwork.

7.6 LOCATION OF THE NOTICE

For visually perceptible works, the copyright notice must be placed in a manner and location so as to give reasonable notice of the claim of copyright.[21] The copyright notice on sound recordings should appear on the surface of the phonorecord, or on the phonorecord label or container, in a manner calculated to give reasonable notice of the claim of copyright.[22]

---

[18] §101

[19] 402(a). The Circle P symbol stands for phonogram and is the international symbol prescribed by the Convention for the Protection of Producers of Phonograms Against Unauthorized Protection of their Phonograms.

[20] ibid.

[21] §401(c). The Copyright Office has issued regulations describing where notice should be placed for various types of works.

[22] §402(c)

Previously, the manner and location of the copyright notice was critical, since the consequences for an incorrect notice could be the loss of copyright. Now, if the form and location of the notice are incorrect, the worse that can happen is that infringers may receive mitigated damages.

7.7 DERIVATIVE WORKS AND COMPILATIONS

For derivative works and compilations, the Copyright Act provides:[23] "... in the case of compilations or derivative works incorporating previously published material, the year date of first publication of the compilation or derivative work is sufficient." Even though the year when the compilation or derivative work was first published is adequate for notice purposes, it is common practice to include the year dates from prior notices when a revision is published.[24] This way, the owner is protected if the work for some reason does not qualify as a compilation or derivative work.

7.8 COLLECTIVE WORKS

A collective work is a form of compilation. It consists of an assemblage of separate works, such as a collection of poems or essays. Each item in the collection may have its own copyright notice.[25] However, a single copyright notice in front of a collective work protects the individual contributions in it.[26]

An exception to the rule concerning notice for collective works is advertisements.[27] Each advertisement must have its own copyright notice.[28] This means that a general copyright notice in a newspaper or magazine does not protect any advertisements contained therein.

---

[23] Section 401(b)(2)

[24] This is why encyclopedias and scientific and legal texts frequently have a string of years listed in their copyright notices.

[25] §404(a)

[26] ibid.

[27] ibid.

[28] Under the 1976 Act, a copyright notice in front of a magazine was insufficient to protect third party advertisements. Now even though the rule is the same, the result is not as disastrous, since the copyright to the advertisement will not be lost.

7.9 GOVERNMENTAL WORKS

If a work consists *predominantly* of one or more works of the U.S. Government, a notice of copyright should specify, either affirmatively or negatively, the portions of the work protected by the Copyright Act.[29] Failure to so designate allows the party being sued for infringement to claim to be an innocent infringer.[30]

7.10 NOTICES ON USEFUL ARTICLES

Certain useful articles are exempted under U.S. copyright law from having a year designation. The motive apparently was to help maintain the market value. The 1976 Act provides that "the year date may be omitted where a pictorial, graphic or sculptural work, with accompanying text material, is reproduced in or on greeting cards, post cards, stationery, jewelry, dolls, toys or any useful articles."[31] A "useful article" is defined as:[32] "an article having an intrinsic utilitarian function that is not merely to portray the appearance of the article or to convey information."

With the passage of the Berne Convention Implementation Act, the year (or even entire copyright notice) can be left off any work without invalidating the copyright. This means the year designation can be deleted from sheet music, maps, T-shirts, mugs and other useful items, without their copyrights being affected.

7.11 INTERNATIONAL NOTICE FORMS

In devising a copyright notice, attention should not only be given to U.S. law, but also to the international copyright conventions to which the U.S. belongs. This requires consideration of the notice requirements of the Universal Copyright Conven-

---

[29] §403

[30] There is not a designation of U.S. governmental material with the notice of copyright in front of this book, since governmental material does not constitute a dominant portion of this book. However, an equivalent statement is made in the disclaimer.

[31] §401(b)(2)

[32] §101

tion (UCC) and the Pan American Convention (PAC).[33] The Berne Convention can be ignored since it has no notice requirements. The UCC requires the "Circle C" form of notice prescribed by U.S. law, the name of the author and the year of first publication.[34] As the PAC has no prescribed notice form, the supplemental claim *"all rights reserved"* is commonly used in the masthead.

7.12 NON-STATUTORY NOTICES

Add-on warnings or "in terrorem" notices, as they are sometimes called, are widely seen. They supplement or add to the statutory notice and warn the reader what will happen if unauthorized reproductions of the work are made. An example is: "Reproduction of this work in whole or in part is strictly prohibited and all violators will be prosecuted to the fullest extent of the law." Legally, add-on notices contribute little, since however strongly their warning is phrased, it is still no more effective than the statutory notice, since you cannot generate rights by tooting your own horn.

7.13 NOTICES FOR PUBLICATIONS

The following form of copyright notice appears in numerous books, journals, and newsletters published by the American Library Association: "Copyright © XXXX, American Library Association" where XXXX is the four digit year of publication, e.g., 1995. Use of the word "copyright" is redundant, but it gets the message across.

7.14 NOTICE ON MANUSCRIPTS

If you are preparing to send a manuscript to a publisher, what kind of notice do you put on it? Under the Berne Convention Implementation Act, lack of notice has no effect on validity

---

[33] Bilateral treaties could also be a factor for some countries, since they could be based on notice requirements.

[34] Although the UCC form of copyright notice and the U.S. copyright notice are the same, sometimes both forms of notice are put on a work, e.g., where the rights are owned by different parties.

of the copyright and, therefore, notice is unnecessary. However, since manuscripts are sometimes circulated without the author's permission, a copyright notice of some form is desirable so the recipient will know whose work it is.[35] So what do you do?

A conventional three-element notice is not proper because there has been no publication. Moreover, by including a year designation, the public could be misled regarding the existence of publication. One approach is to use the year in which the manuscript was first distributed to a third party, even though it was only a limited distribution. Another procedure, where the work has been registered, is to use the year of registration. Alternatively, one can use a non-statutory notice on the work to indicate that copyright rights are being claimed, e.g., "Unpublished Manuscript — Not for Release or Publication." Until legislation is passed providing a form of copyright notice for unpublished works, this problem of notice form will remain. Until then, the author still has a safety net, since whatever form of notice is used, the copyright cannot be forfeited.

7.15 UNAUTHORIZED REMOVAL OF NOTICE

Copyright protection is not affected by the removal, destruction or obliteration of the copyright notice from publicly distributed copies.[36] Anyone who removes a copyright notice is subject to a possible *criminal* fine up to $2500.[37]

7.16 CROSS REFERENCES

Chapter One covers copyright fundamentals. Chapter Two explains the Berne Convention.

---

[35] Putting a copyright notice on the cover sheet of the manuscript does not mean the notice stays with the manuscript. Some agents remove the cover sheets and replace them with their own cover sheets when submitting the manuscripts to publishers. This also occurs when manuscripts are sent out for peer review, when one person bounces it to another.

[36] §405(c)

[37] §506(d). This is something literary agents and others who routinely remove manuscript cover sheets should consider.

Chapter Eight:

COPYRIGHT DURATION

8.1 OVERVIEW

The term or duration of a copyright depends on the type of work and its status as of January 1, 1978. All terms extend until the end of the calendar year in which they would otherwise expire. For individual authors, the copyright term is based on the life of the author plus fifty years. For works made for hire, and anonymous and pseudonymous works, copyright terms are the shorter of seventy-five years from publication or one-hundred years from creation. Special rules cover the terms of joint works and works that were in their first or renewal terms of copyright, or works that were unpublished on January 1, 1978. When a copyright expires, the work enters the public domain.

Copyright terms are important because they measure how long a copyright lasts. Generally, the longer the term, the more valuable the copyright. Copyright terms are now longer than the author's life, but that was not always the case. The Copyright Act of 1790 provided for an initial term of copyright of fourteen years and a renewal term of fourteen years. The 1909 Act doubled the initial and renewal terms to twenty-eight years. However, even fifty-six years seemed short as life spans increased, and when the 1976 Act was passed, the term of copyright was increased again. The Berne standard for individual authors, based on the life of the author plus fifty years, was adopted. For certain works, terms of one-hundred years from creation or seventy-five years from publication were created.

How long can copyright terms be? The Constitution gives Congress the power to extend to authors and inventors for *limited times* the exclusive right to their respective writings and discoveries.[1]

---

[1] Article I, Section 8, Clause 8. See Chapter Two.

HOW LONG IS A LIMITED TERM?

Copyright terms have been increased from twenty-eight years, to fifty-six years, to life plus fifty years, and still the Constitutional limits have not been probed. Seemingly, the only requirement is that a definite term be imposed, i.e., that the term end at some point. This means that, so long as science doesn't establish immortality, any standard based on life will work.

However, if the terms are stretched too far, argument could be made that the quid pro quo an author is receiving for creating a work is beyond the Constitutional mandate. Why should an author be rewarded with an extended term after death? Look for a test in court where a party who is sued for infringement on a fifty year plus life copyright raises a defense that the term is unconstitutional and if the work was not published during the author's lifetime, this would even be a better situation to test.

Already, there is discussion of a new Berne standard of life plus seventy-five years. The longer a copyright lasts, the longer a work can be protected, and, potentially, the greater the value of the copyright.

8.2 TERMS UNDER THE 1976 ACT

The 1976 Copyright Act established a term of copyright for works created after January 1, 1978, based on the life of the author plus fifty years.[2] A "life-plus-fifty-year" measure was chosen because it was the standard of the Berne Convention.[3]

Under the life-plus-fifty rule, all copyrighted works of an author, whenever completed, expire uniformly fifty years after

---

[2] §302(a) of the Copyright Act

[3] Although the U.S. was not a party to the Berne Convention in 1976, the U.S. still had hopes of joining. Establishing a compatible term was seen as a necessary first step.

the author's death.[4] Therefore, by definition an author cannot outlive his or her copyrights. In fact, the term of most copyrights will extend for most of the lives of the author's children.

COPYRIGHT TERM GUIDE FOR INDIVIDUAL AUTHORS BASED ON YEAR OF PUBLICATION

Year Published	Initial Term (ends)	Renewal Term (ends)
1910	1938	1966
1920	1948	1976
1930	1958	1986
1940	1968	1996
1950	1978	2025
1960	1988	2035
1970	1998	2045
1980	Life + 50 Years or 2055	———
1990	Life + 50 Years or 2065	———

In situations where basing a term on the life of the author was not practical, a fixed term system was established. For works made for hire, and for anonymous and pseudonymous works, the copyright term is the shorter of one-hundred years from creation, or seventy-five years from publication. Under these rules, it is necessary to know when an author dies, or when a work is created or published. If a work was created more than one-hundred years ago, or was first published more than seventy-five years ago, the author is presumed to have died more than fifty years ago.[5] This may work for older authors, but is not very useful for authors who die young.

8.3 ANONYMOUS AND PSEUDONYMOUS WORKS

For anonymous and pseudonymous works, the 1976 Act provided terms the shorter of seventy-five years from the year

---

[4] Although all the copyrights of an author will have the same expiration date, the works will have different individual terms depending on when the author completed each work.

[5] §302(e)

of first publication, or one-hundred years from the year of creation. An "anonymous work" is defined as:[6] "A work of which on its copies or phonorecords no natural person is identified as the author." A "pseudonymous work" is defined as:[7] "A work of which on its copies or phonorecords the author is identified under a fictitious name." The author is able to control the term of copyright by the way the authorship is shown.[8] If a writer uses a pen name or publishes a book without being identified as the author, the term is determined by the 75/100 year rule. If the author publishes under his or her own name, the life-plus-fifty rule applies. An author can even publish under a pseudonym and change his or her mind and file notice of authorship with the Copyright Office. However, there seems to be no way to switch at some point from the author's real name to a pseudonym.

The Writer Who Didn't Know When to Die

Jones, age thirty, had just finished the final draft of his latest book. He wanted his sons to retain the copyright to the work for as long as possible. However, his doctor had told him that he only had two years to live.

Rather than using his true name, Jones decided to use a pen name. The publisher had no problem with this since this was Jones' first fictional work. A friend, who was a trademark attorney, advised Jones that the term of copyright was life-plus-fifty years. However, if a pen name was used, the term would be one-hundred years from creation or seventy-five years from publication.

As Jones saw things, the copyright term would likely be fifty percent longer if he used a pen name. This was the route he took, and the book was published eighteen months later. Contrary to all odds, Jones was still living two years later, and his doctor said he could expect to live a normal live span.

Jones' novel did very well and was going to be made into a movie. Jones decided he would be better off with a life-plus-

---

[6] §101

[7] ibid.

[8] In the real world, there would not be much opportunity to play these kind of games. Any author with a track record would use the name that the public would recognize.

fifty-year term and filed a letter with the Copyright Office iden-
tifying himself as the author of the work. This changed the
term to life-plus-fifty years.
At all times, Jones was merely exercising his statutory rights.
However, he should have waited longer before identifying him-
self. Only after the seventy-five year term had been reduced to
less than fifty years, could Jones have been sure that the life
measure was best.

8.4 WORKS MADE FOR HIRE

Another situation where a measure based on the life of the author did not work effectively was for works made for hire. It would be unduly burdensome to determine the actual author-ship of works prepared by employees in the scope of their em-ployment, much less attempt to track employees after they left.

Therefore, for works made for hire, the 75/100 year rule ap-plies. A "work made for hire" is defined in as:[9]

> (1) a work prepared by an employee within the scope of his or her employment; or
> (2) a specially ordered or commissioned work which is a con-tribution to a collective work, a part of a motion picture or other audiovisual work, a translation, a supplementary work, a compilation, an instructional text, a test, answer material for a test, or as an atlas, if the parties expressly agree in a written instrument signed by them that the work shall be considered a work made for hire.

This definition covers works made for hire by employees within the scope of employment and works prepared by con-tractors who prepare specially commissioned works. In both cases, the terms are the shorter of one-hundred years from cre-ation, or seventy-five years from publication.

Whether an employer-employee situation exists, depends upon an analysis of the facts. (See *The Community for Creative Non-Violence v. Reid* in Chapter Three.) In most cases, the answer will be apparent. Nevertheless, studying the tests in the CCNV case will show the author who is involved in borderline situa-tions what to do to slant the job one way or the other.

---

[9] §101

Also, even if the author is clearly acting as a contractor in preparing a commissioned work, that does not mean that the resulting work will be considered as a work made for hire. Commissioned works are restricted to certain designated categories, and in most instances, the work prepared in these situations, unless it is something audiovisual or a supplemental work, will not fit the designated pigeonholes.[10]

Another catch is that even if there is a fit in work categories, the author must have agreed *in writing* that the work was to be made as a work made for hire.[11] Qualifying commissioned works as works made for hire is difficult, and parties cannot arbitrarily decide between them that a work will be treated as a work made for hire.[12]

8.5 JOINT WORKS

Multiple authorship poses special problems. If all the authors die during the same year, determining the term is easy. However, when they die at different times, what term applies then?

The term of a joint work (except for works made for hire) lasts for the life of the *last* surviving author plus fifty years.[13] This provides an opportunity for some more "name your copyright term" game playing by those so inclined. Since the copyright term will extend for the life of the *last* surviving author, the author may legitimately prolong the term of copyright by collaborating with someone younger.[14] If a son or daughter is included as a co-author, thirty to fifty years could potentially be added to the term. The statute does not cover the situation in

---

[10] §101 under "Works made for hire."

[11] ibid.

[12] This is more of a problem for the commissioning party than the author. The commissioning party wants to qualify the work as a work for hire. When that scenario fails, the author, as creator, is left with the copyright. Of course, title can be assigned, you say. Well, yes and no. Any assignment of any copyright interest, including title, is voidable at some point in time. See Chapter Nine on Termination of Grants.

[13] §302(b)

[14] Anyone who is added as an author must be a legitimate contributing co-author.

which the joint authors are a combination of individuals and authors who prepare their contributions as works made for hire. This is another example where a statute tried to deal with specifics but did not cover all the possibilities. [15]

8.6 PRE-EXISTING UNPUBLISHED WORKS

Under the 1909 Act, unpublished works which were not in the public domain were protected at common law for unlimited terms. Since the 1976 Act covered published and unpublished works, it was necessary to limit the terms of the unpublished works.

Works which were not in the public domain when the 1976 Act became effective were dealt with as follows. Unpublished works were designated to expire on December 31, 2002.[16] However, for works which were still unpublished at that time, the expiration date was further extended to December 31, 2027.[17]

8.7 PRE-EXISTING COPYRIGHTED WORKS

Another category of works which have special terms are those which were already published and copyrighted on January 1, 1978. The terms of these works depend on whether the copyright was in its first or second term. If a work was in its first term of copyright, its term is twenty-eight years from publication. If the copyright was renewed, its second term is forty-seven years.[18]

A final group of works which had their terms extended were those which would have expired before the 1976 Act became effective, except for previous term extensions. Works which were in their renewal term between December 31, 1976 and December 31, 1977, or which had their term extended by special act of Congress prior to this time, had their terms extended to a total of seventy-five years.[19]

---

[15] Most likely, the work would be allowed the longer of the two terms.
[16] §303
[17] ibid.
[18] §304(a)
[19] §304(b)

To avoid the necessity of making formal renewals, the Copyright Renewal Act of 1992 automatically extended the renewal terms of all works published between January 1, 1964 and December 31, 1978. Renewal applications may still be filed, but are no longer mandatory. *This means that an author automatically receives the benefit of the renewals and the extended terms without doing anything. No longer will any works subject to renewal be forfeited because the renewals were not made on time.*

8.8   END OF YEAR TERMINATION RULE

Copyrights do not expire at the end of their designated terms; the terms of all copyrights run to *the end of the calendar year* in which they would otherwise expire.[20] This rule applies whether the copyright term is based on the life of the author, or the 75/100 year rule. Therefore, all works of an individual author expire *uniformly* fifty years after the author's death, and works belonging to a company will expire in groups at the end of each year.

There is no need to determine the author's exact date of death, nor to determine exactly when a work was created or published. One only needs to determine the year of death, or the year of creation or publication, as applicable. For example, if a writer died in 1995, the term of copyright for all his/her works will expire on December 31, 2045. It makes no difference whether the he/she died in January or December. Consequently, all the author's works will have different terms depending on the creation dates.

8.9   WORKS IN THE PUBLIC DOMAIN

The "public domain" is used to categorize works which are not protected by copyright and are freely available to the public for copying. When copyrights expire, the works enter the public domain.

---

[20] §304. Depending on when the term would have normally terminated, this can add from one to 364 days to the term. Only authors who die on December 31st receive no benefit from this provision. Those who can survive to New Year's Day will gain 364 days for their heirs.

This is the quid pro quo the public gets for the limited exclusive rights given the author. As copyrights expire, the works go into the public domain where they can be used by anyone without restriction.

Works which were in the public domain on January 1, 1978, e.g., works published without copyright notice prior to that time, are not protectable by copyright. Similarly, if a work's copyright term had expired prior to January 1, 1978, it is in the public domain.[21]

8.10 CROSS REFERENCES

For related subjects, see Chapter Three on ownership and Chapter Eleven on renewals.

---

[21] The line had to be drawn somewhere, and works which were in the public domain prior to January 1, 1978 are uncopyrighted and uncopyrightable. But in view of GATT, this only is correct now for works with U.S. authorship. See Appendix S.

Chapter Nine:

TERMINATION OF GRANTS

9.1 OVERVIEW

Congress has long sought to protect authors from unwise transactions that may have been made before the value of a work became apparent. Under the 1909 Act, this was done by giving the author a right of renewal of copyright. When the original copyright lapsed, the author was supposedly free to start over with the renewed copyright.

As will be seen in Chapter Eleven, because of grantor estoppel, the renewal system did not work as intended. As a result, the 1976 Act eliminated renewals for works made on or after January 1, 1978. Only works that were in their first copyright term on January 1, 1978 are still subject to renewal.

Congress extended the term of copyright and allowed the author a right to terminate grants of copyright rights. The right of termination gives the author the right to selectively terminate specific grants during a designated time period. Two rights of termination were granted. One right covers transfers and licenses made before January 1, 1978 which had their terms extended. The other applies to transfers and licenses of works (except "works made for hire") made on or after January 1, 1978. The former is the "56 year" rule. The latter is the "35/40 year" rule. While these two rights are superficially similar, they have significant differences and should be studied separately.

The Sale That Wasn't

Jerry writes a novel and, after several years of trying to market it, finally gives up. A friend, Anna, reads the manuscript and likes it. She offers Jerry $1000 for all rights to the novel. Jerry decides something is better than nothing and accepts.

Many years pass, and Anna finds a publisher. The work is published and is an immediate success. Can Jerry reclaim the copyright that he assigned?
You bet! If Jerry considered that he made a bad deal, at some point in the future he can terminate the sale to Anna and start over. This is what termination of grants is all about.

Termination of grants is one of the most difficult and complex areas of copyright law. However, because of its application to all grants of all kinds and because this hits home for every author, the subject must be addressed and mastered.[1]

THE AUTHOR'S RIGHTS TO RENEGE

When is a sale not a sale? When a copyright interest is involved. The right of termination gives the author a chance to revoke previous grants that may be unique. In no other area of law can a party unilaterally terminate previous grants of ownership rights and licenses. For example, an author sells the publishing rights to a novel. At some point in the future, the author can exercise a right of termination and may be able to retain any consideration which had been paid. This is definitely a case of having your cake and eating it too.

9.2 THE 56 YEAR RULE

The 1976 Act established a right of termination for grants for works that were in their first or renewal terms of copyright on January 1, 1978.[2] Any agreement that the proprietor concluded *before* January 1, 1978 for works that had their renewal term extended by the 1976 Act can be revoked after the work has been in existence for fifty-six years.[3]

Termination must be made within a five-year period begin-

---

[1] The term "grant" is used to include both transfers (assignments and exclusive licenses) and non-exclusive licenses.

[2] §304(c) of the Copyright Act

[3] Since the 1976 Act added nineteen years to the twenty-eight year renewal term, it was considered that grants could be terminated during this extended period.

ning fifty-six years from the date the copyright was first procured, or on January 1, 1978, whichever is later.[4] Notice of termination cannot be given sooner than two years, or more than ten years in advance.[5]

The author, or other qualified person, has the right to exercise the right of termination in his or her ownership interest. Furthermore, the author's termination rights pass to the author's widow or widower, children or grandchildren who own more than half the termination rights.[6]

The widow or widower owns the termination right if there are no surviving children or grandchildren. The surviving children or grandchildren own the termination right if there is no widow or widower. If there is a widow or widower *and* surviving children or grandchildren, half the termination right goes to the spouse and half to the children and grandchildren on a *per stirpes* basis.[7]

The right of termination under the fifty-six year rule not only applies to grants by the author, but also to grants that may have been made by the party who executed it.[8] In the latter instance, the right of termination is exercisable by the *surviving* grantor(s).[9]

9.2.1 Service of Notice Under the 56 Year Rule

The notice of termination is required to be served *in advance* in writing on the grantee or the grantee's successor in title. The notice should state the date within the designated five-year period when the grant will terminate.[10] The selected termination date cannot be sooner than two years, or later than ten years from when the notice is given. The notice of termination must

---

[4] All termination notices now must be given starting fifty-six years after the copyright was granted.

[5] 304(c)(4)(A)

[6] §304(c)(1) and (2). The statutory definitions of widow, widower and children in §101 do not apply to the fifty-six year rule.

[7] §304(c)(2). *"Per stirpes"* means that the rights are taken on a representative basis. For example, an author's grandchildren would share the rights that their father or mother had.

[8] §304(c)(1)

[9] ibid. There is no equivalent right to terminate grants by non-authors under the 35/40 year rule.

[10] §304(c)(4)

comply with the form, content and manner of service prescribed by the Register of Copyrights. The requirements currently prescribed by the Register of Copyrights are found in the Addendum to this Chapter.

The termination rights do not become vested until the notice of termination has been served.[11] Where an author's rights revert to two or more persons, they vest in proportional shares.[12] Any further grant has to be signed by the same owners in whom the right vested.

9.3 THE 35/40 YEAR RULE

All grants of copyright rights made on or after January 1, 1978 (excluding testamentary grants) are terminable. However, there is no need to rush to serve notice; no agreements are terminable under the 35/40 year rule until at least 2013.[13] All copyright grants made after January 1, 1978, including assignments and licenses, will be terminable after a certain period after the grants were made.

DERIVATIVE WORKS

To avoid the inequities which resulted when a copyright was renewed (see Chapter Eleven), the 56 year and 35/40 year rules provide that derivative works prepared before their underlying grants were terminated can continue to be utilized under the terms of their grants.

For example, a movie based on a novel can continue to be performed even though the sale of the movie rights to the novel is subsequently voided. However, the owner of the derivative work does not have the right to prepare new derivative works based upon the copyrighted work covered by the terminated grant.

---

[11] §304(c)(6)(B)

[12] §304(c)(6)(C)

[13] If a grant was made to a copyrighted work on January 1, 1978, the grant would be subject to termination forty years later or thirty-five years from publication. Assuming that publication took place at the same time as the grant, the earliest possible date of termination would be thirty-five years later, i.e. January 1, 2013.

The author, if living, is entitled to execute the right of termination.[14] If the author is dead, the termination right is exercisable by the author's widow or widower, and his or her children, or surviving children of any dead child.[15]

The statutory definition of "widow" or "widower" which applies in this instance is the following:[16] "The author's surviving spouse under the author's domicile at the time of his or her death, whether or not the spouse later remarried." "Children" are defined as:[17] "That person's immediate offspring, whether legitimate or not, and any children legally adopted by that person." The widow or widower has the entire termination interest if there are no surviving children or grandchildren. If there are surviving children or grandchildren, the spouse has one-half interest.[18]

The author's surviving children and grandchildren own the termination interest if there is no surviving widow or widower. If there is a surviving widow or widower, the surviving children and grandchildren have one-half interest to divide among themselves.[19] The rights of an author's children or grandchildren to terminate are exercised on a *per stirpes* basis.[20]

EXCLUSIONS FROM TERMINATION

Not all grants made after January 1, 1978, can be terminated. Excluded from termination are copyrights prepared as works made for hire. Also, there is no right of termination for transfers or licenses made by parties other than the author.

For example, if the author died after a work was created and the spouse sold rights to the work, the spouse would not have a termination right. However, the spouse may have a termination right in respect to grants made by the author before he or she died.

---

[14] §203(a)(1)
[15] §203(a)(2)(A)
[16] §101
[17] ibid.
[18] §203(a)(2)(A)
[19] §203(a)(2)(B)
[20] §203(a)(2)(C)

9.3.1 Service of Notice Under the 35/40 Year Rule

Under the 35/40 year rule, termination rights apply to grants made on or after January 1, 1978.[21] The termination rights must be exercised within thirty-five years from publication of the work or forty years from when the grant was made.[22]

There are two procedures for giving notice of termination. Under the first procedure, termination must be made during a five year window beginning at the end of thirty-five years from the date of the execution of the grant.[23] Under the second procedure, termination can be made either at the end of forty years from execution of the grant, or thirty-five years from the date of publication, whichever term ends earlier.[24]

Notice of termination must be served at least two years before the selected termination date, and may be given up to ten years before that date.[25] The party giving the notice can specify at what point during the five-year window the termination will occur.[26]

9.4 STATUTORY TERMINATION

Assume an author assigns the rights in his novel to a publisher on March 15, 1980, and the work is published on October 18, 1990. Later, the author hears that he has an inherent right to terminate the agreement and goes to a copyright attorney for advice.

The attorney advises him that his termination right would be exercisable during the five-year period starting the earlier of March 15, 2020 (forty years added to the date of assignment), or October 18, 2025 (thirty-five years from the date of publication).

The author is told that if he wants to terminate on March 15, 2020, he has to give notice of termination between March 15,

---

[21] §203(a)

[22] §203(a)(3)

[23] ibid.

[24] §203(a)(4)(A)

[25] ibid.

[26] If notice of termination is given during the last year of the five year window, it would be too late since a minimum of two years advance notice is required.

2010, and March 15, 2018, i.e., ten to two years in advance of the selected termination date.

A notice of termination must be in writing and be signed by the author.[27] If the author is dead, it must be signed by the person or persons who are entitled to exercise more than one-half of the author's termination interest.[28] The notice must give the date of termination and be served upon the grantee, or the grantee's successor in title.

The notice must comply with the form, content and manner of service prescribed by the Register of Copyrights and be recorded in the Copyright Office. But here explanations cease, since rules on giving a 35/40 year notice have yet to be promulgated.

9.5 VESTING UNDER BOTH RULES

Upon notice of termination under either rule, the rights to the termination vest. This means that without taking any further action, the grant that was notified will terminate at the designated time. This procedure is important since it ensures that anyone who dies *after vesting* will be represented by the person's heirs or designees under the person's will.[29]

A frequently asked question is whether the party giving notice of termination can negotiate with third parties prior to actual termination. This is not allowed. A further grant, or agreement to make a grant, of any right covered by a notice of termination is only valid if it is made *after* the effective date of termination.[30]

However, an agreement to make a future grant may be made after notice of termination and before termination if the agree-

---

[27] § 203(a)(4)

[28] §203(a)(1). Since it takes more than a fifty percent ownership interest to give a valid termination, if one author of a joint work is in favor of the termination and the other author is not, the transfer stands.

[29] A notice of termination is an important document. Just like a will, it should be treated as valuable property and safeguarded. The notice of termination will override any will or agreement to make a will that purports to cover the grant in question.

[30] §203(b)(4)

ment parties are the same as were involved in the notice of termination.[31] Thus, only the grantor and the original grantee, or his or her successor in title, can negotiate before termination.

9.6 CROSS REFERENCES

Chapter Four on transfers of copyright should be reviewed. Chapter Twelve discusses the effect of termination of grants under wills.

---

[31] ibid.

ADDENDUM TO CHAPTER NINE

56 YEAR RULE TERMINATION PROCEDURE

Procedures prescribed by the Copyright Office for making 56 year terminations are given below:

Terminations can currently be made under Section 304(c) in accordance with procedures prescribed in Copyright Office regulations. No special form is required; however, the notice must comply with conditions in respect to contents, signature, service, and recordation:

CONTENTS—

(1) The name of the grantee whose rights are being terminated, or the grantee's successor in title, and the address at which notice is being served.

(2) The title and name of at least one author of, and the date copyright was originally secured in, each work to which the notice of termination applies; and, if possible, the original copyright registration number.

(3) A brief statement reasonably identifying the grant to which the notice of termination applies.

(4) The effective date of termination.

(5) In case of a termination of grant by a person or persons other than the author, a listing of the surviving person or persons who executed the grant. Where the termination is exercised by the successors of a deceased author, a listing of the author's surviving widow or widower, the author's surviving children, and if any of the author's children are dead, the surviving children of such deceased child, together with an indication by the person executing the notice showing that such party has more than one-half of the author's termination interest. (In the alternative the person or persons submitting the notice may say that to their best knowledge and belief the notice has been signed by all persons necessary to terminate the grant and explain why all of the information that was requested was not submitted.)

SIGNATURE—

(1) In case the notice is made by a person or persons other than the author, the notice shall be signed by all surviving person(s) who executed the grant, or by their authorized agents.

(2) In case of termination by one or more of the authors, notice shall be signed by the author or his duly authorized agent. If the author is dead, the notice must be signed by the number and proportion of the author's termination interest required under the statute, or by their duly authorized agents.

(3) Where signature is by an agent, it must clearly identify the persons on whose behalf the agent is acting.

(4) The handwritten signature of each person shall be accompanied by a typewritten or legibly printed full name and address of that person.

SERVICE —

(1) The notice of termination shall be served on each grantee whose rights are being terminated, or the grantee's successor in title, by personal service or by first class mail sent to an address, which, after reasonable investigation, is found to be the last known address of the grantee or successor in title.

(2) The service provisions of the statute will be satisfied if, before notice of termination is served, a reasonable investigation is made as to the current ownership of the rights being terminated and service is based accordingly.

(3) A reasonable investigation should include a search of the Copyright Office records, and if the work is a musical composition, a report from the performing rights society with which the work is registered.

(4) Compliance with paragraphs (2) and (3) above will satisfy the statutory service requirements; however, compliance with these regulations is not necessary so long as the statutory provisions are met.

RECORDATION—

(1) A copy of the notice has to be recorded with the Copyright Office and a recording fee paid.

(i) The copy submitted shall be a complete and exact duplicate of the notice of termination as served with the actual signature(s) appearing on the notice.

(ii) The copy shall be accompanied by a statement setting forth the date on which the notice was served and the manner of service.

(2) A fee is required depending on the length of the document and statement.

(3) The date of recordation is the date that all documents including the fee are received in the Copyright Office. A certified record of the recordal is returned to the sender.

Chapter Ten:

DEPOSIT AND REGISTRATION

10.1 OVERVIEW

Under the 1909 Copyright Act, deposit and registration were prerequisites to obtaining statutory copyright. A copyright did not exist until a work was published with a copyright notice, registered and deposited. Under the 1976 Act, failure to register or deposit after January 1, 1978 no longer had any effect on validity.[1] Registration was optional, and while deposit was required for works published with copyright notice, the only penalty for non-deposit was a monetary fine.[2] Copyright registration was a prerequisite for suing for copyright infringement. Also, registration was necessary before statutory damages and attorney fees could be recovered for infringements.[3]

The Berne Convention Implementation Act made several changes relating to deposit and registration. Deposit is now required for all *published* works, rather than only those published with notice of copyright.[4] Registration of Berne Convention

---

[1] While deposit is a necessary adjunct to registration, a work can be deposited without being registered.

[2] Before a penalty can be imposed, the Copyright Office has to make a written demand for deposit and allow three months for the deposit to be made.

[3] Under the 1909 Act, once a work was registered, statutory damages and attorney fees could be recovered retroactively. However, the 1976 Act registration has no such retroactive effect.

[4] Originally, deposit was keyed to works published with copyright notice. Since The Berne Convention Implementation Act did away with notice as a mandatory requirement, the deposit requirement was expanded to include published works, whether they had a notice or not.

works first published abroad is no longer necessary to bring infringement suits.[5]

10.2 DEPOSIT

Deposit is thought of as being part of registration. However, deposit is an independent requirement to provide source material to the Library of Congress. Deposit is required within *three months* of publication by the copyright owner or publisher.[6]

PENALTIES FOR NON-DEPOSIT

An author or owner of the exclusive right of publication is required to deposit copies or phonorecords of a work upon publication. If the deposit is not made, the Register of Copyrights can demand that deposit.
If the deposit is not made upon demand, the party may be fined. First offenders may be fined up to $250 and be required to pay the total retail price of the copies or phonorecords demanded, or reasonable cost to the Library of Congress acquiring them. Willful or repeated offenders may be fined up to $2500.

The statutory provision covering deposit reads as follows:[7]

... the owner of copyright or of the exclusive right of publication in a work published in the United States shall deposit within three months after the date of such publication —
(1) two complete copies of the best edition; or
(2) if the work is a sound recording, two complete phonorecords of the best edition, together with any printed or other visually perceptible material published with such phonorecords.

---

[5] It was considered sufficient for U.S. compliance with Berne for the registration requirement only to be lifted for Berne Convention works first published abroad. Works first published in the U.S. still must be registered before an infringement action can be brought.
[6] §407(a). An author should make sure that any publisher he or she uses accepts this responsibility so that he or she will not be in violation of the law.
[7] ibid.

"Complete" includes all elements which comprise the work as published. This includes the cover of a book and transparent overlays used in scientific works. Elements that would not, if considered separately, be copyrightable subject matter, i.e., game pieces for a board game, should be included.

10.3 BEST EDITION

The *best edition* of a work must be deposited. If the copies or phonorecords submitted do not comprise the best edition, the application for registration may be rejected. The "best edition" is defined as:[8] "...the edition published in the United States at any time before the date of deposit, that the Library of Congress determines to be most suitable for its purposes."

BEST EDITION GUIDELINES

The "best edition" is fairly self-explanatory. Officially, the best edition is whatever the Library of Congress deems to be most suitable for its purposes. This generally means it is the fanciest, most expensive version of a work that has been published.

For example, if a work is published in paperback and hardcover, the hardcover version is the best edition. If there are two hardcover versions, one illustrated and one without illustrations, the illustrated edition is the best edition. A trade edition rather than a book club edition is the best edition.

A book with thumb notches rather than one without would be the best edition. A larger size book rather than smaller size would be the best edition. If videotape is being deposited, the best edition is usually considered to be the widest tape format that is available. However, if a narrower format is the most widely distributed, that is considered to be the best edition.

The copies or phonorecords are deposited with the Copyright Office.[9] Where a copyright application and fee have been

---

[8] §101
[9] §407(b)

submitted, the deposit satisfies both the registration and deposit requirements.[10]

The Register of Copyrights has authority to exempt deposit, or only require deposit of a single copy or phonorecord.[11] The Register can grant a waiver from filing or accept alternative materials from individual authors of pictorial, graphic or sculptural works where their monetary value would make the deposit of two copies unfair or unreasonable.[12]

The Register has authority to accept material other than a copy or phonorecord of the work for deposit purposes. Identifying material which can be deposited in lieu of copies or phonorecords includes photographs or transparencies showing the work.[13] Finally, the Copyright Office has excused from deposit certain types of works.[14] However, just because mandatory deposit is excused does not preclude deposit if a copyright application is submitted.

---

[10] If deposit was made merely to satisfy the deposit requirement without seeking a registration, a subsequent deposit will still be required if the work is eventually submitted for registration.

[11] §407(c)

[12] ibid. This applies where (1) less than five copies or phonorecords of a work have been published, or (2) the work was published in a limited edition consisting of numbered copies.

[13] In the case of pictorial or graphic works, the material must reproduce the actual colors in the work. In all other cases, the proofs can either be black and white or in color. Photographic transparencies must be 35 mm and mounted if less than 3 by 3 inches. Photographs preferably are 8 by 10 inches. If a copyright notice is present, it should be shown. C.F.R. § 202.21

[14] Excluded from deposit are diagrams and models representing scientific or technical works; architectural or engineering blueprints; greeting cards, picture postcards and stationery; lectures, sermons, speeches and addresses; computer programs and automated databases in machine readable form; three-dimensional sculptural works and works reproduced in or on jewelry, dolls, toys, games, floor coverings, wallpaper, textiles or any useful article; prints, labels and advertising materials in connection with the lease, licensing or sale of articles of merchandise, works of authorship, or services; and test or answer materials when published separately from other literary works. 37 C.F.R. §202.19(c)

Special relief from deposit requirements is available by petition to the Copyright Office.[15] The request must be made in writing and should state the reasons why the applicant cannot submit the required deposit.

10.4 REGISTRATION PROCESS

Registration of copyrights is simple compared to obtaining patent and trademark registrations. A short two-page form is submitted, the examination process is fast-paced, and the Copyright Office will assist you. However, do not be tempted to rush through the form: *errors and mistakes can be used to support allegations of fraud.*

Registration is permissive and can be done at any time during the term of copyright:[16] "At any time during the subsistence of copyright in any published or unpublished work, the owner of copyright or of any exclusive right in the work may obtain registration of the copyright claim by delivering to the Copyright Office the deposit specified ...." To register *unpublished* works, submission of only one complete copy or phonorecord is required. Two copies or phonorecords are normally required to register *published* works.[17] The Register acts as an intermediary for depository purposes with the Library of Congress, and the copies or phonorecords submitted to the Copyright Office must satisfy the "best edition" requirements.[18]

10.5 ADVANTAGES TO REGISTRATION

Even though registration is no longer compulsory, there are several advantages to registering:
- Registration is a condition for commencing an infringement suit in most instances.[19] If you sue for copyright infringement, you either should have a registration, or have submitted a copyright application in complete form. An exception is for Berne

---

[15] 37 C.F.R. §209.19(e)
[16] §408(a)
[17] §408(b)
[18] ibid.
[19] §411(a)

Convention works that were first published abroad, since registration is excused.[20]

• The copyright owner preserves the right to seek an award of *statutory* damages for infringements resulting *after* registration.[21] The option to seek statutory damages is important since actual damages are difficult to prove.

• The copyright owner can seek to recover reasonable attorney fees in bringing an infringement suit for claims resulting *after* registration.[22]

• If a claim of copyright is registered before publication, or within five years after publication, the certificate of registration is *prima facie* evidence of the validity of the copyright and the facts stated in the certificate.[23]

• If copyright notice was omitted from publicly distributed copies or phonorecords, an innocent infringer is not liable for actual or statutory damages unless the work is registered and actual notice thereof is given.[24]

• Registration is a prerequisite for relying upon the copyright transfer recordal and notice provisions[25] (see Chapter Four). Only when a copyright has been registered can a grantee be protected from subsequent improper licenses or transfers by the grantor.

10.6 MECHANICS OF REGISTRATION

Copyright registration before the Copyright Office is fairly easy. It is much less adversarial than the prosecution of patents and trademarks before the U.S. Patent and Trademark Office. Registration can generally be achieved without the assistance of an attorney, and authors who file their own applications will find representatives at the Copyright Office willing to assist them with questions they might have.

---

[20] ibid.

[21] §412

[22] ibid.

[23] §410(c). Registration must be made within five years of publication for this presumption to apply.

[24] §504(b)

[25] §205(c)(2)

Registration involves completing a copyright application form (or photocopy) and filing it with the Copyright Office, together with the required number of copies or phonorecords of the "best edition" of the work. Payment of an application fee is required at the time of submission.[26] All payments sent to the Copyright Office should be in the form of a money order, check or bank draft payable to the Register of Copyrights. Uncertified checks are accepted subject to collection. Authors who file numerous applications may open a deposit account with the Copyright Office to simplify matters.

CAUTION: Be sure to submit everything pertaining to an application to the Copyright Office in one packet, and, to avoid confusion, do not combine applications. If the deposit copies are sent separately from the payment and application form, the application will be rejected. Deposit materials are retained or disposed of by the Copyright Office and will not be returned to the applicant and cannot be used to support a subsequent application.

10.7 REGISTRATION FORMS

Registration forms are furnished free of charge by the Copyright Office. Even though the copyright registration forms are relatively simple and straightforward, care should be taken in completing them.[27] The forms available (excluding the supplemental registration form which is discussed subsequently in this Chapter) are:[28]

1. FORM TX (nondramatic literary works)
2. FORM VA (visual arts)
3. FORM PA (performing arts)
4. FORM GR/CP (group periodicals)

---

[26] Until 1991 the fee was $10. It has now been increased to $20. Nevertheless, registration remains a bargain.

[27] Fraud may be found where the applicant fails to disclose prior works on which the subject work was based or provides incorrect information.

[28] In addition to the forms listed in this chapter, there are Renewal forms and a cover sheet used for recording agreements.

5. FORM SE (individual serial)
6. FORM SE Group
7. Short Form SE
8. FORM SR (sound recordings)
9 FORM G/DN (group daily newspapers)
10. FORM CON (continuation sheet)

COPYRIGHT APPLICATION FORMS

Copyright application forms are available free of charge from the Copyright Office. The forms and information kits on related subjects can be ordered by contacting the Copyright Office at the following address:
Publications Section
Copyright Office
Library of Congress
Washington, D.C. 20559
A hot line is maintained for ordering forms at 202-287-9100. For further information, an information specialist may be contacted at 202-707-3000.
NOTE: The Copyright Office is not permitted to give legal advice or information and guidance on matters pertaining to disputes over copyright ownership, suits against possible infringers, procedures for getting a work published or methods for obtaining royalty payments.

• Form TX, Appendix B, is used to register "textual" works, and covers a broad range of published and unpublished literary works. Fiction, non-fiction, poetry, periodicals, textbooks, reference works, dictionaries, catalogs, advertising copy, compilations of information and computer programs are all registered with this form.

• Form VA, Appendix C, is used to register works of "visual arts." It is used for works which are primarily pictorial, graphic or sculptural in nature. Included in this group are two- and three-dimensional works of fine, graphic and applied art, photographs, prints and art reproductions, maps, globes, charts, technical drawings, diagrams and models. If a work comprises mostly pictures, drawings or illustrations, the VA form should be used.

• Form PA, Appendix D, stands for "performing arts." It is used to register musical works (including accompanying words), dramatic works (including accompanying music), pantomimes and choreographic works and motion pictures and other audio-visual works.

• Form GR/CP, Appendix E, "group copyright," is used to register a group of related works that can be registered separately. It is limited to registration of a group of works by the same individual author which is first published as a contribution to a periodical within a twelve month period.[29]

• Form SE, Appendix F, is used to register "serials." This class includes periodicals, newspapers, annuals, journals, transactions, etc., published by societies.

• Form SE/Group, Appendix G, is a specialized form used for group registration of certain serials within a three-month period within the same calendar year. Short Form SE, Appendix H, is for a collective work made for hire.

• Form SR, Appendix I, is used to register "sound recordings." This category has increased importance to authors in view of the numerous books that are being recorded on cassette.

• Form G/DN, Appendix J, is used for group registration of daily newspapers.

• Form CON, Appendix K, is a continuation sheet for other application forms.

If a work contains copyrightable material falling into two or more classes, it should be placed in the class most appropriate for the work as a whole. For example, if a work contains textual material and graphics, determination should be made as to whether the TX or VA form is the most appropriate.

10.8 THE EXAMINATION PROCESS

Copyright examination is straightforward. The application is initially examined to ensure that the work has been properly characterized and to determine that all the required information has been provided. If the application, the deposit and the fee are

---

[29] §408(c)(2)

all found to be proper, the applicant is given a registration date as of the application (filing) date.[30]

Processing time from filing a copyright application to obtaining the registration certificate is normally three to six months. Most objections, excepting lack of copyrightable subject matter, are curable. The applicant is given a time limit of 120 days to respond to any communications. No special form is required. Upon registration, a registration certificate is provided to the copyright applicant.

SPECIAL HANDLING

Expedited processing of a copyright application or recordal of a document pertaining to copyright can be obtained upon paying a special handling fee. Special circumstances must be shown. The requestor must show pending or threatened litigation, customs matters or a contract or publishing deadline. If special handling is approved, processing can be done within five working days.

The request for special handling may be made by mail or in person. The Copyright Office has a form to be filled out by those who come in person. Applicants by mail must provide a letter explaining the need for special handling. A special handling fee of $200 is required, plus the standard application or recordal filing fee.

10.9 SUPPLEMENTAL REGISTRATIONS

Supplemental registration Form CA, Appendix L, is used to correct information in a previous registration.[31] Information can be added or items corrected where information previously provided was wrong or incomplete, or to reflect a change in circumstance, e.g., a change of address.

---

[30] Suit can be filed after an application has been submitted since the registration is effective upon filing. Of course, this assumes the application was filed in proper form.

[31] To fill out Form CA, the party merely states what information is wrong or needs to be corrected in the basic registration and adds whatever new information is appropriate.

Supplemental registrations are useful, they should not be used as a substitute for recording an interest under an agreement. Recordal of copyright agreements gives constructive notice of the facts in the recorded documents (see Chapter Four); supplemental registrations do not have a notice effect.

10.10 RULE AGAINST MULTIPLE REGISTRATIONS

After a work has been registered with the Copyright Office, additional registrations of the same work by the same party or others are precluded. This rule was developed because a registration is considered to inure to the benefit of all the owners of exclusive rights, present and future.

10.11 VISUAL ARTS REGISTRY

The Visual Arts Registry is new (see Chapter Two). The Copyright Office does not provide special forms for use by visual artists or the owners of buildings. Any statement which is designated as a "Visual Arts Regulatory Statement" and which pertains to a work which has been incorporated in or made a part of a building may be recorded upon paying a recording fee.[32]

SURFING THE INTERNET

Want to connect with the Copyright Office on the Internet? Telnet to marvel.loc.gov and login "marvel." Select the copyright menu. COHM is a record of all works, except serials, since 1978. COHS is a record of all serials since 1978. COHD is an index of all documents recorded. Access is available on a twenty-four hour basis.

10.12 CROSS REFERENCES

Renewals are covered in Chapter Eleven. The copyright registration forms are found in Appendices B through P. Appendix R includes basic information on copyright filings and procedures, and information about contacting the Copyright Office.

---

[32] §113(c)(3)

ADDENDUM TO CHAPTER TEN

COMPLETION OF APPLICATION FORM

Instructions on completing Application Form TX are given, as a guide to the reader. Completing most of the other forms is similar.

Step-by-step instructions for filling out the TX Application Form follow:

SPACE 1:

The work is given a title (space 1, line 1), and if desired, an alternative title can be included for cross reference purposes (space 1, line 2). If the work being registered is published as part of another work, e.g., a contribution to a periodical or collective work, information about the work should be given (space 1, line 3).

SPACE 2:

The author's name and years of birth and death go in area 2, line 1. Spaces are available to enter information on three authors. (Additional sheets can be added, if necessary.)

If the work is a work made for hire, the party who acted as the employer, or who commissioned the work, should be designated as the author. If the work is not a work made for hire, the actual creator or creators are the authors.

A problem area is joint ownership. Before listing any co-authors, the applicant should be sure that the parties qualify for joint authorship. For there to be joint ownership, the parties must have intended that their respective contributions be merged into a unitary whole.

Another authorship question which is addressed in line 2 is whether the work was anonymous or pseudonymous. If anonymous, no author is listed. If pseudonymous, a fictional name is given as the author.

The author's contribution must be stated in line 2 and his or her nationality or domicile given. The contribution made by the author should be specifically stated.

SPACE 3:

The year in which the work was completed must be given, and if the work has been published, information is requested regarding the date and nation of first publication. If the work is unpublished, there is no publication date.

SPACE 4:

The names and addresses of the copyright claimants are entered here. This may be different from the authorship, since certain exclusive rights may have been assigned. (If the names are different from the authorship, an explanation should be made.)

SPACE 5:

The applicant must state whether the work has previously been registered and, if so, give the registration number and year of registration.

SPACE 6

The applicant is required to state whether the work which is being registered is a compilation or derivative work. This only comes into play if the work is based on or incorporates a pre-existing work.

SPACE 7:

If the work is nondramatic and printed in English, the applicant is required to state who printed the work and give the place of manufacture (printing). This provision is a carry-over from when the U.S. had a manufacturing control law to ensure U.S. or Canadian printing.

SPACE 8:

The applicant can indicate his or her willingness to license the work for the benefit of the blind and handicapped. This space can be left blank if desired.

SPACE 9:

The applicant may list a deposit account (if there is one) and is required to give the name and the address of the person with whom correspondence should be directed.

SPACE 10:

The applicant is required to sign the form, certify that the statements made are correct and confirm the basis on which the application was submitted, i.e., as author, copyright claimant or owner of exclusive rights.

SPACE 11:

The applicant must include a return address for receiving the certificate.

Chapter Eleven:

RENEWAL OF COPYRIGHTS

11.1 OVERVIEW

U.S. copyright laws have always had copyright renewal provisions. By renewing a copyright, an author was able to secure a copyright for a second term. This resulted in a longer terms of copyright and provided the author with a second chance to sell rights to the work. Under the 1909 Copyright Act, the original term of copyright was twenty-eight years. By renewal, the term of protection could be extended for a second term of twenty-eight years.

The 1976 Copyright Act continued renewals for works that were in their first term of copyright prior to January 1, 1978, but abolished the system for works published afterwards. The reasons behind the abolishment of the renewal system were two-fold. First, the copyright terms under the 1976 Act were considered sufficiently long so that renewal terms were unnecessary, and second, because of the ability to terminate grants (Chapter Nine), renewals were not needed for authors to reclaim rights to the copyrights.

11.2 RENEWALS UNDER THE 1909 ACT

Under the 1909 Act, if a copyright to a work was not renewed within the year prior to the expiration of the original term, it lapsed upon expiration of the original term. Works which were renewed were copyrighted for another twenty-eight years. A number of works not subject to control by the author were renewable by the copyright owners. These works are listed below:[1]

---

[1] §304(a) of the Copyright Act. The same provision was in the 1909 Act.

(1) posthumous works,[2]

(2) periodical, cyclopedic or other composite works upon which the copyright was originally secured by the proprietor thereof,

(3) any work copyrighted by a corporate body, or

(4) any work by an employee for whom such work is made for hire.

Other works, including a contribution by an individual author to a periodical or to a cyclopedic or other composite work, could only be renewed by the author.[3] If the author was dead, renewal could be done by a statutorily designated representative.[4] This procedure proved unfair to the individual author, since the renewal rights could not be freely assigned.

PURPOSES OF RENEWALS

Historically, renewals were considered to serve three purposes:

(1) Copyrights to works which were of little value were eliminated because of non-renewal.

(2) The term of copyright for viable works was extended because of renewal.

(3) The author was given the opportunity to regain control of the copyright being renewed.

11.3 THE "REAR WINDOW" CASE

The *Abend* or "Rear Window" case, discussed below, illustrates the complications and inequities that often resulted under the old renewal system.

In *Abend*,[5] the Supreme Court ruled that the re-release of the

---

[2] This is construed in cases to mean a work in which no assignment occurred during the author's lifetime.

[3] §304(a)

[4] If the author was not living, the widow, widower or children of the author could exercise the right of renewal. If there was no one in this group, the author's executors, or if there was no will, the author's next of kin, had renewal rights.

[5] *Stewart et al. v. Abend, dba Authors Research Co.*, No. 88-2102 S.Ct. (April 24, 1990), 18 USPQ 3d 1614.

film "Rear Window" infringed the renewal copyright in the underlying story. In 1945, film rights to the short story "It Had to be Murder" were assigned by the author, Cornell Woolrich, to a production company. In conjunction with the assignment, the author agreed to renew his copyright and to assign the renewal to the production company. The story was subsequently used as the basis for Alfred Hitchcock's motion picture "Rear Window," starring Jimmy Stewart. After the movie was released and before the copyright was renewed, Woolrich died.

Woolrich left no survivors, and Woolrich's executor renewed the copyright in the story and assigned the renewal rights to Abend. After the movie "Rear Window" was re-released, Abend sued Stewart, Hitchcock and various other parties for copyright infringement.

The district court found for the defendants, relying on a fair use defense that the owner of a derivative copyright could continue to use the work during the renewal term of the underlying copyright. The circuit court reversed, holding that the assignment of the renewal rights by the author did not defeat the statutory rights of the author's successor. Justice O'Connor, speaking for the Supreme Court, confirmed the circuit court's decision, holding that the author's successor to the renewal copyright is free and clear of any restrictions on the author.

What was particularly harsh about this decision was that the motion picture was a derivative work prepared legitimately under the original copyright. However, Judge O'Connor argued that if Congress had felt it necessary to make an exception for derivative works in renewal cases, it would have done so.

11.4 WHY THE RENEWAL SYSTEM FAILED

An author's ability to renew was often restricted. Formalities had to be complied with rigorously. Renewals had to be made during a limited period of time, long after a work was made. To make matters worse, often someone other than the author was charged with the duty.[6] Also, it was sometimes unclear who had renewal rights, since this depended on the state where the author was domiciled. As a result, if the renewal application was

[6] It has been estimated that eighty-five percent of all works were never renewed so that their copyrights expired after one term.

not submitted by the proper party within a prescribed period, the work entered the public domain.

The killing blow to renewals was rendered by the courts.[7] Utilizing principles of equitable estoppel, authors were prevented from disowning their previous contractual commitments if the right of renewal was sold with the first term of copyright. If the author was alive at the time of renewal, the original grant was confirmed. This thwarted one of the purposes for which renewals were put in the law, i.e., to give authors whose works had appreciated in value a chance to renegotiate.

The Writer and the Publisher

In the 1950's, Smith wrote and published a novel which achieved modest sales. Copyright title, including rights to make derivative works and all renewal rights, was assigned to the publisher. When the work came up for renewal in the 1980's, Fanfare Movies was interested in acquiring rights to make the novel into a motion picture.

The way the renewal should have worked was that Smith, who was still living, would have the right to the renewal and would be able to deal with Fanfare.

However, because of the estoppel rule, Smith's right of renewal inured to the benefit of the publisher. If Smith had been dead at the time of renewal and had been survived by a wife, the renewal right would have inured to her benefit. The inequities and unpredictability are evident since there was no way in telling who was going to own the renewal rights.

11.5 RENEWALS UNDER THE 1976 ACT

The 1976 Copyright Act discontinued renewals for works that were prepared on or after January 1, 1978. However, the renewal right was carried over for works in their first term of copyright on January 1, 1978.[8] Additionally, the renewal term of copyright was extended from twenty-eight to forty-seven years.[9]

---

[7] A leading case is *Fred Fisher Music Co. v. Witmark & Sons*, 318 U.S. 643 (1943) where it was held that the renewal rights may be assigned even though not expressly transferred.

[8] §304(a)

[9] ibid.

Under the 1976 Act, if a renewable work was posthumous, copyrighted by a corporate body, made as a work for hire or was a periodical, cyclopedic or other composite work, the copyright proprietor had renewal rights.[10] Works which did not fall within these groupings were renewable only by the author.[11] If the author was not alive, the renewal rights were owned by designated dependents of the author or the author's estate.[12] Renewals were required to maintain copyright protection and had to be made within *one year* prior to the expiration of the original copyright.

Renewal Too Soon

Cowboy Joe writes a western novel. The work was published November 30, 1960. Therefore, the twenty-eighth year of the copyright began on November 30, 1987. Cowboy Joe was told that the sooner he renewed the better, but that he had to wait until the last year of the copyright.

Cowboy Joe applied for a renewal copyright on December 15, 1987. The application was rejected as untimely. What Cowboy Joe forgot was that all copyright terms were extended by the 1976 Act, so that they all uniformly expire on December 31. Therefore, Cowboy Joe was two weeks too soon.

11.6 COPYRIGHT RENEWAL ACT OF 1992

Even after the 1976 Act, complaints continued about the formalities of renewals. As a result, sixteen years after the 1976 Copyright Act, the Copyright Renewal Act of 1992 was signed into law.[13] This Act extended first term copyrights for the renewal term and made application of renewal optional. The effect was that works published between January 1, 1964 and December 31, 1977 were automatically renewed for a renewal term of forty-seven years.[14] To encourage voluntary renewal, the law provides

---

[10] §304(B)

[11] §304(C)

[12] ibid.

[13] This legislation was signed by President Bush on June 26, 1992. P.L. 102-307, 106 Stat. 264.

[14] §304(a)(2)(A)

that renewal within the last year of the copyright constitutes *prima facie* evidence of the validity of the copyright:[15]

> If an application to register a claim to the renewed and extended term of copyright in a work is made within one year before its expiration, and the claim is registered, the certificate of such registration shall constitute *prima facie* evidence as to the validity of the copyright during its renewed and extended term and of the facts stated in the certificate....

If a work is renewed later, the evidentiary weight accorded the registration is at the discretion of the court.[16] This provision erodes the presumption of validity by filing a renewal.

The 1992 Act provided that the basic renewal procedures of the 1909 and 1978 Acts were to be followed.[17] Certain works can be renewed by the copyright owner, whoever that is, and other works can only be renewed by individual authors or their statutorily designated representative.[18]

If a renewal application is filed within one year prior to the expiration of the original term, the renewal right rests in the person who was entitled to renew when the application for renewal was made.[19] Otherwise, the renewal right rests in the person entitled to the renewal on the last day of the original term of copyright.

Also, the 1992 Act clarified the status of derivative works prepared under grants of the original copyright. If no renewal application was filed within the year preceding the expiration of the original term, the derivative work may continue to be used during the renewal term.[20]

Published works whose copyright terms were extended can be renewed even though the works were not originally registered. Since "registration" is defined to include both original registrations and renewal registrations, statutory damages and attorney fees are recoverable for both.

---

[15] §304(a)(4)(B)
[16] ibid.
[17] §304(a)(B) and (C)
[18] ibid.
[19] §304(a)(4)(A)
[20] ibid.

11.7 PARTIES HAVING RENEWAL RIGHTS

Where works are subject to the exclusive renewal rights, the order of the parties entitled to renew is:[21]

(i) the author of such work, if the author is still living,

(ii) the widow, widower, or children of the author, if the author is not living,

(iii) the author's executors, if such author, widow, widower, or children are not living, and

(iv) the author's next of kin, in the absence of a will.

The author's spouse and children comprise one class for renewal purposes and share the interest in the work proportionally according to the number of members in the class.[22] This is different than under the termination of grants rules (see Chapter Nine).

RENEWAL DEFINITIONS: WIDOW, WIDOWER AND CHILDREN

Do not make the mistake of assuming that the definitions of "widow," "widower" and "children" in Section 101 of Copyright Act apply to renewals. These definitions were intended for terminations of grants. The common law interpretations of terms "surviving spouse" and "children" developed under the 1909 law apply to renewals. A surviving spouse and children are construed to constitute one class and share the renewal right proportionally. Also, illegitimate and adopted children, although provided for under the 1976 Act, may not be allowed inheritance rights since this was the rule under common law.

---

[21] §304(a) amended.

[22] Thus, if the survivors are a spouse and three children, each party is entitled to a twenty-five percent ownership interest. If only the spouse and one child survive, each would have a fifty percent interest.

11.8 RENEWAL APPLICATION

The designated party must submit Form RE, Appendix M, together with the proper fee to the Copyright Office.[23] This form is used regardless of which class was originally registered. The renewal can be filed during the last year of the initial term, or at anytime during the renewal term.[24]

No new deposit of the copyrighted work is required when making a renewal. The effective date of the renewal is the date on which an acceptable renewal application and fee are received by the Copyright Office.

11.9 CROSS REFERENCES

See Chapter Eight on copyright terms. Chapter Nine deals with termination of grants and Chapter Fourteen presents problems of renewals relative to wills. Copies of Renewal Form RE, Addendum to RE and Form RE CON are also included in Appendices M, N and O.

---

[23] At the time of publication of this book, the fee was $20.
[24] §304(a)(3)(A)

Chapter Twelve:

COPYRIGHT INFRINGEMENT

12.1 OVERVIEW

Litigation is the engine that drives our legal system. Laws are passed, but their interpretation is left to the courts. Little would be known about the scope of the copyright or other laws, or their application to particular situations, if it was not for legal actions.

The Copyright Act provides two grounds for copyright infringement actions.[1] The plaintiff can allege that the defendant infringed one or more of the plaintiff's exclusive rights of copyright. Alternatively, the plaintiff can claim that copies or phonorecords of the work were imported by the defendant into the U.S. without the plaintiff's consent.

Federal district courts have *original and exclusive* jurisdiction of any civil copyright infringement action.[2] Jurisdiction exists without regard to the amount of the dispute or citizenship. Venue lies wherever the defendant can be found for the purpose of serving a complaint.

12.2 PREREQUISITES OF SUIT

Copyright infringement suits cannot be brought without *standing*. The plaintiff must have been the legal or the beneficial owner at the time that the exclusive right of copyright was infringed.[3] The defendant must have violated one of the plaintiff's exclusive rights of copyright or must have authorized or provided means for the infringement (contributory infringer).

A condition precedent for bringing a suit for copyright infringement is that the copyright must have been registered with

---

[1] §501(a) of the Copyright Act.
[2] 28 U.S.C. § 1338(a)
[3] §501(b)

119

the U.S. Copyright Office.[4] The registration requirement is satisfied by filing a complete copyright application with the proper deposit and fee.[5] Another condition of bringing a copyright infringement suit is that the suit must be brought within the prescribed time period. The statute of limitations for bringing a civil infringement action is *three* years from when the claim accrued.[6] This means that the plaintiff must sue within three years of the last infringement. Usually this will not be a problem since the infringement will likely be ongoing, and, if anything, the plaintiff will only lose some damages.

STATE COURT ACTIONS

Although Federal courts have exclusive jurisdiction for copyright infringement actions, state courts handle a number of copyright claims. Contracts, transfers and licenses regarding copyrights are construed under state law and may be litigated in state courts.

If a copyright license or transfer is litigated in a state court, the court must apply applicable federal law. For example, the requirement that copyright transfers must be in writing cannot be ignored.

The interplay between federal and state law and courts is complicated. Sometimes it is difficult to determine which court has jurisdiction. When an agreement is executed in one state and is litigated in another state, even determining the applicable state law may be difficult.

---

[4] §411(a). This requirement is excused for Berne Convention works which have a foreign country as the country of origin.

[5] By paying an extra processing fee of $200 and adequately explaining the reason for urgency, examination can be requested on a priority basis.

[6] §507(b). In a case where a work is published, the claim for unauthorized reproduction would accrue upon publication. A claim for distribution, however, would not accrue until copies or phonorecords of the work had been sold.

Multiple defendants can be joined in an action.[7] The court is required to give notice of the suit to other parties whose interests may be affected. Any party claiming an interest in the copyright who desires to join the suit may do so.[8]

12.3 ELEMENTS OF PROOF

The plaintiff must prove that the defendant infringed one or more of the copyright owner's exclusive rights e.g., reproduction, distribution, preparation of derivative works, public performance or pubic display. Unauthorized copying can be proven from the defendant's admissions or testimony, or by witnesses who testify that they saw the defendant do the copying. Usually, however, copying is established circumstantially by showing (1) that the defendant had access to the work and (2) that there was "substantial similarity" between the two works. Access may be implied if the works are "strikingly similar."

In determining substantial similarity, both ideas and expressions are considered. A two-part test for determining infringement has been established by the courts:

(1) Do the works have substantial similarity in the general ideas?

(2) Do the works have substantial similarity in expression?

The former goes to the total concept, or fundamental essence of the work, excluding the mere idea of the underlying work.[9] The latter represents the traditional approach to copyright infringement where a portion or portions of a work is duplicated in another work.

In determining *substantial similarity* between two works, it is the similarities that are most important. If sufficient similarities exist, the differences will usually not preclude a finding of infringement.

---

[7] Actual and contributory infringers are jointly and severally liable. This allows the plaintiff to collect an award of damages from any of the defendants that have assets.

[8] §501(b)

[9] An example sometimes given is *The West Side Story* and *Romeo and Juliet*. Even though the settings are vastly different, the events and interplay of the characters are substantially identical.

12.4 PLEADINGS AND DISCOVERY

A suit is commenced by filing a complaint with the proper court. A copy and summons are served by the court on each defendant. The complaint identifies the parties and explains the basis for jurisdiction and venue. The rights of the plaintiff that were violated are usually stated as alternative counts of action with the strongest counts first. The complaint ends with a prayer for relief. The certificate of registration should be attached to any complaint.

The defendant responds by filing an answer. The answer generally denies the counts raised by the plaintiff and pleads any special defenses. If desired, the answer may include counterclaims.

Unless there is a motion for a temporary restraining order or preliminary injunction, the next step is discovery. Discovery allows the parties to gauge the strength of the other party's case. After the parties have tested each other during discovery, settlement is often possible.

There are several varieties of discovery. There are written interrogatories and oral depositions. Written interrogatories are inexpensive and easy to do, but can easily be sidestepped. Oral depositions are taken before a court reporter under oath and allow the deposer to reframe questions and probe for inconsistencies. The parties can ask for admission of facts. A request for admissions is a useful adjunct to oral depositions since, even if the party being deposed does not know the facts, reasonable efforts must be taken to find them.[10]

Also, the parties can be asked to provide copies of various documents, or to be allowed to inspect pertinent goods or properties. All relevant documents except those that represent privileged communications between the client and attorney may be requested.[11]

A note of caution should be heeded by the parties to an infringement suit. Discovery is like a boomerang. What you throw

---

[10] Thus, if a question is asked in a deposition, the answer could always be that the party does not know or does not remember.

[11] Even documents that are not directly relevant but which are reasonably calculated to lead to relevant documents can be discovered.

at the other party tends to return in kind. The Golden Rule of Discovery is, "Do not unto others what you would not want done unto you."

12.5 DEFENSES

There are a number of ways that a defendant can defend against a suit for copyright infringement. The defendant can allege that:

• The plaintiff was not the owner of the copyright of the exclusive rights being infringed at the time of the alleged infringement.

• The defendant's use was fair use and therefore not an infringement. Because fair use allows such a wide latitude, this defense is almost automatic.

• The work was independently created by the defendant. If there was an earlier work that both the plaintiff and defendant utilized, this argument can be fairly effective.

• The copyright was void because of lack of originality. Again, this works best when there are pre-existing works.

• The copyright has not been registered with the Copyright Office. This is generally little more than a delaying tactic since the defect can usually be cured.

• The defendant had a license from the plaintiff or another party. In these days of multiple ownership, being able to establish a license from another source is a distinct possibility.

• The plaintiff abandoned or forfeited the copyright. This is getting to be a harder defense to rely upon. However, for copyrights that were published pre-Berne Convention with lack of notice, this can be a good defense.

• The plaintiff violated the antitrust laws or otherwise misused the copyright laws. Success depends on the facts and what smoking guns the plaintiff left.

• The action being complained of occurred outside the three-year statute of limitations.

• The plaintiff is estopped to bring the action because the defendant was misled into believing that his actions would not constitute an infringement. This line of defense arises from the fact that while assignments have to be in writing, licenses can be oral or *implied from a course of conduct*.

The above listing of defenses is exemplary rather than inclusive, and inventive counsel will be able to develop many additional arguments. No case is perfect, and whatever flaws exist will soon become painfully apparent.

COMPUTER PROGRAMS

The standard tests of substantial similarly do not work very well for computer programs. Line by line copying is unlikely, and there are no plots, characterization or dialogue patterns to compare.

What has evolved with computer programs is a "total concept and feel" test. If two programs have the same concept and feel, or look and feel, they are treated as being substantially similar.

In determining look and feel, the courts look for similarities in data structure files, in screen outputs and in sub-routines. What was taken, not what was added to the program, is generally determinative.

12.6 TAKING THE INFRINGEMENT TO TRIAL

Some copyright infringement cases go to trial, where testimony is taken in court. The case can either be decided by a judge, or either party can demand a jury trial. At trial, both sides will present their case. Burden of proof of infringement is originally on the plaintiff. However, burden is on the defendant to overcome the presumed validity of the copyright. Usually, each side will have expert witnesses to address the issue of substantial similarity.

Most copyright cases are fact driven, and the law sometimes takes some strange twists as the courts try to do justice. Witnesses can make or break a case, and their selection is critical. Everything else being equal, the side which has the best attorneys and best witnesses and which devotes the most effort to pre-trial preparation will usually prevail.

12.7 REMEDIES

The Copyright Act provides for a wide range of remedies. The plaintiff can seek monetary damages, the defendant's profits, an injunction, or to have the infringing articles impounded and destroyed. Statutory damages, attorney fees and court costs may also be recoverable.

12.7.1 Injunctions

A temporary restraining order can be sought and both preliminary and final injunctions may be granted. A temporary restraining order may be granted upon proof that the plaintiff is likely to be injured pending a hearing on a preliminary injunction.[12] A preliminary injunction may be granted upon proof that the plaintiff is likely to prevail on the merits at trail. A final injunction issues at the time of final judgment when the plaintiff wins.[13]

Injunctions may be enforced against the defendant anywhere in the U.S. If the defendant fails to comply with an injunction, the plaintiff can file a motion against the defendant for contempt of court.[14]

12.7.2 Damages

Monetary damages are intended to compensate the copyright proprietor for losses incurred by the unauthorized taking

---

[12] To seek a temporary restraining order, the plaintiff has to post a bond.

[13] The court does not have to grant an injunction even if infringement is found. In the "Rear Window" case, the court in effect issued a compulsory license. The plaintiff was compensated, but the defendant could show the picture. See *Stewart v. Abend*, No. 88-2102 S.Ct. (April 24, 1990), 18 USPQ 2d 1614.

[14] Sometimes the plaintiff will go after a defendant who agrees to stop the infringement; however, knowing that the defendant is untrustworthy, the plaintiff files suit and gets a consent decree where the defendant admits infringement and agrees to cease. This allows the plaintiff to file a contempt of court action if the defendant violates the injunction.

of his or her copyrighted work. Damages can be actual or statutory.[15] Actual damages are those which are proven by the plaintiff to be attributable to the infringement, e.g., loss of profits. Since proving actual damages is difficult, the law provides for the recovery of statutory damages, if certain conditions are met.

Statutory damages are discretionary with the plaintiff and can be elected any time before final judgment.[16] Statutory damages can be awarded over a wide range, i.e., $500-$20,000, as the court considers just.[17] If the infringement was innocent, the court may award damages as little as $200; if done willfully, the damages may be increased to as much as $100,000.[18] There are several problems with statutory damages. The election to take statutory damages relates to *all* infringements of any one work.[19] Furthermore, statutory damages are only available for infringements that take place after the copyright to the work was registered.[20] The copyright owner can not do anything about infringements that take place before registration, since this is controlled by the defendant. However, registration is a controllable process. *Where a work has potential commercial value, as a rule of thumb, it should be registered before or concurrently with publication.*

If a copyright notice was omitted from some copies of published works to which the defendant had access, the defendant can raise an innocent infringer defense to mitigate actual or statutory damages.[21] In the case of statutory damages, the plaintiff will receive damages from the lower end of the allowable range.

12.7.3 Profits

The plaintiff can also seek to recover the defendant's profits.[22] Profits are prorated so that the plaintiff only receives prof-

---

[15] §504(a)

[16] §504(c)(1). All parts of a derivative work or a compilation constitute one work.

[17] ibid.

[18] §504(c)(2)

[19] This means that the same range of statutory damages would apply whether someone made ten copies of a work or a thousand copies.

[20] For published works, a three-month grace period is provided.

[21] §401(d) and 402(d)

[22] §504(b)

its attributable to the infringement. There cannot be a double recovery of both the defendant's profits and the plaintiff's damages. Moreover, treble damages or profits are not available for copyright infringements, as they are in trademark infringement suits.

In establishing the defendant's profits, the plaintiff only has to provide proof of the defendant's gross revenues. The burden is on the defendant to establish any deductible expenses.[23] If the defendant is unable to prove any expenses, the plaintiff will take everything.

The Nude Photograph

Suppose that a nude photograph is taken by Joe photographer of an unknown lady. Years later, the subject of the photograph becomes famous, and the photograph is published in a prominent men's magazine without Joe's consent. Joe sues the publisher for copyright infringement.
The court finds in favor of Joe, and Joe decides to forego statutory damages and go for the publishers' profits. Joe proves the gross revenues associated with the issue of the magazine that included the infringing picture.
If the publisher fails to establish costs, Joe will recover everything. What the publisher needs to do is prove production costs and also put into evidence that the profits were attributable to a number of articles and photographs. This way, the net profits will be allocated, and Joe's recovery will be limited.

12.7.4 Impounding and Disposition

Impounding of the infringing works and duplicating equipment can be requested at any time during the pendency of an action.[24] The court can order the impounding of "all copies and phonorecords claimed to have been made or used in violation of the copyright owner's exclusive rights." Also subject to impoundment are "all plates, molds, masters, tapes, film negatives or other

---

[23] ibid.
[24] §503(a)

articles by means of which such copies or phonorecords may be reproduced."[25]

As part of its judgment, the court may order the "destruction or other reasonable disposition" of "all copies and phonorecords found to have been made in violation of the copyright owner's exclusive rights, and the articles by means of which such copies and phonorecords may be reproduced."[26]

CRIMINAL SANCTIONS FOR INFRINGEMENT OF COPYRIGHT (§2319 OF Title 18)

According to copyright law, any person who commits an offense willfully and for purposes of commercial advantage or private financial gain:
(1) shall be imprisoned not more than five years, or fined in the amount set forth in this title, or both, if the offense consists of the reproduction or distribution, during any 180-day period, of at least ten copies or phonorecords, or one or more copyrighted works, with a retail value of more than $2,500;
(2) shall be imprisoned not more than ten years, or fined in the amount set forth in this title, or both, if the offense is a second or subsequent offense under paragraph (1); and
(3) shall be imprisoned not more than one year, or fined in the amount set forth in this title, or both, in any other case.

12.7.5 Attorney Fees and Court Costs

The award of attorney fees and court costs is discretionary with the court.[27] Recovery of costs may be allowed against any party other than the U.S.[28] Attorney fees only go to the prevailing party and must be reasonable in amount.[29] Attorney fees,

---

[25] ibid.

[26] §503(b)

[27] §505

[28] ibid. Costs were mandatory to the prevailing party under the 1909 Act.

[29] ibid. The courts are divided on whether bad faith or irresponsibility on the part of the losing party is required.

like statutory damages, can only be recovered for acts of infringements that take place after registration.[30]

12.8 CRIMINAL SANCTIONS

The Copyright Act was amended in 1992 to make criminal sanctions applicable to infringements of all types of copyrighted works.[31] Before passage of this Act, criminal actions could only be brought where sound recordings, motion pictures or other audiovisual works were infringed. Now, any person who infringes a copyright owner's rights willfully and for purposes of commercial advantage or private financial gain is a potential criminal infringer.[32] The enhanced sanctions under Section 2319 are limited to the rights of *reproduction and distribution*. As in the case of civil infringements, there is a three-year statute of limitation.[33]

12.9 CROSS REFERENCES

Reference is made to Chapter Six for key cases on fair and unfair use. A landmark case on derivative works is found in Chapter Eleven.

---

[30] The copyright owner should not be under a delusion that his or her attorney fees will be fully recovered. That never happens. Judges are reluctant to award attorney fees, and when awarded, they generally represent only a fraction of the total costs.

[31] The sanctions allow for up to five years imprisonment if at least ten copies are made within a 180-day period worth $2500. Up to ten years imprisonment can result for a second or subsequent offense. Up to one year imprisonment and $2500 fine are provided in other cases. Fines are set according to Federal Uniform Sentencing Guidelines. Maximum for an individual is $250,000, and for a corporation, $500,000.

[32] §506(a)

[33] §507(a)

Chapter Thirteen:
PROTECTION OF TITLES AND CHARACTERS

13.1 OVERVIEW

The courts have held that the copyright laws do not protect titles to literary works, and the Copyright Office has concurred with this position. Logically, there is no reason for a work to be protected by copyright and for its title not to be, but that is the law.

Lack of copyright protection aside, protection for titles may be found in trademark and unfair competition law. If a title is distinctive, it may be protectable under Federal or state trademark laws, or under unfair competition laws. The possibility of trademark protection for titles is strongest where the work belongs to a series. Titles to unitary (stand alone) works require secondary meaning.

Depending on the characterization, literary characters, including their appearances, may be protected. Character protection is especially important for merchandise licensing. In the entertainment industry, it is often the case that more money is made from product licensing than from the motion picture itself.

Protecting titles and characters under the trademark laws has several advantages. One advantage is that infringers cannot use the defense that they did not know about a previous work, since liability for trademark infringement is based on likelihood of confusion, not conscious copying. Also, intent to use trademark applications, which relate back to the filing date, can be filed before the name is in use, to protect future merchandisable names.

COPYRIGHTS AND TRADEMARKS

Copyrights and trademarks are overlapping forms of protection. Authors need to understand and differentiate between them. Copyrights have limited, albeit long, terms. Trademarks, if used, can last forever. Copyrights result automatically when a tangible work is created. Trademarks result by selling a product or supplying a service under a distinctive name or mark.

Example: Mary Jane writes a computer program, which she refers to as "Cal Calc," to plan meals whereby the caloric content of food is displayed once the portions of the ingredients in a meal are designated. As she writes the program, it is automatically copyrighted. Mary Jane files an intent to use trademark application on "Cal Calc" to protect the name. However, in order for the trademark registration to issue, she will have to sell the program under the Cal Calc mark in commerce.

13.2 PROTECTION OF LITERARY TITLES

Protection for titles of literary works depends on the type of work and whether a title is inherently distinctive.[1] Under trademark law, if a title is non-descriptive of a work, it is protectable. If the title is descriptive, it can only be protected if it has "secondary meaning." Secondary meaning is achieved when a work is associated with a particular source by a significant portion of the public. Examples of highly successful works which have non-descriptive titles are *Gone with the Wind* and *Roots*. For these titles, proving secondary meaning is quite easy. However, if a title is descriptive of the work, or the public exposure of the work is minimal, establishing secondary meaning may be difficult.

For example, in one case the publishers of *PT 109 — John F. Kennedy In World War II* failed in an effort to prevent use of the title, *John F. Kennedy & PT-109*. Secondary meaning could not be

---

[1] The term "literary works" is used to refer to titles to books, plays, periodicals, motion pictures, television shows, etc.

established since these were about the only words one could use to describe the subject matter.[2]

SECONDARY MEANING

Secondary meaning can be established by introducing evidence of the following kinds:
(1) The length and continuity of public use;
(2) The amount of money spent on advertising;
(3) The total sales that have been made;
(4) The geographical and product market areas; or
(5) The dissimilarity of the title to other titles.
To show public usage, the author can prove prior sales of the work or show pre-release information and press releases. The more open and widespread the usage and the greater the advertising and sales promotion, the better the chances for proving that the title is distinctive. Another way to establish secondary meaning is through surveys. Surveys can be conducted by means of personal or telephone interviews. Surveys are best performed by reputable survey organizations utilizing proper survey techniques.

13.2.1 Unitary Works

Since the title for a unitary work is deemed to be descriptive of the work it represents, trademark protection is not presumed. The author must prove secondary meaning by showing commercial success. The greater the sales and advertising, the more likely that secondary meaning can be shown.

13.2.2 Series of Works

Titles for series of works, if distinctive, are protectable as trademarks. The titles for a series of works, e.g., magazine or newsletter titles, may be registered with the U.S. Patent and Trademark Office as periodicals. Proof of secondary meaning is

---

[2] *McGraw-Hill Book Co. v. Random House, Inc.*, 132 USPQ 530, 32 Misc. 2d 704, 225 N.Y.S. 2d 646 (1962).

only required in instances where the title is descriptive of the work.[3]

13.2.3 Titles in Different Mediums

Based on an apparent sponsorship theory, it is possible to extend the use of literary titles to articles of merchandise such as clothing, games and toys. The Trademark Act protects against false designation of origin and gives the author leverage to prevent others from expanding into collateral product areas.[4]

13.3 PROTECTION OF CHARACTERS

Contrary to titles, characters are not automatically precluded from copyright protection. However, copyright protection for characters is not assured, and authors may have to seek protection under the trademark laws, as is the case with titles.

Whether the copyright to a work will protect a character apart from the elements of the plot depends on several factors. Key considerations are the development of the character in the original work, the similarity of the appropriated work to the original work and the use to which the appropriated work is put.

The legal issues for protection of a literary character are (1) whether the character is sufficiently described to command copyright protection and (2) whether the alleged infringer copies such characterization, as opposed to a broader idea. If a character is developed sufficiently by the author, an image will be created in the mind of the reader, and copyright infringement may be found.

In a Second Circuit case, Judge Augustus Hand set forth the premise that characters, if sufficiently developed, can be protected independently of a story's plot.[5] However, the Ninth Circuit found that Sam Spade in *The Maltese Falcon* was not copyrighted. In this particular case, the court ruled that rights to the

---

[3] The applicant can avoid a descriptiveness rejection by amending to the Supplemental Register. Therefore, even if a title is descriptive, it can be registered, provided that there have been sales in commerce.

[4] §43(a) of the Lanham Act.

[5] *Nichols v. Universal Corp.*, 45 F.2d 110 (2nd Cir. 1930), *cert. denied*, 282 U.S. 905 (1931).

independent use of the character had not been conveyed when the copyright to the movie was sold.[6] While the Sam Spade decision is still followed in California, other jurisdictions tend to follow Judge Hand's view of predictability.

Although court decisions differ, the general rule is that even if a character is protected, subsequent authors may use general ideas and concepts associated with the character, but not the specific expression of the original character. For example, in a case between the creators of Superman and the creators of the Great American Hero, the court found that even though Superman was sufficiently developed to be copyrighted, only the idea and not the expression was taken by the Greatest American Hero characterization.[7]

13.3.1 Cartoon Characters

The copying of cartoon characters generally results in a copyright violation since the drawings are subject to copyright protection independent of the overall work. In the *Air Pirates* case, Mickey Mouse and other Disney cartoon characters were granted protection independently from the stories in which they appeared on the basis that the primary appeal of the works lay with the characters.[8]

13.3.2 Characters in Audiovisual Works

Characters in audiovisual works fall between literary characters and cartoon characters with regard to protectable interests. The characters are not subject to automatic copyright protection as cartoons characters are, but because of their visual aspect, they are easier to protect than literary characters.

In a landmark case involving the movie "Star Wars," the producers of the movie and the licensee, Kenner, sued Ideal Toy for infringement of the characters Darth Vader, C-3PO and R2-D2.

---

[6] *Warner Bros. Pictures v. Columbia Broadcasting Systems Inc.*, 216 F.2d 945 (9th Cir. 1954), *cert. denied*, 348 U.S. 971 (1955).

[7] *Warner Bros. v. American Broadcasting Cos.*, 530 F. Supp. 1187 (S.D.N.Y 1982), *aff'd.* 720 F.2d 751 (9th Cir. 1978).

[8] *Walt Disney Productions v. Air Pirates*, 345 F. Supp. 108 (1972), *aff'd* 581 F.2d 751 (9th Cir. 1978), *cert. denied*, 439 U.S. 1132 (1979).

The court accepted that characters could be protected separate from a work and allowed that three-dimensional designs could infringe a two-dimensional design, but in holding for the defendant, found that the physical similarities were not substantial.[9]

13.3.3 Characters Promoting Products

Literary or cartoon characters that have been delineated sufficiently to have a life of their own are protected against wrongful appropriation in the sale of collateral products. However, where the characters are being reproduced without any elements of plot or personality, the copying has to be extremely close for there to be infringement.

For example, in a case involving the well-known Pink Panther character, United Artists sued Ford for using an animated cougar in advertisements for its Cougar motor cars.[10] The plaintiff lost because the court found that the cougar did not physically resemble the Pink Panther character enough for there to be infringement.

However, any additional associations beyond the basic reference to the original source may be fatal. In a case involving the main character from the movie "E.T.," the court held that E.T. was a copyrightable character and that use of the E.T. name in conjunction with phrases associated with the movie such as "I Love You" and "Phone Home" constituted infringement.[11]

13.4 SELECTING TITLES AND NAMES

For marketing purposes, publishers and producers usually prefer short descriptive titles, but from a legal standpoint they are usually undesirable. The less descriptive a title and the more arbitrary and unique it is, the better the chances of protecting it, which dictates the use of longer non-descriptive titles.

Not only should writers and publishers consider whether a title is proper from a marketing standpoint, but also whether the title is free from conflicts with other names and titles. Once a

---

[9] *Ideal Toy Co. v. Kenner Products*, 443 F. Supp. 291 (S.D.N.Y. 1977)

[10] *United Artists Corp. v. Ford Motor Co.*, 483 F.Supp. 89 (S.D.N.Y. 1980)

[11] *Universal City Studios v. Kamar Industries, Inc.*, 212 USPQ 1162 (S.D. Tex. 1982)

tentative name for a book or periodical has been selected, the title should be searched to determine if it has been used or claimed by others. A search can be made through the card indexes or computerized databases at the library. Alternatively, on-line database searches through a service like Dialog, which offers books in print and trademark database searching, can be very helpful. If cost is no problem, an outside specialist or law firm can be hired to do the search.

THOMSON & THOMSON COPYRIGHT RESEARCH GROUP

Title searches determine the availability of a literary title. Titles can be researched for books, motion pictures, plays, television programs, etc. Character names and names of musical or other performing groups can also be searched.

Copyright searches can be ordered to determine if a specific work is copyrighted and to trace copyright ownership. A copyright search for a book includes information on the author, the publisher, copyright registration and renewal data, as well as a listing of derivative works such as motion pictures and plays.

Thomson & Thomson's Copyright Research Group in Washington, D.C. specializes in title searches. Searches can be ordered by calling 800-356-8630 (in D.C. 202-546-8046).

Names of major characters in fictional works should also be searched. In addition to making sure that the character names do not infringe the rights of another party, the author has to be concerned whether a character name of a real person was used.

Considerable experience is required to determine whether a title or name would infringe a reference. While it is more costly for a trademark attorney to do the search, an opinion generally comes with it.

Another option is to leave the searching to the publisher. This is an acceptable risk for large publishers, but there is no telling what the quality of the search would be if performed by some of the small presses.

13.5 INTENT TO USE TRADEMARKS

A new tool is available that can be used to protect titles for periodical works, e.g., magazines or a series of books. Previously, a title had to be used *in commerce* before a trademark application could be filed. However, since 1989, it has been possible to file intent to use trademark applications protecting marks in advance of actual use.

In an intent to use situation, an application is filed claiming the mark and specifying the goods, e.g., "a periodical publication." Filing is constructive use and is equivalent to actual use throughout the U.S.

Once filed, the application is examined by the U.S. Patent and Trademark office, and if there are no conflicting federal registrations, the mark is published for opposition. If no opposition is filed during the opposition period (30 days, extendible to 120 days), a notice of allowance will issue.

The applicant then has six months from the notice of allowance to provide proof of use of the mark. However, upon petition, one or more additional extensions may be taken. Once proof of use is shown, the application will be registered.

This procedure offers writers, publishers and producers a means to get vested rights to titles and names which will be used for merchandising products. If a trademark application issues as a registration, the title or name relates back to its filing date for priority purposes.

13.6 CROSS REFERENCES

See Chapter Twelve for a review of copyright litigation.

Chapter Fourteen:

WILLS AND INHERITANCE

14.1 OVERVIEW

Copyright is a species of intangible personal property which is testamentarily transferable by the author to designated beneficiaries by will. If there is no will, the deceased person's property passes, by operation of law, to his or her heirs according to the laws of the state where the party resided.

Logically, an author should be able to grant copyright interests upon his or her death in the same manner as other property rights. However, what the author would like to do with his or her copyright interests and what can be done may differ significantly.

Because of renewal and termination of grant provisions (Chapters Nine and Eleven), the author may make certain bequeaths or enter into contracts only to have them overridden by parties outside his or her will. "Will bumping" can take place so that the author's copyrights are controlled by parties not of the author's choice.

Additionally, many states regulate income and property acquired or earned during marriage by giving each spouse certain property rights. Examples are community property states and states which give surviving spouses election rights against the decedent's will.

14.2 RENEWALS UNDER THE 1909 ACT

The right to renew copyrights under the 1909 Act for a second twenty-eight year term belonged exclusively to the author and certain statutorily designated parties. Any testamentary grants or grants made by an author while living that conflicted with the statutory order prescribed for renewal rights were void.

Because of a line of cases which held that the author was estopped to disavow previous grants (see Chapter Nine), the statute was overridden where the author was living at the time of renewal. However, if the author died before the renewal term commenced, any previous grantees of renewal rights received nothing. If the author died without a will, the renewal rights followed the statutory order in the copyright laws.

The Grant That Failed

Suppose that Carol assigned the original term of copyright to her pre-1978 published work on "The History of Indians in The Southwest" to Little Boy Blue Press. Renewal interests were assigned to the publisher.

Carol leaves the renewal rights in her will to her husband. She dies before the work is renewed. The publisher is the loser, since only a statutorily designated party can renew the registration, and Carol's husband was the next party in line.

In another scenario, assume that Carol had willed the renewal rights to her favorite niece, Sue, and then died before the renewal term starts. The renewal rights will still belong to her husband. In this case, both the publisher and the niece are losers. However, what if Carol survived until the renewal was made? Then, the publisher will own the renewal right since Carol would not be allowed to deny her grant.

14.3 RENEWALS UNDER THE 1976 ACT

The good news is that the 1976 Copyright Act did away with renewals for works published on or after January 1, 1978. The bad news is that the renewal system was continued for works which were in their first term of copyright on January 1, 1978.[1] The renewal process was designed to terminate once the first-term copyrights had completed a 28-year cycle.[2]

In accordance with the statutory order under the 1909 Act, renewal rights initially belonged to the author. If the author was dead, the renewal rights belonged to the author's widow, wid-

---

[1] §304(a) of the Copyright Act.
[2] This means that after December 31, 2006 there will no longer be any renewals. Until then, they are still around.

ower or children. Next in line were the author's executors acting in a fiduciary capacity for the legatees of copyright under the author's will. If the author died without a will, the author's next of kin acquired the renewal rights.

Any efforts by the author to grant the renewal rights to others, e.g., a publisher, were ineffective. However, not all works were restricted from transfer. Posthumous works, composite works where the copyright was originally secured by the proprietor, works copyrighted by a corporate body and works made for hire were renewable by the *copyright owner*.[3]

14.4 COPYRIGHT RENEWAL ACT OF 1992

The Copyright Renewal Act of 1992 made registration of renewals voluntary. The copyright renewal term for works subject to renewal between December 31, 1977 and January 1, 1964 was extended to forty-seven years. Therefore, the copyright term for qualifying works was extended to seventy-five years, whether a work was formally renewed.

If a copyright renewal application is submitted, it has to be submitted by the properly prescribed parties.[4] However, even if a renewal application is not filed, it still renews. In this case, it is owned by the statutory party or parties who owned the renewal rights on the last day of the original term.

The Novelist's Lover

In 1980, romance novelist, Joy, conveys the derivative work rights to her best selling novel, Fire in Her Eyes, *including rights of renewal, to Top Star Movie Studio. The copyright is due for renewal in 1995. Joy dies in 1990 and is survived by her husband. Her will leaves all her interests in the renewal copyright to her lover. Who has rights to the renewal term? The movie studio? The lover? Her husband?*
What the author did prior to her death and what she left in her will do not make any difference. The Copyright Act prescribes who will have the renewal right — the husband. Transferring

---

[3] §304(a)
[4] These parties are the same ones as were discussed in connection with the 1909 Act.

the renewal interest during her life and willing the rights in her will were meaningless transactions. The only way Top Star would have acquired the renewal right was if Joy were alive at the time the renewal was made.

14.5 RENEWAL CLASSES

An obvious question is whether the "widow, widower or children" constitute a single class, or whether the widow or widower have rights preferential to the children. This issue was addressed in *DeSylva*.[5]

The widow of songwriter George DeSylva, trying to exclude an illegitimate son, argued that the "widow or widower" constituted a separate class which would have priority over the author's children. The Ninth Circuit and the Supreme Court rejected this argument holding that the widow and children constituted a single class and that the widow and son shared the renewal interest. The argument that an illegitimate son did not qualify as a son for statutory purposes was rejected, since California allowed illegitimate children to inherit rights from a parent.

In *DeSylva*, the sharing was fifty-fifty, but what would happen if there were two children? Would the spouse get fifty percent and each child twenty-five percent, or would each party receive a one-third interest? There is no set answer, since it depends on the inheritance law where the author was domiciled.

14.6 GRANTS OF RENEWAL RIGHTS

Certain safeguarding actions can be taken to minimize the risks associated with acquiring copyrights rights of works that are still subject to renewal. The assignee, e.g., the publisher, can acquire the expectancy rights of the other parties who are in line to receive the renewal rights. For this to work, the assignee must take an assignment from each of the parties who are potential recipients of the renewal rights. Care should be taken to ensure that the agreements are supported by fees, or the transactions will fail.

---

[5] *DeSylva v. Ballentine*, 351 U.S. 570, 580 (1956)

Even if the assignee is willing to expend time and money acquiring rights, the effort may prove futile. If there are no widow, widower or children, the next of kin may be difficult to track down. Also, if the author moves to a different state, different parties could be involved.

14.7 TERMINATION OF GRANTS

The 1976 Act introduced a system of termination of grants (see Chapter Nine). Under it, the author and certain other statutorily designated parties can, by serving a notice of termination in a prescribed five-year window, terminate any previous transfers and licenses. The 1976 Act provides that the right of termination only pertains to *in vivo* grants by the author.[6] Therefore, testamentary grants are not revocable under the termination of grant provisions. However, the termination of grant rules are still important when drafting a will, since certain parties will be able to revoke the author's *in vivo* grants after the author is dead and may be able to re-acquire effective control of the author's copyrights.

The Author's Dilemma

Tom, a successful writer who incorporated his business, assigned the copyrights to all his works to the corporation. The corporation licenses various publishers to publish the assigned works.

Tom dies, and his heirs receive stock in the corporation. Normally, in this kind of situation, the corporation could carry on as before. But because copyrights are involved, there may be problems.

If Tom's heirs are different than the parties who have the statutory right of termination, not only may they find that the grants to the publishers are terminated, but also that the assignments to the corporation are voided. Normal estate planning procedures are kaput. Even the old reliable standby — trusts — is likely to fail. Setting up a trust, even an irrevocable trust, is a grant that would be terminable like anything else.

---

[6] §203(a) and 304(c). The latter provision covers the termination of rights with respect to renewals.

The parties who are entitled to exercise the right of termination depend on which right of termination is being exercised. One group has the termination rights with respect to transfers made before January 1, 1978 for works whose renewal terms were extended. Another group has termination rights for transfers made on or after January 1, 1978.

For pre-1978 transfers, the parties having termination rights are the same as those who have the right to renew the copyrights for a second term.[7] The order is: (1) the author, if living; (2) the widow, widower or children of the author, if the author is not living; (3) the author's executors, if the author, widow, widower or children are not living; and (4) the author's next of kin, in the absence of a will of the author.

For post-1978 transfers, a different statutory order is prescribed.[8] The right to terminate grants is initially vested in the author. If the author is dead and there are no surviving children or grandchildren, the right vests in the author's surviving spouse. If there is no surviving spouse, it vests in the author's surviving children and the surviving children of any dead child of the author on a *per stirpes* basis. If there are a surviving spouse and surviving children or grandchildren, the author's termination interest is owned one-half by the surviving spouse and one-half by the surviving children and the surviving children of any dead child, on *per stirpes* basis.

14.8 COMMUNITY PROPERTY RIGHTS

In the community property states, an author may be restricted in making testamentary grants of copyright interests.[9] The premise in these states is usually that any income received from earnings during marriage is jointly owned and, upon divorce or death, should be divided equally.[10]

---

[7] §304(c).

[8] §203

[9] A husband or wife can only give away what he or she owns. The spouse's part of the community property remains intact.

[10] Among the states there are differences in what is considered community property so that offering more precise guidelines is beyond the scope of this book.

> ### COMMUNITY PROPERTY RIGHTS
>
> Authors living in the eight community property states, i.e., Arizona, California, Idaho, Louisiana, New Mexico, Nevada, Texas and Washington, should exercise particular caution. They may not have full enjoyment to the copyrights to their works. Furthermore, authors should not conclude that there are no spousal copyright ownership problems because they do not reside in one of the above states.
> Under the Uniform Marital Property Act ("UMPA"), ownership of property acquired during marriage is shared, rights vest at creation, and title is non-determinative of ownership. So far, only Wisconsin has subscribed to UMPA.

This would seem to be compatible with the copyright laws. However, any requirement that royalties be shared for works published before marriage, or suggestion that the copyrighted works be jointly owned seems to be carrying protectionism too far in this age of equality.

To add to the authors' misfortune, some states, such as Texas, consider that income on personal property is community property. A liberal California case (which gets more press than it deserves) can be found on joint ownership.[11]

In *Worth*, a California divorce case, the husband argued that under the Copyright Act, the copyrights to several works he had authored during marriage belonged solely to him because copyright ownership initially vests in the author. However, the court considered the husband's authorship non-determinative and noted that the spousal contributions need not be identical. Then, seizing on the word "initially," the court noted that irrespective of the initial vesting, copyright interest is transferred by operation of law to the spouse.

To minimize potential problems, authors can try to preserve their rights of copyright by entering into prenuptial or postnuptial agreements. The author may seek a denouncement

---

[11] *In re Marriage of Susan and Frederick Worth*, Cal. Ct. of Appeals, 1st Appellate District, Oct. 25, 1987.

of any rights to any works prepared during the marriage and also obtain a conveyance back by the non-author spouse.

It is not only in the community property states where the author may have problems. Some states have adopted the principle of equitable distribution of property upon dissolution of marriage so that property acquired during marriage is divided regardless of its ownership. Also, other states may allow the surviving spouse to elect against the decedent's will.

Authors who have valuable works should seek professional estate planning assistance from advisors who are knowledgeable about copyrights. Copyright ownership introduces a number of complications, and it would be prudent to test the estate planner's knowledge about copyrights. It may take both a copyright attorney and an estate planning attorney working together to adequately deal with the situation.

14.9 CROSS REFERENCES

Chapter Three on ownership, Chapter Nine on termination of grants, and Chapter Eleven on renewals should be reviewed.

Chapter Fifteen:
INTERNATIONAL ASPECTS

15.1 OVERVIEW

As copyrights are the product of national laws, they are necessarily limited in their application to the territorial jurisdiction claimed by each country. Protection in a country depends upon compliance with the copyright laws of that country. There is no single international copyright that covers the U.S. and other countries. Nevertheless, copyright protection is often available for U.S. nationals in countries which are parties to common conventions, or have reciprocity agreements with the U.S.

Copyright interests of citizens and residents of the U.S. are protected internationally by bilateral treaties or under various copyright conventions. Bilateral treaties usually are negotiated between countries on a one-on-one basis. Conventions, on the other hand, usually have several different versions and are open to any qualifying countries that subscribe.

15.2 BILATERAL TREATIES

Copyright protection in the U.S. for works of foreign authors and works of U.S. authors abroad may be obtained by bilateral treaties. This procedure can be as simple as exchanging diplomatic notes, indicating that the U.S. and the other country will grant copyright protection to each other's nationals. Usually, a treaty for the reciprocal treatment of copyright rights is negotiated.

The U.S. has entered into over thirty bilateral treaties.[1] It is important to consider these treaties as adjuncts to the copyright conventions to be relied upon if needed. With respect to older works, a bilateral treaty may be the only form of protection which

---

[1] Circular 38(a), Appendix Q

is available. For example, although Canada did not join the UCC until 1962, a certification was made effective January 1, 1924 that the U.S. accords national treatment to Canadian citizens with respect to copyrighted works. Conversely, any U.S. work since that date has been protected in Canada.

Even where one or several of the copyright conventions are applicable, bilateral treaties should be considered. A copyright owner seeking to enforce rights abroad should look at the total package of rights that may be available.

15.3 THE PAN AMERICAN CONVENTION

Early in the twentieth century, the U.S. and seventeen Latin American countries ratified a series of treaties referred to as the Pan American Convention (PAC). The U.S. ratified the PAC in 1911. The PAC is a regional copyright treaty that provides protection to authors of the contracting countries who have secured an acknowledgment of copyright in their own country. To qualify a work for the PAC, a statement "indicating a reservation of the property right" should be put on the work concerned.

PAN AMERICAN CONVENTION NOTICE

The statement generally seen on works is "All Rights Reserved" or its Spanish equivalent "Todos los derechos reservados." This statement usually follows the U.S. statutory form of copyright notice. Arguably, the U.S. notice would in itself be a valid reservation of rights, but a careful claimant would include an additional reservation as noted above.

By using appropriate language of reservation, a U.S. author automatically has copyright protection for his or her works in PAC member countries without having to comply with local formalities such as registration.

15.4 THE UNIVERSAL COPYRIGHT CONVENTION

Early in the twentieth century, the U.S. and Europe went separate ways with regard to their copyright laws. The U.S.

adopted a highly structured copyright system, while most other countries followed the Berne Convention and had non-conditional copyright procedures. Because of the importance of U.S. works in the global marketplace, a mechanism for providing international copyright protection was needed. The Universal Copyright Convention (UCC) was devised following World War II to meet this need.

UCC NOTICE

Universal Copyright Convention rights result by compliance with copyright formalities in the author's country and inclusion of a notice on published works in the following form:

© OWNER'S NAME, YEAR

This is like the "Circle C" form of U.S. notice except that the "year of first publication" and "the copyright owner's name" are in reverse order. However, this difference is not considered substantive, and either format can be used.

Under U.S. law, the author has an option whether to use the "Circle C" form of notice, the word "Copyright," or the abbreviation "Copr." The "Circle C" form of notice is preferred since it conforms with both U.S. and UCC requirements.

The UCC, which was formed in 1954, was adhered to by the U.S. in 1955. Its principal feature was *nondiscrimination*. The UCC mandated that member nation must provide works by nationals of member countries, or works first published in member countries, the same copyright protection it grants to works of its own nationals. However, equality of protection alone would not offer any advantage over existing bilateral treaties if the foreign parties still had to comply with local formalities. Therefore, the UCC excused compliance with all formalities in respect to unpublished works.

For published works, the only formality that was required was use of the "Circle C" notice form which had been used under U.S. copyright law. Works first published in a UCC member country with the "Circle C" copyright symbol, accompanied by the name of the copyright owner and the year of first publication, were excused from all other copyright formalities such as publication, registration and payment of fees.

To ensure a minimum term of copyright protection for UCC participants, each signatory was required to provide copyright protection for at least twenty-five years.[2] The UCC has remained a fluid vehicle for change and has been amended at various times.

Berne availability notwithstanding, U.S. authors and publishers continue to use the "Circle C" form of notice to qualify for the UCC where international protection is desired.[3] Having both Berne and the UCC to rely on provides U.S. authors and publishers with the best of both worlds.

15.5 THE BERNE CONVENTION

Instead of an author or publisher having to copyright a work in a number of countries, under the Berne Convention, copyright protection is automatic. All published and unpublished Berne Convention works are protected in all member countries without complying with any formalities and without regard to the country of creation.

An unpublished work is a Berne Convention work if one or more of the authors is a national of a nation adhering to Berne. A published work is a Berne Convention work if written by a national of a nation adhering to Berne, or if the work was first published in, or was simultaneously (within thirty days) published in, a nation adhering to the Berne Convention.

During the years of debate that preceded the passage of the 1976 Copyright Act, a strong push was made to modify the U.S. laws to be Berne compatible. Although the effort failed, significant strides were made.

Under the 1976 Act, published and unpublished works were protected, registration was made permissive, a copyright term compatible with Berne was introduced and a number of previously incompatible formalities were eliminated. However, the goal of achieving Berne compatibility had to wait another de-

---

[2] This is for the first term if the country has more than one term.

[3] The major drawback to UCC protection is the compulsory licenses. If this is a sensitive subject, then UCC protection should be rethought.

cade. It wasn't until the Berne Convention Implementation Act was passed in 1988, that U.S. laws were sufficiently changed for the U.S. to adhere to Berne. There was still some question whether the U.S. really met Berne standards, and in 1990, moral rights and architectural rights for buildings were granted to conform to Berne requirements.

CONCURRENT CANADIAN PUBLICATION

Prior to adherence to Berne, U.S. publishers qualified under the Berne Convention using a "back door" approach. A procedure was developed where a work by a U.S. author was "simultaneously published" in the U.S. and Canada. Publication within thirty days was considered to meet the simultaneous publication requirement under the Berne Convention. Therefore, protection under the Berne Convention was obtained in member countries by co-publication in Canada. Now that the U.S. is a direct party to Berne, co-publication is no longer necessary.

Because of U.S. participation, Berne is now clearly the dominant copyright convention in the world. The key to Berne's success has been its simplicity. A copyright results when a work is prepared, and all formalities or conditions of copyright, e.g., publication, registration, deposit and copyright notice, have been eliminated. As far as the future is concerned, it is important to note that, as with the case of the UCC, changes in Berne are on the horizon. Among other things, there is discussion of a longer minimum term.

However, copyright formalities are not a thing of the past just because the U.S. has finally joined the Berne Convention. Registration is still required in the U.S. as a condition of bringing infringement suits for Berne Convention works first published in the U.S. Also, various other formalities, while not conditions of copyright, give the owner certain legal advantages.[4]

---

[4] For example, registration results in liquidated damages and attorney fees, and use of a copyright notice forecloses an innocent infringer defense.

15.6 FOREIGN REGISTRATION

Despite international copyright conventions and bilateral treaties, the copyright owner or publisher should not rule out registration in countries of interest. Depending on the importance of the work, registration may be advantageous in selected foreign countries. Certainly, if a work is going to be published in a country, local registration should be considered. Also, consideration should be given to registering in countries where significant sales are anticipated. Finally, some countries do not belong to Berne or the UCC, which means that protection is only attainable via local registration. An example of such a country is Taiwan.

15.7 ENFORCEMENT OF RIGHTS

Determining whether copyright rights exist in a selected foreign country is simple. All one has to do is determine if the U.S. has treaty rights relating to copyrights with the country.[5] However, determining the *scope of protection* that exists in a given country can be a difficult matter.

Other countries may have entered into different versions of the copyright conventions than the U.S., which means that authors have to ascertain which versions of the conventions are applicable. Also, the effect of any bilateral treaties will have to be considered. Finally, one has to determine the local copyright law at the time of alleged infringement.

The rights accorded the copyright owner may be substantially different in foreign countries than in the U.S. For example, while there generally is no right of display abroad, moral rights of the author are, as a rule, more developed than in the U.S. Foreign countries may have special broadcast rights, while the U.S. does not. Even if it is known what laws apply, they may be enforced differently than in the U.S., and the courts may be subject to local influences.

The foregoing discussion illustrates the issues that can be raised and shows that the scope of foreign protection is nebulous and unpredictable. There are many questions and few definite answers. If authors wish to determine what copyright rights

[5] See Circular R38a, Appendix Q.

exist with respect to a specific work in a given country or countries, the best way to proceed is to engage an intellectual property firm that specializes in international trademark and copyright practice. The largest concentration of these firms is in the New York City area.

15.8 CROSS REFERENCES

Chapter Two reviews the changes in law leading up to U.S. adherence to Berne. Circular 38a in Appendix Q, on International Copyright Relations of the U.S. contains a wealth of information. A report of the GATT Copyright Regulations is in Appendix S.

Chapter Sixteen:

PUBLICATION

16.1 OVERVIEW

Following the 1976 Copyright Act, publishers have generally received exclusive licenses from their authors, leaving copyright title with the author. However, authors who contribute to periodicals are usually required to assign their copyrights to the publisher. If copyright ownership is retained by the author, certain rights must be licensed to the publisher. Conversely, if title is assigned to the publisher, certain rights should be retained by the author.

While neither the author nor publisher can do without the other, their interests often conflict. Nowhere is this more evident than in drafting provisions to publishing agreements. The agreements must balance the needs of the publisher to obtain rights necessary to publish a work against the author's interests to protect the work and maximize his or her return.

The process of formulating clauses for publishing agreements is ongoing. As changes are made in the copyright laws and as court cases are decided interpreting the law, refinements in the agreement clauses are made and new strategies are developed.

NEGOTIATING STRATEGY

When negotiating with publishers, one has to consider the overall picture and not get hung up on particular clauses. Another thing to remember is that the ultimate purpose of an agreement is to resolve future conflicts. The author wants to be published and receive an appropriate monetary reward. The publisher wants whatever publication rights it considers necessary and various legal safeguarding provisions. Within these parameters, there is a lot of room for negotiation.

Each publisher has standard form agreements which will be tendered to the author. These agreements, while obviously biased in the publisher's favor, address topics which, from experience, need to be covered. The author generally should be more concerned about what is missing than what is there.

A useful negotiating tactic is to draft an addendum of changes and attach these to the agreement tendered by the publisher. Frequently this will be found less objectionable by the publisher than if the agreement is rewritten.

16.2 ASSIGNMENT OR LICENSE

In any proposed publishing contract the question that must be addressed at the outset is which party — author or publisher — will be title holder of the copyright. This determination is fundamental to structuring the agreement.[1]

Under pre-1978 law, copyright title and the right to sue could only be in one party. Also, publication and registration were necessary for a statutory copyright. In this context, it made sense to assign title to the publisher, as normal operating procedure.

However, for works created after January 1, 1978, copyright title automatically vested in the author on creation, irrespective of whether the work is published.[2] Also, the owners of any *exclusive rights* have all the attributes of a copyright owner, which means that publishers can sue without having title. Finally, because of the possibility of defamation, right of privacy suits and other actions, publishers want the authors to absorb some of the possible exposure. The result has been that most book publishers now allow authors to retain the copyright for unitary works. They have found that with exclusive license rights, they can still publish the same as in pre-1978 days when they had legal title.[3] Because of the termination of grant provisions (see Chapter

---

[1] This author has seen agreements in which the publisher has tried to take rights both by assignment and exclusive license, apparently not realizing that the two procedures are mutually exclusive.

[2] With the passage of the Copyright Renewal Act of 1992, even works published before January 1, 1978 which are subject to renewal have had their terms automatically extended.

[3] Both assignments of title and exclusive license rights are considered to be transfers of copyright ownership.

Nine), no non-terminable assignment of the copyright rights could have been made anyway.

By leaving copyright title with the author, the author remains directly exposed if suit is brought by a third party. If the author is brought into the suit by the plaintiff, it is easier for the publisher to defend any claims or seek cross-indemnity.

From an author's perspective, granting an exclusive license is generally preferable to making an assignment. All rights which are not expressly licensed are retained. Although exclusive licenses can present problems of their own, it is better to have problems than not to have any rights.

Where the work is part of a composite work, e.g., periodical articles, the rules change. In these cases, publishers usually rightfully demand title. Therefore, authors of works which are combined with or incorporated into other works are still generally required to assign title of copyright.[4]

16.3 PRIMARY RIGHTS

Present day publishing agreements define the terms and conditions under which licensing rights are extended to the publisher. The rights given are a matter of negotiation. Certain rights are viewed by the publisher as being essential to market a work, while others are merely sought because they have been obtained in other agreements and the author does not object.

An exclusive right to print, publish, sell and license the work in the English language in the U.S. and Canada with non-exclusive rights in other countries is typical. An exclusive license gives the licensee the right to sue to enforce the licensed rights against others. This is all the publisher generally needs.

However, rights can not be decided in a vacuum; there must be a consideration of the work and where and how it will be marketed. Exclusive rights for other English speaking countries, e.g., the Philippines, the Commonwealth (excluding Canada), the Irish Republic and South Africa may be included. Grants of

---

[4] Basically, it is too difficult for a publisher to deal with people who contribute articles to magazines the same way as authors of novels or trade books. Also, where there is either no consideration or there is only a front-end payment, the effort involved in negotiating a publishing agreement is not justified.

exclusive rights for countries, other than the U.S. and Canada, are often conditioned so that they are revocable for nonperformance. Foreign language (translation) rights are often handled separately from the English language grants. The agreement should be structured so that any translation exclusives are revocable by the author for any language or country where rights have not been granted by the publisher after a designated period of time.

Publishers usually wait for a year to eighteen months to publish a work after acceptance. Authors normally would like to see things happen within a year or less of delivery of the completed manuscript. However, publishers frequently have such a large backlog that, except for works where current publication is critical, little can be done to move publication forward. This is when to check out the small publishers who are just getting started.

16.4 ROYALTIES

Royalties are usually on the order of ten to fifteen percent for hardcover editions and six to twelve percent for paperbacks (based on list price). A sliding scale royalty scale may be used which rewards the authors of popular works. Advances on royalties may be paid which are deducted from future royalty payments. Accounting is typically semi-annual with payment being made within ninety days after the designated date. However, the author may be able to negotiate for the immediate payment of royalties for the Commonwealth publication rights, foreign language rights or subsidiary rights, as they are pass through items. Advances of royalties may be possible, particularly for subsequent books.

16.5 SUBSIDIARY RIGHTS AND ROYALTIES

Subsidiary rights are secondary rights to the principal rights which are being granted. They include, for example:
- Publication by book clubs
- Publication of paperback reprints
- Publication in serial form
- Dramatic rights (including movies)

- Merchandising and ancillary rights

Book club, paperback rights and merchandising rights are normally split fifty-fifty between the author and publisher. The author usually obtains a proportionately larger share of the first serialization rights (pre-publication serial rights). Second serialization rights (post-publication serial rights) are usually shared fifty-fifty.

16.6 BOOBY TRAPS FOR THE AUTHOR

Some potential negotiating traps for the author to be aware of are noted below:
- The author should be careful about licensing the foreign language rights. Unless the publisher is going to actively pursue the placing of the work with foreign publishers, the author should retain the foreign language rights.[5]
- The author should generally favor granting licenses over making assignments. There should be a reversionary clause in licenses returning copyright rights to the author a reasonable period of years after publication.
- The author should not relinquish film rights to the publisher unless hired in the first instance to write a screen play. If the book is later converted into a movie, this generally has little to do with the publisher, and in any event, the publisher will likely benefit by having increased book sales.
- The author should not give up more than fifty percent of the paperback rights when the book is originally published in hardcover. A fifty-fifty split is standard if the publisher does some promotion.
- The author should not accept an option clause that gives the publisher the right to publish the author's next book under the *same* terms. If the first book is successful, the author is generally entitled to more favorable terms for the second.
- The author should limit the time the publisher has to consider the author's outline or manuscript or to exercise a publication option. It is a law of physics that matters come to rest on an editor's desk, and the more time allowed the publisher to respond the longer the wait for an answer.

---

[5] If the author has an agent, the agent may be better able to place the foreign rights than the U.S. publisher.

- The author should refuse conditional advances and should never agree to pay back an advance if projected sales are not achieved. The publisher should know his own business and not overestimate the sales.
- The author should not routinely grant subsidiary rights to the publisher. Often, these are worth more than the original work. Also, the characters may become licensable entities and have utility separate and apart from the book and any sequels.

16.7 PERIODICAL PUBLICATIONS

Agreements relating to publishing articles in periodical works tend to be simple, if not non-existent. The author normally assigns copyright title to the publisher and makes certain minimal representations. Often there is no royalty payment, or only a nominal lump-sum fee upon acceptance or publication of the article.

Any rights of copyright that the author wishes to retain should be expressly reserved at the time of assignment. If this is not done, the author may be in the position of an infringer.

Authors who are employees of companies should be careful to reserve all rights to the work that the company may require. Most companies have publication review committees or legal staff to advise the authors.

16.8 THE AUTHOR'S WARRANTY

When a publisher receives a manuscript from a author, the publisher generally has no assurances except from the author about where the work came from or how it was derived. Therefore, the publisher may seek a warranty containing various representations from the author as a condition of publication.

The following represent warranty statements that have been sought by some publishers:

- That the author is the sole author of the work and that the work is original.
- That the work has not previously been published and is not in the public domain.
- That the author owns the copyright to the work and has not granted any prior licenses or assigned the work to others.

- That the work does not infringe the copyright of any third party.
- That the work does not defame or invade the privacy of any person or organization.
- That the work does not contain any matter that is scandalous, obscene or libelous.

While warranties vary, basically the publisher is seeking safeguarding language to show good faith in publishing the work. Some publishers may go a step further and seek an indemnity from the author to pay the publisher's damages and attorney fees in defending the work. *This kind of commitment is generally not in the author's best interest.*

CHECKLIST OF RETAINED RIGHTS FOR PERIODICAL PUBLICATIONS

Title to periodical publications usually must be assigned. Rights that the author or his or her company may wish to retain are noted below:

(1) The right to reproduce the work or excerpts thereof for personal or internal use by the author or his company.

(2) The right to prepare adaptations or compilations of the work. Without this reservation it would be an infringement for the author to prepare a derivative work.

(3) The right to give talks or lectures based on the work. If the author intends to make any oral presentations of the work, the right should be reserved.

(4) The right to display or perform the work or portions thereof (if applicable).

(5) All intellectual property rights other than copyright. The publisher does not need these rights and they should be expressly disclaimed.

(6) The right to approve requests that the publisher may subsequently receive from other parties to publish the work.

(7) Any moral rights that the author wants to claim in association with the work should be clearly stated.

16.9 WARRANTY CHECKLIST

The author's warranty should have a cap or maximum liability limit which is low enough so that the author will not be too adversely affected. Traditionally, in intellectual property agreements, a limitation is put on the licensor's liability which is based on a percent of the net royalties received by the licensor. A similar arrangement should be sought in publishing agreements. If an indemnification is required, if possible it should be limited to fifty percent of the royalties received by the author, net of any agent commissions or other deductions. Of course, if an absolute dollar limit can be negotiated, this should also be acceptable.

In addition to negotiating a cap, the author can further limit warranties by:

• having the publisher agree to assume a certain amount of initial expense (e.g., $10,000) if the indemnification is triggered.

• requiring that any royalties withheld by the publisher pending a claim be placed in an interest-bearing escrow account.

• expressly excluding any indemnification responsibility for material added or provided by the publisher. The book cover will normally come in this category.

• conditioning the applicability of the warranty against a final court judgment.

• requiring prompt written notice of any claim or action as a condition of the warranty.

• obtaining the rights to appoint an attorney of his or her choice to defend legal actions together with the right to approve any settlements.

• excluding from the publisher's indemnification any liability for consequential or indirect damages, including loss of profits.

• excluding risks assumed by the publisher. If the author brings a potential problem to the publisher's attention, and the publisher is willing to accept the risk, this item should be excluded.

• limiting the indemnification to actions brought for infringements or other causes of actions accruing in the U.S. so as to exclude foreign liability.

• limiting the indemnification to royalties earned for the

work in question. In no event should the author allow the pooling of royalties from other works that the publisher has published for indemnification purposes.

16.10 COPYRIGHT NOTICE AND REGISTRATION

The publishing agreement should require that a notice of copyright consistent with U.S. law and the Universal Copyright Convention appear on the work in the author's name. Also, the publisher should be required to provide the author with proof that the work has been registered in the author's name with the U.S. Copyright Office.[6]

16.11 DELIVERY OF MANUSCRIPT

The author is usually required to deliver two copies of the complete manuscript in a content and form satisfactory to the publisher.[7] This normally is interpreted to mean that all supplemental materials including attachments and indices will be required, as well any permissions that the author obtained.[8]

There may be a dispute between authors and publishers as to whether a submission is complete. To defend against subsequent claims by the publisher, the author should require that any deficiencies be notified in writing within a reasonable period of time.

16.12 PUBLISHING INSURANCE

Normally, the publisher will have insurance covering media perils, e.g., libel, defamation, invasion of privacy, right of publicity, trademark and copyright infringement and errors and admissions. Therefore, if sued, the publisher is protected by insurance.

---

[6] Registration offers a number of advantages and the author should make sure his or her work is properly registered with the U.S. Copyright Office.

[7] Sometimes computer diskettes are required as part of the delivery package.

[8] It is generally the author's duty, to obtain all necessary permissions or consents; however, for technical works, this burden can often be pushed off on the publisher.

Where, however, does this leave the author? Unless the author has insurance coverage, he or she may be out on a limb. Not only would the author likely have direct liability to the plaintiff, but if the insurance company settles a claim on behalf of the publisher, restitution could be sought against the author. The safest solution is for the author to be listed as a *named insured* on the publisher's policy. This protects the author to the same extent as the publisher, and the author and does not have to be concerned about being sued by the insurance company in subrogation to the publisher.

16.13 LITERARY AGENTS

There are three things to know about literary agents. First, there is nothing sacred about them since anyone can be one. Second, it is very hard for new authors to find agents willing to represent them. Third, there is little uniformity in literary agents' terms and conditions.

Therefore, if you use an agent, find out the agent's background. How long has the agent been in business and how many books has the agent placed? What authors does the agent represent? What publishers has the agent placed books with? What expenses are charged? What is the agent's share of royalties? Is the agent a member of any literary agents associations? The author should add to this list questions of his or her own.

In addition to providing a hand-holding service to the author, agents are considered to perform two primary functions: (1) finding a publisher and (2) negotiating the publishing agreement. Authors who have their publisher already lined up usually have no trouble finding an agent to represent them.

Agents function as a screening service for the publishers. Agents usually have connections with certain publishers, and as a direct result, publishers more readily review submissions from those agents than those received directly from authors. Agents are supposed to know the ins and outs of the publishing business and, like sports agents, be able to get their clients the best deals possible.

Authors who have placed their own books with publishers sometimes will solicit an agent to represent them during negotiations. Whether an agent is needed depends on the status of the author, the type of work and the services that the author needs the agent to perform. An author who prepares a first novel would find an agent useful, assuming that one can be obtained. An author of a trade book may be able to place it better without the help of an agent, since the agent would likely know little about the subject matter.

Agency agreements can be oral or written.[9] They can be limited to a single work, cover a defined field of works or be restricted to the author's output over a period of time. Agent commissions are usually between ten and fifteen percent of royalties and advances.

Some agents charge a fee for reading a work, others do not. The higher the reading fee, the more wary the author should be of the agent since some agents make their living this way. Usually, agents who are members of one of the literary agent's associations are required to follow certain standards and do not charge a reading fee.

The agent's commission is based on what the publisher pays the author so if there is no payment, there is no commission. From the author's standpoint, the agent's commission should be made pro rata out of each payment received. Sometimes, however, agents try to front-load commissions or expenses.

Usually the author's royalties and advances (if any) are paid to the agent. This way the agent is assured of receiving payment. The agent should redistribute the payments promptly to the author, less the agent's commission. If payments are deferred, a trust account should be considered.

16.14 CROSS REFERENCES

See Chapter Three on transfers and Chapter Nine on termination of grants.

---

[9] Some states have laws controlling agency agreements.

APPENDICES

APPENDIX A:
TABLE OF CASES

Salinger v. Random House, 811 F.2d 90 (2nd Cir. 1987), *cert. denied* 108 S.Ct. 213 (1987), p. 55-56

Stewart et al. v. Abend, dba Authors Research Co., No. 88-2102 S.Ct. (April 24, 1990), 18 USPQ 2d 1614, p. 112-113, 125

Universal City Studios v. Kamar Industries, Inc., 212 USPQ 1162 (S.D. Tex. 1982), p. 136

United Artists Corp. v. Ford Motor Co., 483 F. Supp. 89 (S.D. N.Y. 1980), p. 136

Walt Disney Productions v. Air Pirates, 345 F. Supp. 108 (1972), aff'd 581 F.2d 751 (9th Cir. 1978), *cert. denied* 439 U.S. 1132 (1979), p. 135

Warner Bros. Pictures, Inc. v. Columbia Broadcasting Systems Inc., 216 F.2d 945 (9th Cir. 1954), *cert. denied* 348 U.S. 971 (1955), p. 135

Warner Bros. Pictures, Inc. v. American Broadcasting Cos., 530 F. Supp. 1187 (S.D. N.Y. 1982), *aff'd.* 720 F.2d 751 (9th Cir. 1978), p. 135

APPENDIX B:
APPLICATION FORM TX (LITERARY WORKS)

FORM TX
For a Literary Work
UNITED STATES COPYRIGHT OFFICE

REGISTRATION NUMBER

_____

TX _____ TXU _____
EFFECTIVE DATE OF REGISTRATION

_____

Month _____ Day _____ Year _____

DO NOT WRITE ABOVE THIS LINE. IF YOU NEED MORE SPACE, USE A SEPARATE CONTINUATION SHEET.

1

TITLE OF THIS WORK ▼

PREVIOUS OR ALTERNATIVE TITLES ▼

PUBLICATION AS A CONTRIBUTION If this work was published as a contribution to a periodical, serial, or collection, give information about the collective work in which the contribution appeared. **Title of Collective Work ▼**

If published in a periodical or serial give: **Volume ▼**   **Number ▼**   **Issue Date ▼**   **On Pages ▼**

2   **a**

NAME OF AUTHOR ▼

DATES OF BIRTH AND DEATH
Year Born ▼   Year Died ▼

Was this contribution to the work a "work made for hire"?
☐ Yes
☐ No

AUTHOR'S NATIONALITY OR DOMICILE
Name of Country
OR { Citizen of ▶_____
Domiciled in▶_____

WAS THIS AUTHOR'S CONTRIBUTION TO THE WORK
Anonymous? ☐ Yes ☐ No
Pseudonymous? ☐ Yes ☐ No
If the answer to either of these questions is "Yes," see detailed instructions.

NATURE OF AUTHORSHIP Briefly describe nature of material created by this author in which copyright is claimed. ▼

NOTE

Under the law, the "author" of a "work made for hire" is generally the employer, not the employee (see instructions). For any part of this work that was "made for hire" check "Yes" in the space provided, give the employer (or other person for whom the work was prepared) as "Author" of that part, and leave the space for dates of birth and death blank.

b

NAME OF AUTHOR ▼

DATES OF BIRTH AND DEATH
Year Born ▼   Year Died ▼

Was this contribution to the work a "work made for hire"?
☐ Yes
☐ No

AUTHOR'S NATIONALITY OR DOMICILE
Name of Country
OR { Citizen of ▶_____
Domiciled in▶_____

WAS THIS AUTHOR'S CONTRIBUTION TO THE WORK
Anonymous? ☐ Yes ☐ No
Pseudonymous? ☐ Yes ☐ No
If the answer to either of these questions is "Yes," see detailed instructions.

NATURE OF AUTHORSHIP Briefly describe nature of material created by this author in which copyright is claimed. ▼

c

NAME OF AUTHOR ▼

DATES OF BIRTH AND DEATH
Year Born ▼   Year Died ▼

Was this contribution to the work a "work made for hire"?
☐ Yes
☐ No

AUTHOR'S NATIONALITY OR DOMICILE
Name of Country
OR { Citizen of ▶_____
Domiciled in▶_____

WAS THIS AUTHOR'S CONTRIBUTION TO THE WORK
Anonymous? ☐ Yes ☐ No
Pseudonymous? ☐ Yes ☐ No
If the answer to either of these questions is "Yes," see detailed instructions.

NATURE OF AUTHORSHIP Briefly describe nature of material created by this author in which copyright is claimed. ▼

3   **a**

YEAR IN WHICH CREATION OF THIS WORK WAS COMPLETED This information must be given ◀Year in all cases.

b **DATE AND NATION OF FIRST PUBLICATION OF THIS PARTICULAR WORK**
Complete this information ONLY if this work has been published.
Month▶ _____ Day▶ _____ Year▶ _____ ◀ Nation

4

See instructions before completing this space.

COPYRIGHT CLAIMANT(S) Name and address must be given even if the claimant is the same as the author given in space 2. ▼

TRANSFER If the claimant(s) named here in space 4 is (are) different from the author(s) named in space 2, give a brief statement of how the claimant(s) obtained ownership of the copyright. ▼

APPLICATION RECEIVED

ONE DEPOSIT RECEIVED

TWO DEPOSITS RECEIVED

REMITTANCE NUMBER AND DATE

DO NOT WRITE HERE OFFICE USE ONLY

MORE ON BACK ▶ • Complete all applicable spaces (numbers 5-11) on the reverse side of this page.
• See detailed instructions. • Sign the form at line 10.

DO NOT WRITE HERE
Page 1 of _____ pages

169

EXAMINED BY	FORM TX
CHECKED BY	

□ CORRESPONDENCE
Yes

FOR
COPYRIGHT
OFFICE
USE
ONLY

DO NOT WRITE ABOVE THIS LINE. IF YOU NEED MORE SPACE, USE A SEPARATE CONTINUATION SHEET.

PREVIOUS REGISTRATION Has registration for this work, or for an earlier version of this work, already been made in the Copyright Office?
□ Yes □ No If your answer is "Yes," why is another registration being sought? (Check appropriate box) ▼
a. □ This is the first published edition of a work previously registered in unpublished form.
b. □ This is the first application submitted by this author as copyright claimant.
c. □ This is a changed version of the work, as shown by space 6 on this application.
If your answer is "Yes," give: **Previous Registration Number** ▼   **Year of Registration** ▼

5

DERIVATIVE WORK OR COMPILATION Complete both space 6a and 6b for a derivative work; complete only 6b for a compilation.
a. **Preexisting Material** Identify any preexisting work or works that this work is based on or incorporates. ▼

b. **Material Added to This Work** Give a brief, general statement of the material that has been added to this work and in which copyright is claimed. ▼

6

See instructions
before completing
this space.

—space deleted—

7

REPRODUCTION FOR USE OF BLIND OR PHYSICALLY HANDICAPPED INDIVIDUALS A signature on this form at space 10 and a check in one of the boxes here in space 8 constitutes a non-exclusive grant of permission to the Library of Congress to reproduce and distribute solely for the blind and physically handicapped and under the conditions and limitations prescribed by the regulations of the Copyright Office: (1) copies of the work identified in space 1 of this application in Braille (or similar tactile symbols); or (2) phonorecords embodying a fixation of a reading of that work; or (3) both.

a □ Copies and Phonorecords   b □ Copies Only   c □ Phonorecords Only

8

See instructions.

DEPOSIT ACCOUNT If the registration fee is to be charged to a Deposit Account established in the Copyright Office, give name and number of Account.
Name ▼   Account Number ▼

CORRESPONDENCE Give name and address to which correspondence about this application should be sent. Name/Address/Apt/City/State/ZIP ▼

9

Be sure to
give your
daytime phone
◄ number

Area Code and Telephone Number ►

CERTIFICATION* I, the undersigned, hereby certify that I am the
Check only one ►
{ □ author
□ other copyright claimant
□ owner of exclusive right(s)
□ authorized agent of _____

of the work identified in this application and that the statements made
by me in this application are correct to the best of my knowledge.   Name of author or other copyright claimant, or owner of exclusive right(s) ▲

Typed or printed name and date ▼ If this application gives a date of publication in space 3, do not sign and submit it before that date.

_____ date ► _____

Handwritten signature (X) ▼

10

**MAIL
CERTIFI-
CATE TO**

Name ▼

**Certificate
will be
mailed in
window
envelope**

Number/Street/Apartment Number ▼

City/State/ZIP ▼

YOU MUST:
• Complete all necessary spaces
• Sign your application in space 10
SEND ALL 3 ELEMENTS
IN THE SAME PACKAGE
1. Application form
2. Nonrefundable $20 filing fee
   in check or money order
   payable to *Register of Copyrights*
3. Deposit material
MAIL TO
Register of Copyrights
Library of Congress
Washington, D.C. 20559

11

The Copyright Office
has the authority to ad-
just fees at 5-year intervals, based on changes
in the Consumer Price
Index. The next adjust-
ment is due in 1996.
Please contact the
Copyright Office after
July 1995 to determine
the actual fee schedule.

February 1993—100,000   ☆U.S. GOVERNMENT PRINTING OFFICE: 1993-342-581/60,504

APPENDIX C:
APPLICATION FORM VA (VISUAL ARTS)

FORM VA
For a Work of the Visual Arts
UNITED STATES COPYRIGHT OFFICE

REGISTRATION NUMBER

VA   VAU

EFFECTIVE DATE OF REGISTRATION

Month   Day   Year

DO NOT WRITE ABOVE THIS LINE. IF YOU NEED MORE SPACE, USE A SEPARATE CONTINUATION SHEET.

1

TITLE OF THIS WORK ▼   NATURE OF THIS WORK ▼ See instructions

PREVIOUS OR ALTERNATIVE TITLES ▼

PUBLICATION AS A CONTRIBUTION If this work was published as a contribution to a periodical, serial, or collection, give information about the collective work in which the contribution appeared.   **Title of Collective Work ▼**

If published in a periodical or serial give: Volume ▼   Number ▼   Issue Date ▼   On Pages ▼

2 a

NAME OF AUTHOR ▼   DATES OF BIRTH AND DEATH
Year Born ▼   Year Died ▼

Was this contribution to the work a   **AUTHOR'S NATIONALITY OR DOMICILE**   WAS THIS AUTHOR'S CONTRIBUTION TO
"work made for hire"?   Name of Country   THE WORK   If the answer to either
☐ Yes   OR ⎰ Citizen of ▶_____   Anonymous?   ☐ Yes ☐ No   of these questions is
☐ No   ⎱ Domiciled in▶_____   Pseudonymous?   ☐ Yes ☐ No   "Yes," see detailed instructions.

NOTE

Under the law, the "author" of a "work made for hire" is generally the employer, not the employee (see instructions). For any part of this work that was "made for hire" check "Yes" in the space provided, give the employer (or other person for whom the work was prepared) as "Author" of that part, and leave the space for dates of birth and death blank.

NATURE OF AUTHORSHIP Check appropriate box(es). **See instructions**
☐ 3-Dimensional sculpture   ☐ Map   ☐ Technical drawing
☐ 2-Dimensional artwork   ☐ Photograph   ☐ Text
☐ Reproduction of work of art   ☐ Jewelry design   ☐ Architectural work
☐ Design on sheetlike material

b NAME OF AUTHOR ▼   DATES OF BIRTH AND DEATH
Year Born ▼   Year Died ▼

Was this contribution to the work a   **AUTHOR'S NATIONALITY OR DOMICILE**   WAS THIS AUTHOR'S CONTRIBUTION TO
"work made for hire"?   Name of Country   THE WORK   If the answer to either
☐ Yes   OR ⎰ Citizen of ▶_____   Anonymous?   ☐ Yes ☐ No   of these questions is
☐ No   ⎱ Domiciled in▶_____   Pseudonymous?   ☐ Yes ☐ No   "Yes," see detailed instructions.

NATURE OF AUTHORSHIP Check appropriate box(es). **See instructions**
☐ 3-Dimensional sculpture   ☐ Map   ☐ Technical drawing
☐ 2-Dimensional artwork   ☐ Photograph   ☐ Text
☐ Reproduction of work of art   ☐ Jewelry design   ☐ Architectural work
☐ Design on sheetlike material

3 a b

YEAR IN WHICH CREATION OF THIS   DATE AND NATION OF FIRST PUBLICATION OF THIS PARTICULAR WORK
WORK WAS COMPLETED This information   Complete this information Month ▶ _____ Day▶ _____ Year▶ _____
◀Year must be given in all cases.   ONLY if this work has been published.   ◀ Nation

4

COPYRIGHT CLAIMANT(S) Name and address must be given even if the claimant is the same as the author given in space 2. ▼

See instructions before completing this space.

TRANSFER If the claimant(s) named here in space 4 is (are) different from the author(s) named in space 2, give a brief statement of how the claimant(s) obtained ownership of the copyright. ▼

APPLICATION RECEIVED

ONE DEPOSIT RECEIVED

TWO DEPOSITS RECEIVED

FUNDS RECEIVED

DO NOT WRITE HERE OFFICE USE ONLY

MORE ON BACK ▶ • Complete all applicable spaces (numbers 5-9) on the reverse side of this page.   **DO NOT WRITE HERE**
• See detailed instructions.   • Sign the form at line 6.   Page 1 of ___ pages

EXAMINED BY	FORM VA
CHECKED BY	

☐ CORRESPONDENCE
Yes

FOR
COPYRIGHT
OFFICE
USE
ONLY

DO NOT WRITE ABOVE THIS LINE. IF YOU NEED MORE SPACE, USE A SEPARATE CONTINUATION SHEET.

PREVIOUS REGISTRATION Has registration for this work, or for an earlier version of this work, already been made in the Copyright Office?

☐ Yes   ☐ No   If your answer is "Yes," why is another registration being sought? (Check appropriate box) ▼

a. ☐ This is the first published edition of a work previously registered in unpublished form.

b. ☐ This is the first application submitted by this author as copyright claimant.

c. ☐ This is a changed version of the work, as shown by space 6 on this application.

If your answer is "Yes," give: **Previous Registration Number** ▼   **Year of Registration** ▼

5

DERIVATIVE WORK OR COMPILATION Complete both space 6a and 6b for a derivative work; complete only 6b for a compilation.

a. **Preexisting Material** Identify any preexisting work or works that this work is based on or incorporates. ▼

b. **Material Added to This Work** Give a brief, general statement of the material that has been added to this work and in which copyright is claimed. ▼

6

See instructions
before completing
this space.

DEPOSIT ACCOUNT If the registration fee is to be charged to a Deposit Account established in the Copyright Office, give name and number of Account.

Name ▼   Account Number ▼

7

CORRESPONDENCE Give name and address to which correspondence about this application should be sent.   Name/Address/Apt/City/State/ZIP ▼

Area Code and Telephone Number ▶

Be sure to
give your
daytime phone
◀ number

CERTIFICATION* I, the undersigned, hereby certify that I am the

check only one ▼

☐ author

☐ other copyright claimant

☐ owner of exclusive right(s)

☐ authorized agent of _____

Name of author or other copyright claimant, or owner of exclusive right(s) ▲

of the work identified in this application and that the statements made
by me in this application are correct to the best of my knowledge.

Typed or printed name and date ▼ If this application gives a date of publication in space 3, do not sign and submit it before that date.

Date▶ _____

☞   **Handwritten signature (X)** ▼

8

Mail certificate to:	Name ▼
Certificate will be mailed in window envelope	Number/Street/Apt ▼
	City/State/ZIP ▼

YOU MUST:
• Complete all necessary spaces
• Sign your application in space 8

SEND ALL 3 ELEMENTS
IN THE SAME PACKAGE:
1. Application form
2. Nonrefundable $20 filing fee
   in check or money order
   payable to *Register of Copyrights*
3. Deposit material

MAIL TO:
Register of Copyrights
Library of Congress
Washington, D.C. 20559-6000

9

*17 U.S.C. § 506(e): Any person who knowingly makes a false representation of a material fact in the application for copyright registration provided for by section 409, or in any written statement filed in connection with the application, shall be fined not more than $2,500.

March 1995—300,000   ♲ PRINTED ON RECYCLED PAPER

☆U.S. GOVERNMENT PRINTING OFFICE: 1995-387-237/41

APPENDIX D:
APPLICATION FORM PA (PERFORMING ARTS)

FORM PA
For a Work of the Performing Arts
UNITED STATES COPYRIGHT OFFICE

REGISTRATION NUMBER

PA   PAU

EFFECTIVE DATE OF REGISTRATION

Month   Day   Year

DO NOT WRITE ABOVE THIS LINE. IF YOU NEED MORE SPACE, USE A SEPARATE CONTINUATION SHEET.

1

TITLE OF THIS WORK ▼

PREVIOUS OR ALTERNATIVE TITLES ▼

NATURE OF THIS WORK ▼ See instructions

2 **a**

NAME OF AUTHOR ▼

DATES OF BIRTH AND DEATH
Year Born ▼   Year Died ▼

Was this contribution to the work a "work made for hire"?
☐ Yes
☐ No

AUTHOR'S NATIONALITY OR DOMICILE
Name of Country
OR { Citizen of ▶_____
Domiciled in▶_____

WAS THIS AUTHOR'S CONTRIBUTION TO THE WORK
Anonymous? ☐ Yes ☐ No
Pseudonymous? ☐ Yes ☐ No
If the answer to either of these questions is "Yes," see detailed instructions.

NATURE OF AUTHORSHIP Briefly describe nature of material created by this author in which copyright is claimed. ▼

NOTE

Under the law, the "author" of a "work made for hire" is generally the employer, not the employee (see instructions). For any part of this work that was "made for hire" check "Yes" in the space provided, give the employer (or other person for whom the work was prepared) as "Author" of that part, and leave the space for dates of birth and death blank.

b

NAME OF AUTHOR ▼

DATES OF BIRTH AND DEATH
Year Born ▼   Year Died ▼

Was this contribution to the work a "work made for hire"?
☐ Yes
☐ No

AUTHOR'S NATIONALITY OR DOMICILE
Name of Country
OR { Citizen of ▶_____
Domiciled in▶_____

WAS THIS AUTHOR'S CONTRIBUTION TO THE WORK
Anonymous? ☐ Yes ☐ No
Pseudonymous? ☐ Yes ☐ No
If the answer to either of these questions is "Yes," see detailed instructions.

NATURE OF AUTHORSHIP Briefly describe nature of material created by this author in which copyright is claimed. ▼

c

NAME OF AUTHOR ▼

DATES OF BIRTH AND DEATH
Year Born ▼   Year Died ▼

Was this contribution to the work a "work made for hire"?
☐ Yes
☐ No

AUTHOR'S NATIONALITY OR DOMICILE
Name of Country
OR { Citizen of ▶_____
Domiciled in▶_____

WAS THIS AUTHOR'S CONTRIBUTION TO THE WORK
Anonymous? ☐ Yes ☐ No
Pseudonymous? ☐ Yes ☐ No
If the answer to either of these questions is "Yes," see detailed instructions.

NATURE OF AUTHORSHIP Briefly describe nature of material created by this author in which copyright is claimed. ▼

3 **a**

YEAR IN WHICH CREATION OF THIS WORK WAS COMPLETED This information must be given
◀Year in all cases.

b Complete this information ONLY if this work has been published.

DATE AND NATION OF FIRST PUBLICATION OF THIS PARTICULAR WORK
Month▶_____ Day▶_____ Year▶_____
◀ Nation

4

See instructions before completing this space.

COPYRIGHT CLAIMANT(S) Name and address must be given even if the claimant is the same as the author given in space 2. ▼

TRANSFER If the claimant(s) named here in space 4 is (are) different from the author(s) named in space 2, give a brief statement of how the claimant(s) obtained ownership of the copyright. ▼

DO NOT WRITE HERE
OFFICE USE ONLY

APPLICATION RECEIVED

ONE DEPOSIT RECEIVED

TWO DEPOSITS RECEIVED

FUNDS RECEIVED

MORE ON BACK ▶ • Complete all applicable spaces (numbers 5-9) on the reverse side of this page.
• See detailed instructions. • Sign the form at line 8.

DO NOT WRITE HERE
Page 1 of _____ pages

EXAMINED BY	FORM PA
CHECKED BY	
☐ CORRESPONDENCE Yes	FOR COPYRIGHT OFFICE USE ONLY

DO NOT WRITE ABOVE THIS LINE. IF YOU NEED MORE SPACE, USE A SEPARATE CONTINUATION SHEET.

PREVIOUS REGISTRATION Has registration for this work, or for an earlier version of this work, already been made in the Copyright Office?

☐ Yes ☐ No If your answer is "Yes," why is another registration being sought? (Check appropriate box) ▼

a. ☐ This is the first published edition of a work previously registered in unpublished form.

b. ☐ This is the first application submitted by this author as copyright claimant.

c. ☐ This is a changed version of the work, as shown by space 6 on this application.

If your answer is "Yes," give: **Previous Registration Number ▼**   **Year of Registration ▼**

5

DERIVATIVE WORK OR COMPILATION Complete both space 6a and 6b for a derivative work; complete only 6b for a compilation.

a. Preexisting Material Identify any preexisting work or works that this work is based on or incorporates. ▼

b. Material Added to This Work Give a brief, general statement of the material that has been added to this work and in which copyright is claimed. ▼

6

See instructions before completing this space.

DEPOSIT ACCOUNT If the registration fee is to be charged to a Deposit Account established in the Copyright Office, give name and number of Account.

Name ▼   **Account Number ▼**

CORRESPONDENCE Give name and address to which correspondence about this application should be sent.   Name/Address/Apt/City/State/ZIP ▼

Area Code and Telephone Number ▶

7

Be sure to give your daytime phone number ◀

CERTIFICATION* I, the undersigned, hereby certify that I am the

Check only one ▼

☐ author

☐ other copyright claimant

☐ owner of exclusive right(s)

☐ authorized agent of _____

Name of author or other copyright claimant, or owner of exclusive right(s) ▲

of the work identified in this application and that the statements made by me in this application are correct to the best of my knowledge.

Typed or printed name and date ▼ If this application gives a date of publication in space 3, do not sign and submit it before that date.

date ▶

☞ Handwritten signature (X) ▼

8

MAIL CERTIFI-CATE TO	Name ▼
Certificate will be mailed in window envelope	Number/Street/Apartment Number ▼
	City/State/ZIP ▼

YOU MUST:
• Complete all necessary spaces
• Sign your application in space 8

SEND ALL 3 ELEMENTS IN THE SAME PACKAGE:
1. Application form
2. Nonrefundable $20 filing fee in check or money order payable to *Register of Copyrights*
3. Deposit material

MAIL TO:
Register of Copyrights
Library of Congress
Washington, D.C. 20559-6000

9

The Copyright Office has the authority to adjust fees at 5-year intervals, based on changes in the Consumer Price Index. The next adjustment is due in 1996. Please contact the Copyright Office after July 1995 to determine the actual fee schedule.

*17 U.S.C. § 506(e): Any person who knowingly makes a false representation of a material fact in the application for copyright registration provided for by section 409, or in any written statement filed in connection with the application, shall be fined not more than $2,500.

July 1993—300,000   ♻ PRINTED ON RECYCLED PAPER   ✡U.S. GOVERNMENT PRINTING OFFICE: 1993-342-582/80,017

APPENDIX E:
APPLICATION FORM GR/CP (GROUP OF
CONTRIBUTIONS TO PERIODICALS)

ADJUNCT APPLICATION
for Copyright Registration for a
Group of Contributions to Periodicals

 **FORM GR/CP**

UNITED STATES COPYRIGHT OFFICE

- Use this adjunct form only if you are making a single registration for a group of contributions to periodicals, and you are also filing a basic application on Form TX, Form PA, or Form VA. Follow the instructions, attached.

- Number each line in Part B consecutively. Use additional Forms GR/CP if you need more space.

- Submit this adjunct form with the basic application form. Clip (do not tape or staple) and fold all sheets together before submitting them.

REGISTRATION NUMBER
TX   PA   VA

EFFECTIVE DATE OF REGISTRATION

. . . .
(Month)   (Day)   (Year)

FORM GR/CP RECEIVED

Page _____ of _____ pages

DO NOT WRITE ABOVE THIS LINE. FOR COPYRIGHT OFFICE USE ONLY

(A)

Identification of Application

IDENTIFICATION OF BASIC APPLICATION:
● This application for copyright registration for a group of contributions to periodicals is submitted as an adjunct to an application filed on: (Check which)

☐ Form TX   ☐ Form PA   ☐ Form VA

IDENTIFICATION OF AUTHOR AND CLAIMANT: (Give the name of the author and the name of the copyright claimant in all of the contributions listed in Part B of this form. The names should be the same as the names given in spaces 2 and 4 of the basic application.)

Name of Author: . . . .

Name of Copyright Claimant: . . . .

(B)

Registration for Group of Contributions

COPYRIGHT REGISTRATION FOR A GROUP OF CONTRIBUTIONS TO PERIODICALS: (To make a single registration for a group of works by the same individual author, all first published as contributions to periodicals within a 12-month period (see instructions), give full information about each contribution. If more space in needed, use additional Forms GR/CP.)

☐
Title of Contribution: . . . .
Title of Periodical: . . . . Vol. . . . . No. . . . . Issue Date . . . . Pages . . . .
Date of First Publication: . . . . Nation of First Publication . . . .
        (Month)   (Day)   (Year)   (Country)

☐
Title of Contribution: . . . .
Title of Periodical: . . . . Vol. . . . . No. . . . . Issue Date . . . . Pages . . . .
Date of First Publication: . . . . Nation of First Publication . . . .
        (Month)   (Day)   (Year)   (Country)

☐
Title of Contribution: . . . .
Title of Periodical: . . . . Vol. . . . . No. . . . . Issue Date . . . . Pages . . . .
Date of First Publication: . . . . Nation of First Publication . . . .
        (Month)   (Day)   (Year)   (Country)

☐
Title of Contribution: . . . .
Title of Periodical: . . . . Vol. . . . . No. . . . . Issue Date . . . . Pages . . . .
Date of First Publication: . . . . Nation of First Publication . . . .
        (Month)   (Day)   (Year)   (Country)

☐
Title of Contribution: . . . .
Title of Periodical: . . . . Vol. . . . . No. . . . . Issue Date . . . . Pages . . . .
Date of First Publication: . . . . Nation of First Publication . . . .
        (Month)   (Day)   (Year)   (Country)

☐
Title of Contribution: . . . .
Title of Periodical: . . . . Vol. . . . . No. . . . . Issue Date . . . . Pages . . . .
Date of First Publication: . . . . Nation of First Publication . . . .
        (Month)   (Day)   (Year)   (Country)

☐
Title of Contribution: . . . .
Title of Periodical: . . . . Vol. . . . . No. . . . . Issue Date . . . . Pages . . . .
Date of First Publication: . . . . Nation of First Publication . . . .
        (Month)   (Day)   (Year)   (Country)

FOR
COPYRIGHT
OFFICE USE
ONLY

DO NOT WRITE ABOVE THIS LINE. FOR COPYRIGHT OFFICE USE ONLY

Title of Contribution: . . . . Title of Periodical: . . . . Vol. . . . . No. . . . . Issue Date . . . . Pages . . . . . . Date of First Publication: . . . . Nation of First Publication . . . . (Month) (Day) (Year) (Country)	**B** **Continued**

Title of Contribution: . . .
Title of Periodical: . . . . . Vol. . . . . No. . . . . Issue Date . . . . Pages . . . . . .
Date of First Publication: . . . . . Nation of First Publication . . .
(Month)   (Day)   (Year)   (Country)

Title of Contribution: . . .
Title of Periodical: . . . . . Vol. . . . . No. . . . . Issue Date . . . . Pages . . . . . .
Date of First Publication: . . . . . Nation of First Publication . . .
(Month)   (Day)   (Year)   (Country)

Title of Contribution: . . .
Title of Periodical: . . . . . Vol. . . . . No. . . . . Issue Date . . . . Pages . . . . . .
Date of First Publication: . . . . . Nation of First Publication . . .
(Month)   (Day)   (Year)   (Country)

Title of Contribution: . . .
Title of Periodical: . . . . . Vol. . . . . No. . . . . Issue Date . . . . Pages . . . . . .
Date of First Publication: . . . . . Nation of First Publication . . .
(Month)   (Day)   (Year)   (Country)

Title of Contribution: . . .
Title of Periodical: . . . . . Vol. . . . . No. . . . . Issue Date . . . . Pages . . . . . .
Date of First Publication: . . . . . Nation of First Publication . . .
(Month)   (Day)   (Year)   (Country)

Title of Contribution: . . .
Title of Periodical: . . . . . Vol. . . . . No. . . . . Issue Date . . . . Pages . . . . . .
Date of First Publication: . . . . . Nation of First Publication . . .
(Month)   (Day)   (Year)   (Country)

Title of Contribution: . . .
Title of Periodical: . . . . . Vol. . . . . No. . . . . Issue Date . . . . Pages . . . . . .
Date of First Publication: . . . . . Nation of First Publication . . .
(Month)   (Day)   (Year)   (Country)

Title of Contribution: . . .
Title of Periodical: . . . . . Vol. . . . . No. . . . . Issue Date . . . . Pages . . . . . .
Date of First Publication: . . . . . Nation of First Publication . . .
(Month)   (Day)   (Year)   (Country)

Title of Contribution: . . .
Title of Periodical: . . . . . Vol. . . . . No. . . . . Issue Date . . . . Pages . . . . . .
Date of First Publication: . . . . . Nation of First Publication . . .
(Month)   (Day)   (Year)   (Country)

Title of Contribution: . . .
Title of Periodical: . . . . . Vol. . . . . No. . . . . Issue Date . . . . Pages . . . . . .
Date of First Publication: . . . . . Nation of First Publication . . .
(Month)   (Day)   (Year)   (Country)

Title of Contribution: . . .
Title of Periodical: . . . . . Vol. . . . . No. . . . . Issue Date . . . . Pages . . . . . .
Date of First Publication: . . . . . Nation of First Publication . . .
(Month)   (Day)   (Year)   (Country)

▲ October 1991—25,000

☆U.S. GOVERNMENT PRINTING OFFICE: 1991: 312-432/40,008

APPENDIX F:
APPLICATION FORM SE (SERIAL)

FORM SE
For a Serial
UNITED STATES COPYRIGHT OFFICE

REGISTRATION NUMBER

_____ U

EFFECTIVE DATE OF REGISTRATION

_____ _____ _____
Month   Day   Year

DO NOT WRITE ABOVE THIS LINE. IF YOU NEED MORE SPACE, USE A SEPARATE CONTINUATION SHEET.

1

TITLE OF THIS SERIAL ▼

Volume ▼ | Number ▼ | Date on Copies ▼ | Frequency of Publication ▼

PREVIOUS OR ALTERNATIVE TITLES ▼

2 **a**

NAME OF AUTHOR ▼

DATES OF BIRTH AND DEATH
Year Born ▼   Year Died ▼

Was this contribution to the work a "work made for hire"?
☐ Yes
☐ No

AUTHOR'S NATIONALITY OR DOMICILE
Name of Country
OR { Citizen of ▶_____
      Domiciled in▶_____

WAS THIS AUTHOR'S CONTRIBUTION TO THE WORK
Anonymous?   ☐ Yes ☐ No
Pseudonymous? ☐ Yes ☐ No
If the answer to either of these questions is "Yes," see detailed instructions.

NATURE OF AUTHORSHIP   Briefly describe nature of material created by this author in which copyright is claimed. ▼
☐ Collective Work   Other:

NOTE

Under the law, the "author" of a "work made for hire" is generally the employer, not the employee (see instructions). For any part of this work that was "made for hire" check "Yes" in the space provided, give the employer (or other person for whom the work was prepared) as "Author" of that part, and leave the space for dates of birth and death blank.

b

NAME OF AUTHOR ▼

DATES OF BIRTH AND DEATH
Year Born ▼   Year Died ▼

Was this contribution to the work a "work made for hire"?
☐ Yes
☐ No

AUTHOR'S NATIONALITY OR DOMICILE
Name of Country
OR { Citizen of ▶_____
      Domiciled in▶_____

WAS THIS AUTHOR'S CONTRIBUTION TO THE WORK
Anonymous?   ☐ Yes ☐ No
Pseudonymous? ☐ Yes ☐ No
If the answer to either of these questions is "Yes," see detailed instructions.

NATURE OF AUTHORSHIP   Briefly describe nature of material created by this author in which copyright is claimed. ▼
☐ Collective Work   Other:

c

NAME OF AUTHOR ▼

DATES OF BIRTH AND DEATH
Year Born ▼   Year Died ▼

Was this contribution to the work a "work made for hire"?
☐ Yes
☐ No

AUTHOR'S NATIONALITY OR DOMICILE
Name of Country
OR { Citizen of ▶_____
      Domiciled in▶_____

WAS THIS AUTHOR'S CONTRIBUTION TO THE WORK
Anonymous?   ☐ Yes ☐ No
Pseudonymous? ☐ Yes ☐ No
If the answer to either of these questions is "Yes," see detailed instructions.

NATURE OF AUTHORSHIP   Briefly describe nature of material created by this author in which copyright is claimed. ▼
☐ Collective Work   Other:

3 **a**

YEAR IN WHICH CREATION OF THIS ISSUE WAS COMPLETED This information must be given ◀Year in all cases.

b DATE AND NATION OF FIRST PUBLICATION OF THIS PARTICULAR ISSUE
Complete this information ONLY if this work has been published.   Month▶ _____ Day▶ _____ Year▶ _____ ◀ Nation

4

COPYRIGHT CLAIMANT(S) Name and address must be given even if the claimant is the same as the author given in space 2. ▼

See instructions before completing this space.

TRANSFER If the claimant(s) named here in space 4 is (are) different from the author(s) named in space 2, give a brief statement of how the claimant(s) obtained ownership of the copyright. ▼

APPLICATION RECEIVED

ONE DEPOSIT RECEIVED

TWO DEPOSITS RECEIVED

REMITTANCE NUMBER AND DATE

DO NOT WRITE HERE
OFFICE USE ONLY

MORE ON BACK ▶
· Complete all applicable spaces (numbers 5-11) on the reverse side of this page.
· See detailed instructions.   · Sign the form at line 10.

DO NOT WRITE HERE
Page 1 of _____ pages

EXAMINED BY	FORM SE
CHECKED BY	
☐ CORRESPONDENCE Yes	FOR COPYRIGHT OFFICE USE ONLY

DO NOT WRITE ABOVE THIS LINE. IF YOU NEED MORE SPACE, USE A SEPARATE CONTINUATION SHEET.

PREVIOUS REGISTRATION Has registration for this issue, or for an earlier version of this particular issue, already been made in the Copyright Office?

☐ **Yes** ☐ **No** If your answer is "Yes," why is another registration being sought? (Check appropriate box) ▼

a. ☐ This is the first published edition of an issue previously registered in unpublished form.

b. ☐ This is the first application submitted by this author as copyright claimant.

c. ☐ This is a changed version of this issue, as shown by space 6 on this application.

If your answer is "Yes," give: **Previous Registration Number** ▼   **Year of Registration** ▼

5

DERIVATIVE WORK OR COMPILATION Complete both space 6a and 6b for a derivative work; complete only 6b for a compilation.

a. **Preexisting Material** Identify any preexisting work or works that this work is based on or incorporates. ▼

b. **Material Added to This Work** Give a brief, general statement of the material that has been added to this work and in which copyright is claimed. ▼

6

See instructions before completing this space.

—space deleted—

7

REPRODUCTION FOR USE OF BLIND OR PHYSICALLY HANDICAPPED INDIVIDUALS A signature on this form at space 10 and a check in one of the boxes here in space 8 constitutes a non-exclusive grant of permission to the Library of Congress to reproduce and distribute solely for the blind and physically handicapped and under the conditions and limitations prescribed by the regulations of the Copyright Office: (1) copies of the work identified in space 1 of this application in Braille (or similar tactile symbols); or (2) phonorecords embodying a fixation of a reading of that work; or (3) both.

a ☐ Copies and Phonorecords   b ☐ Copies Only   c ☐ Phonorecords Only

8

See instructions.

DEPOSIT ACCOUNT If the registration fee is to be charged to a Deposit Account established in the Copyright Office, give name and number of Account.
Name ▼   **Account Number** ▼

9

CORRESPONDENCE Give name and address to which correspondence about this application should be sent.   Name/Address/Apt/City/State/ZIP ▼

Area Code and Telephone Number ▶

Be sure to give your daytime phone ◀ number

CERTIFICATION* I, the undersigned, hereby certify that I am the

Check only one ▶

☐ author
☐ other copyright claimant
☐ owner of exclusive right(s)
☐ authorized agent of _____

of the work identified in this application and that the statements made by me in this application are correct to the best of my knowledge.

Name of author or other copyright claimant, or owner of exclusive right(s) ▲

10

Typed or printed name and date ▼ If this application gives a date of publication in space 3, do not sign and submit it before that date.

_____ **date** ▶ _____

☞ Handwritten signature (X) ▼

MAIL CERTIFICATE TO

Certificate will be mailed in window envelope

Name ▼

Number/Street/Apartment Number ▼

City/State/ZIP ▼

YOU MUST:
• Complete all necessary spaces
• Sign your application in space 10

SEND ALL 3 ELEMENTS IN THE SAME PACKAGE:
1. Application form
2. Nonrefundable $20 filing fee in check or money order payable to *Register of Copyrights*
3. Deposit material

MAIL TO:
Register of Copyrights
Library of Congress
Washington, D.C. 20559-6000

11

The Copyright Office has the authority to adjust fees at 5-year intervals, based on changes in the Consumer Price Index. The next adjustment is due in 1996. Please contact the Copyright Office after July 1995 to determine the actual fee schedule.

*17 U.S.C. § 506(e): Any person who knowingly makes a false representation of a material fact in the application for copyright registration provided for by section 409, or in any written statement filed in connection with the application, shall be fined not more than $2,500.

April 1993—100,000

☆U.S. GOVERNMENT PRINTING OFFICE: 1993-342-581/60,511

APPENDIX G:
APPLICATION FORM SE/GROUP

FORM SE/GROUP ☑
UNITED STATES COPYRIGHT OFFICE

REGISTRATION NUMBER

EFFECTIVE DATE OF REGISTRATION
(Assigned by Copyright Office)

Month	Day	Year

APPLICATION RECEIVED

ONE DEPOSIT RECEIVED

EXAMINED BY   CORRESPONDENCE ☐

DO NOT WRITE ABOVE THIS LINE.

1

List in order of publication

No previous registration under identical title ☐

TITLE ▼   ISSN▼

Volume▼	Number▼	Issue date on copies▼	Month, day and year of publication ▼
1.			
2.			
3.			
4.			
5.			
6.			
7.			
8.			
9.			
10.			
11.			
12.			
13.			
14.			

2

NAME AND ADDRESS OF THE AUTHOR/COPYRIGHT CLAIMANT IN THESE COLLECTIVE WORKS MADE FOR HIRE

FOR NON-U.S. WORKS: Author's citizenship ▼   Domicile ▼   Nation of publication ▼

CERTIFICATION*:   I, the undersigned, hereby certify that I am the copyright claimant or the authorized agent of the copyright claimant of the works identified in this application, that all the conditions specified in the instructions on the back of this form are met, that I have deposited two complimentary subscription copies with the Library of Congress, and that the statements made by me in this application are correct to the best of my knowledge.

Signature (X) _____   Typed or printed name _____

PERSON TO CONTACT FOR CORRESPONDENCE ABOUT THIS CLAIM

Name ▶ _____

Daytime telephone number ▶ _____

Address (if other than given below) ▶ _____

DEPOSIT ACCOUNT

Account number ▶ _____

Name of account ▶ _____

MAIL CERTIFI-CATE TO

Certificate will be mailed in window envelope

Name▼

Number/Street/Apartment Number▼

City/State/ZIP▼

REPRODUCTION FOR USE OF BLIND OR PHYSICALLY HANDICAPPED INDIVIDUALS

a ☐ Copies and Phonorecords

b ☐ Copies Only

c ☐ Phonorecords Only

MAIL TO
Register of Copyrights
Library of Congress
Washington, D.C. 20559

*17 U.S.C. §506(e): Any person who knowingly makes a false representation of a material fact in the application for copyright registration provided for by section 409, or in any written statement filed in connection with the application, shall be fined not more than $2,500.

April 1991—100,000

☆ U.S. GOVERNMENT PRINTING OFFICE: 1991–282-170/20,016

APPENDIX H:
APPLICATION SHORT FORM SE

SHORT FORM SE
For a Serial
UNITED STATES COPYRIGHT OFFICE

REGISTRATION NUMBER

EFFECTIVE DATE OF REGISTRATION
(Assigned by Copyright Office)

Month	Day	Year

APPLICATION RECEIVED

ONE DEPOSIT RECEIVED

TWO DEPOSITS RECEIVED

EXAMINED BY

CORRESPONDENCE ☐

DO NOT WRITE ABOVE THIS LINE.

1 TITLE OF THIS SERIAL AS IT APPEARS ON THE COPY

Volume▼   Number▼   Date on Copies▼   ISSN▼

2 NAME AND ADDRESS OF THE AUTHOR AND COPYRIGHT CLAIMANT IN THIS COLLECTIVE WORK MADE FOR HIRE

3 DATE OF PUBLICATION OF THIS PARTICULAR ISSUE
Month▼   Day▼   Year▼

YEAR IN WHICH CREATION OF
THIS ISSUE WAS COMPLETED
(IF EARLIER THAN THE YEAR OF
PUBLICATION):
Year▼

CERTIFICATION*: I, the undersigned, hereby certify that I am the copyright claimant or the authorized agent of the copyright claimant of the work identified in this application, that all the conditions specified in the instructions on the back of this form are met, and that the statements made by me in this application are correct to the best of my knowledge.

☞ Handwritten signature (X) _____

Typed or printed name of signer _____

PERSON TO CONTACT FOR CORRESPONDENCE ABOUT THIS CLAIM

Name ▶ _____
Daytime telephone number ▶ _____
Address (if other than given below) ▶ _____

DEPOSIT ACCOUNT
Account number ▶ _____
Name of account ▶ _____

MAIL CERTIFICATE TO

Certificate will be mailed in window envelope

Name▼

Number/Street/Apartment Number▼

City/State/ZIP▼

YOU MUST
• Complete all necessary spaces
• Sign your application

SEND ALL 3 ELEMENTS IN THE SAME PACKAGE:
1. Application form
2. Nonrefundable $20 filing fee in check or money order payable to *Register of Copyrights*
3. Deposit material

MAIL TO:
Register of Copyrights
Library of Congress
Washington, D.C. 20559

Copyright fees are adjusted at 5-year intervals, based on increases or decreases in the Consumer Price Index. The next adjustment is due in 1995. Contact the Copyright Office in January 1995 for the new fee schedule.

*17 U.S.C. §506(e): Any person who knowingly makes a false representation of a material fact in the application for copyright registration provided for by section 409, or in any written statement filed in connection with the application, shall be fined not more than $2,500.

June 1992—50,000

☆U.S. GOVERNMENT PRINTING OFFICE: 1992—312-432/60,001

APPENDIX I:
APPLICATION FORM SR (SOUND RECORDING)

FORM SR
For a Sound Recording
UNITED STATES COPYRIGHT OFFICE

REGISTRATION NUMBER

_____

SR   SRU

EFFECTIVE DATE OF REGISTRATION

_____

Month   Day   Year

DO NOT WRITE ABOVE THIS LINE. IF YOU NEED MORE SPACE, USE A SEPARATE CONTINUATION SHEET.

1

TITLE OF THIS WORK ▼

PREVIOUS OR ALTERNATIVE TITLES ▼

NATURE OF MATERIAL RECORDED ▼ See instructions
☐ Musical   ☐ Musical-Dramatic
☐ Dramatic   ☐ Literary
☐ Other _____

2

a

NAME OF AUTHOR ▼

DATES OF BIRTH AND DEATH
Year Born ▼   Year Died ▼

Was this contribution to the work a "work made for hire"?
☐ Yes
☐ No

AUTHOR'S NATIONALITY OR DOMICILE
Name of Country
OR { Citizen of ▶_____
Domiciled in▶_____

WAS THIS AUTHOR'S CONTRIBUTION TO THE WORK
Anonymous? ☐ Yes ☐ No
Pseudonymous? ☐ Yes ☐ No

If the answer to either of these questions is "Yes," see detailed instructions.

NATURE OF AUTHORSHIP Briefly describe nature of material created by this author in which copyright is claimed. ▼

NOTE

Under the law, the "author" of a "work made for hire" is generally the employer, not the employee (see instructions). For any part of this work that was "made for hire," check "Yes" in the space provided, give the employer (or other person for whom the work was prepared) as "Author" of that part, and leave the space for dates of birth and death blank.

b

NAME OF AUTHOR ▼

DATES OF BIRTH AND DEATH
Year Born ▼   Year Died ▼

Was this contribution to the work a "work made for hire"?
☐ Yes
☐ No

AUTHOR'S NATIONALITY OR DOMICILE
Name of Country
OR { Citizen of ▶_____
Domiciled in▶_____

WAS THIS AUTHOR'S CONTRIBUTION TO THE WORK
Anonymous? ☐ Yes ☐ No
Pseudonymous? ☐ Yes ☐ No

If the answer to either of these questions is "Yes," see detailed instructions.

NATURE OF AUTHORSHIP Briefly describe nature of material created by this author in which copyright is claimed. ▼

c

NAME OF AUTHOR ▼

DATES OF BIRTH AND DEATH
Year Born ▼   Year Died ▼

Was this contribution to the work a "work made for hire"?
☐ Yes
☐ No

AUTHOR'S NATIONALITY OR DOMICILE
Name of Country
OR { Citizen of ▶_____
Domiciled in▶_____

WAS THIS AUTHOR'S CONTRIBUTION TO THE WORK
Anonymous? ☐ Yes ☐ No
Pseudonymous? ☐ Yes ☐ No

If the answer to either of these questions is "Yes," see detailed instructions.

NATURE OF AUTHORSHIP Briefly describe nature of material created by this author in which copyright is claimed. ▼

3

a YEAR IN WHICH CREATION OF THIS WORK WAS COMPLETED This information must be given in all cases. ◀ Year

b DATE AND NATION OF FIRST PUBLICATION OF THIS PARTICULAR WORK
Complete this information ONLY if this work has been published.
Month ▶_____ Day ▶_____ Year ▶_____ ◀ Nation

4

See instructions before completing this space.

COPYRIGHT CLAIMANT(S) Name and address must be given even if the claimant is the same as the author given in space 2. ▼

TRANSFER If the claimant(s) named here in space 4 is (are) different from the author(s) named in space 2, give a brief statement of how the claimant(s) obtained ownership of the copyright. ▼

DO NOT WRITE HERE OFFICE USE ONLY

APPLICATION RECEIVED

ONE DEPOSIT RECEIVED

TWO DEPOSITS RECEIVED

REMITTANCE NUMBER AND DATE

MORE ON BACK ▶
• Complete all applicable spaces (numbers 5-9) on the reverse side of this page.
• See detailed instructions.   • Sign the form at line 8.

DO NOT WRITE HERE
Page 1 of _____ pages

	EXAMINED BY	FORM SR
	CHECKED BY	
	☐ CORRESPONDENCE Yes	FOR COPYRIGHT OFFICE USE ONLY

DO NOT WRITE ABOVE THIS LINE. IF YOU NEED MORE SPACE, USE A SEPARATE CONTINUATION SHEET.

PREVIOUS REGISTRATION Has registration for this work, or for an earlier version of this work, already been made in the Copyright Office?
☐ **Yes** ☐ **No** If your answer is "Yes," why is another registration being sought? (Check appropriate box) ▼
a. ☐ This is the first published edition of a work previously registered in unpublished form.
b. ☐ This is the first application submitted by this author as copyright claimant.
c. ☐ This is a changed version of the work, as shown by space 6 on this application.
If your answer is "Yes," give: **Previous Registration Number** ▼   **Year of Registration** ▼

5

DERIVATIVE WORK OR COMPILATION Complete both space 6a and 6b for a derivative work; complete only 6b for a compilation.
a. Preexisting Material Identify any preexisting work or works that this work is based on or incorporates. ▼

b. Material Added to This Work Give a brief, general statement of the material that has been added to this work and in which copyright is claimed. ▼

6

See instructions
before completing
this space.

DEPOSIT ACCOUNT If the registration fee is to be charged to a Deposit Account established in the Copyright Office, give name and number of Account.
Name ▼   **Account Number** ▼

7

CORRESPONDENCE Give name and address to which correspondence about this application should be sent.   Name/Address/Apt/City/State/ZIP ▼

Area Code and Telephone Number ▶

Be sure to
give your
◀ daytime phone
number

CERTIFICATION* I, the undersigned, hereby certify that I am the
Check only one ▼
☐ author
☐ other copyright claimant
☐ owner of exclusive right(s)
☐ authorized agent of ——————————————————————————
             Name of author or other copyright claimant, or owner of exclusive right(s) ▲

8

of the work identified in this application and that the statements made
by me in this application are correct to the best of my knowledge.

Typed or printed name and date ▼ If this application gives a date of publication in space 3, do not sign and submit it before that date.
—————————————————————————————— date ▶ ——————————————

☞ Handwritten signature (X) ▼

**MAIL
CERTIFI-
CATE TO**

Name ▼

Number/Street/Apartment Number ▼

City/State/ZIP ▼

**Certificate
will be
mailed in
window
envelope**

YOU MUST:
• Complete all necessary spaces
• Sign your application in space 8
**SEND ALL 3 ELEMENTS
IN THE SAME PACKAGE:**
1. Application form
2. Nonrefundable $20 filing fee
   in check or money order
   payable to *Register of Copyrights*
3. Deposit material
MAIL TO:
Register of Copyrights
Library of Congress
Washington, D.C. 20559

The Copyright Office
has the authority to ad-
just fees at 5-year intervals, based on changes
in the Consumer Price
Index. The next adjust-
ment is due in 1996.
Please contact the
Copyright Office after
July 1995 to determine
the actual fee schedule.

9

*17 U.S.C. § 506(e): Any person who knowingly makes a false representation of a material fact in the application for copyright registration provided for by section 409, or in any written statement filed in connection
with the application, shall be fined not more than $2,500.
December 1993—75,000

☆U.S. GOVERNMENT PRINTING OFFICE: 1993-301-241/80,051

APPENDIX J:
APPLICATION FORM G/DN (GROUP/DAILY NEWSPAPERS)

FORM G/DN
For Group/Daily Newspapers
UNITED STATES COPYRIGHT OFFICE

REGISTRATION NUMBER

EFFECTIVE DATE OF REGISTRATION
(Assigned by Copyright Office)

Month	Day	Year

APPLICATION RECEIVED

ONE MICROFILM DEPOSIT RECEIVED

EXAMINED BY   CORRESPONDENCE ☐

DO NOT WRITE ABOVE THIS LINE.

1

TITLE OF THIS NEWSPAPER AS IT APPEARS ON THE COPIES ▼   City/State▼

Month and year date on copies ▼   Number of issues in this group ▼   ISSN▼   Edition▼

2

NAME AND ADDRESS OF THE AUTHOR/COPYRIGHT CLAIMANT IN THESE COLLECTIVE WORKS MADE FOR HIRE

3

DATE OF PUBLICATION OF THE FIRST AND LAST ISSUES IN THIS GROUP
Month▼   Day▼   Year▼

(First) _____

(Last)

REPRODUCTION FOR USE OF BLIND OR PHYSICALLY HANDICAPPED INDIVIDUALS
a ☐ Copies and Phonorecords
b ☐ Copies Only
c ☐ Phonorecords Only

CERTIFICATION*:   I, the undersigned, hereby certify that I am the copyright claimant or the authorized agent of the copyright claimant of the works identified in this application, that all the conditions specified in the instructions on the back of this form are met, and that the statements made by me in this application are correct to the best of my knowledge.

Handwritten   Typed or printed
signature (X) _____   name of signer _____

PERSON TO CONTACT FOR CORRESPONDENCE ABOUT THIS CLAIM   DEPOSIT ACCOUNT

Name ▶ _____   Account number ▶ _____

Daytime telephone number ▶ _____   Name of account ▶ _____

Address (if other than given below) ▶ _____

MAIL CERTIFI-CATE TO

Name▼

Number/Street/Apartment Number▼

Certificate will be mailed in window envelope

City/State/ZIP▼

YOU MUST:
• Complete all necessary spaces
• Sign your application

SEND ALL 3 ELEMENTS IN THE SAME PACKAGE:
1. Application form
2. Nonrefundable $40.00 filing fee in check, money order, or bank draft payable to *Register of Copyrights*
3. Deposit material

MAIL TO:
Register of Copyrights
Library of Congress
Washington, D.C. 20559

The Copyright Office has the authority to adjust fees at 5-year intervals, based on changes in the Consumer Price Index. The next adjustment is due in 1995. Please contact the Copyright Office after July 1995 to determine the actual fee schedule.

APPENDIX K:
FORM _____/CON
(CONTINUATION SHEET FOR APPLICATION FORMS)

CONTINUATION SHEET
FOR APPLICATION FORMS

- This Continuation Sheet is used in conjunction with Forms CA, PA, SE, SR, TX, and VA **only**. Indicate which basic form you are continuing in the space in the upper right-hand corner.

- If at all possible, try to fit the information called for into the spaces provided on the basic form.

- If you do not have space enough for all the information you need to give on the basic form, use this continuation sheet and submit it with the basic form.

- If you submit this continuation sheet, clip (do not tape or staple) it to the basic form and fold the two together before submitting them.

- **Part A of this sheet is intended to identify the basic application.**
  Part B is a continuation of Space 2.
  Part C (on the reverse side of this sheet) is for the continuation of Spaces 1, 4, or 6.

DO NOT WRITE ABOVE THIS LINE. FOR COPYRIGHT OFFICE USE ONLY

FORM _____ /CON
UNITED STATES COPYRIGHT OFFICE

REGISTRATION NUMBER

PA PAU SE SEG SEU SR SRU TX TXU VA VAU

EFFECTIVE DATE OF REGISTRATION

(Month)   (Day)   (Year)
CONTINUATION SHEET RECEIVED

Page _____ of _____ pages

A
Identification of Application

IDENTIFICATION OF CONTINUATION SHEET: This sheet is a continuation of the application for copyright registration on the basic form submitted for the following work:
- TITLE: (Give the title as given under the heading "Title of this Work" in Space 1 of the basic form.)

- NAME(S) AND ADDRESS(ES) OF COPYRIGHT CLAIMANT(S) : (Give the name and address of at least one copyright claimant as given in Space 4 of the basic form.)

B
Continuation of Space 2

d

NAME OF AUTHOR ▼

DATES OF BIRTH AND DEATH
Year Born▼   Year Died▼

Was this contribution to the work a "work made for hire"?
☐ Yes
☐ No

AUTHOR'S NATIONALITY OR DOMICILE
Name of Country
OR { Citizen of ▶ _____
Domiciled in ▶ _____

WAS THIS AUTHOR'S CONTRIBUTION TO THE WORK
Anonymous?   ☐ Yes ☐ No
Pseudonymous? ☐ Yes ☐ No
If the answer to either of these questions is "Yes" see detailed instructions.

NATURE OF AUTHORSHIP Briefly describe nature of the material created by the author in which copyright is claimed. ▼

e

NAME OF AUTHOR ▼

DATES OF BIRTH AND DEATH
Year Born▼   Year Died▼

Was this contribution to the work a "work made for hire"?
☐ Yes
☐ No

AUTHOR'S NATIONALITY OR DOMICILE
Name of Country
OR { Citizen of ▶ _____
Domiciled in ▶ _____

WAS THIS AUTHOR'S CONTRIBUTION TO THE WORK
Anonymous?   ☐ Yes ☐ No
Pseudonymous? ☐ Yes ☐ No
If the answer to either of these questions is "Yes" see detailed instructions.

NATURE OF AUTHORSHIP Briefly describe nature of the material created by the author in which copyright is claimed. ▼

f

NAME OF AUTHOR ▼

DATES OF BIRTH AND DEATH
Year Born▼   Year Died▼

Was this contribution to the work a "work made for hire"?
☐ Yes
☐ No

AUTHOR'S NATIONALITY OR DOMICILE
Name of Country
OR { Citizen of ▶ _____
Domiciled in ▶ _____

WAS THIS AUTHOR'S CONTRIBUTION TO THE WORK
Anonymous?   ☐ Yes ☐ No
Pseudonymous? ☐ Yes ☐ No
If the answer to either of these questions is "Yes" see detailed instructions.

NATURE OF AUTHORSHIP Briefly describe nature of the material created by the author in which copyright is claimed. ▼

Use the reverse side of this sheet if you need more space for continuation of Spaces 1, 4, or 6 of the basic form.

CONTINUATION OF (Check which): ☐ Space 1   ☐ Space 4   ☐ Space 6

C
Continuation
of other
Spaces

MAIL TO	Name ▼		YOU MUST: • Complete all necessary spaces • Sign your application	**D**
Certificate will be mailed in window envelope	Number/Street/Apt ▼		SEND ALL 3 ELEMENTS IN THE SAME PACKAGE: 1. Application form 2. Nonrefundable $20 filing fee in check or money order payable to *Register of Copyrights*	**Address for return of certificate**
	City/State/ZIP ▼		MAIL TO: Register of Copyrights Library of Congress Washington, D.C. 20559-6000	

November 1994–100,000   ♻ PRINTED ON RECYCLED PAPER

☆U.S.GOVERNMENT PRINTING OFFICE: 1994-387-237/18

APPENDIX L:
APPLICATION FORM CA
(SUPPLEMENTARY REGISTRATION)

FORM CA
For Supplementary Registration
UNITED STATES COPYRIGHT OFFICE

REGISTRATION NUMBER

TX	TXU	PA	PAU	VA	VAU	SR	SRU	RE

EFFECTIVE DATE OF SUPPLEMENTARY REGISTRATION

Month   Day   Year

DO NOT WRITE ABOVE THIS LINE. IF YOU NEED MORE SPACE, USE A SEPARATE CONTINUATION SHEET.

A

TITLE OF WORK ▼

REGISTRATION NUMBER OF THE BASIC REGISTRATION ▼   YEAR OF BASIC REGISTRATION ▼

NAME(S) OF AUTHOR(S) ▼   NAME(S) OF COPYRIGHT CLAIMANT(S) ▼

B

LOCATION AND NATURE OF INCORRECT INFORMATION IN BASIC REGISTRATION ▼

Line Number . . . . Line Heading or Description . . . .

INCORRECT INFORMATION AS IT APPEARS IN BASIC REGISTRATION ▼

CORRECTED INFORMATION ▼

EXPLANATION OF CORRECTION ▼

C

LOCATION AND NATURE OF INFORMATION IN BASIC REGISTRATION TO BE AMPLIFIED ▼

Line Number . . . . Line Heading or Description . . . .

AMPLIFIED INFORMATION ▼

EXPLANATION OF AMPLIFIED INFORMATION ▼

MORE ON BACK ▶ • Complete all applicable spaces (D -G) on the reverse side of this page.
• See detailed instructions.   • Sign the form at space F.

DO NOT WRITE HERE
Page 1 of _____ pages

FORM CA RECEIVED		**FORM CA**
FUNDS RECEIVED DATE		
EXAMINED BY		FOR COPYRIGHT OFFICE USE ONLY
CHECKED BY		
CORRESPONDENCE ☐		
REFERENCE TO THIS REGISTRATION ADDED TO BASIC REGISTRATION ☐ YES ☐ NO		

DO NOT WRITE ABOVE THIS LINE. IF YOU NEED MORE SPACE. USE A SEPARATE CONTINUATION SHEET.

CONTINUATION OF: (Check which) ☐ PART B OR ☐ PART C

D

DEPOSIT ACCOUNT: If the registration fee is to be charged to a Deposit Account established in the Copyright Office, give name and number of Account.

Name _____

_____

Account Number _____

CORRESPONDENCE: Give name and address to which correspondence about this application should be sent.

Name _____

Address _____ (Apt)

(City) (State) (ZIP)

Area Code and Telephone Number ▶ _____

Be sure to give your daytime phone number ◀

E

CERTIFICATION* I, the undersigned, hereby certify that I am the: (Check one)

☐ author ☐ other copyright claimant ☐ owner of exclusive right(s) ☐ duly authorized agent of _____
(Name of author or other copyright claimant, or owner of exclusive right(s) ▲

of the work identified in this application and that the statements made by me in this application are correct to the best of my knowledge.

Typed or printed name ▼ _____ Date ▼ _____

☞ Handwritten signature (X) ▼ _____

F

MAIL TO		YOU MUST:
	Name ▼	• Complete all necessary spaces • Sign your application in space F
Certificate will be mailed in window envelope	Number/Street/Apt ▼	SEND ALL ELEMENTS IN THE SAME PACKAGE: 1. Application form 2. Nonrefundable $20 filing fee in check or money order payable to *Register of Copyrights*
	City/State/ZIP ▼	MAIL TO: Register of Copyrights Library of Congress Washington, D.C. 20559-6000

G

*17 U.S.C. § 506(e): Any person who knowingly makes a false representation of a material fact in the application for copyright registration provided for by section 409, or in any written statement filed in connection with the application, shall be fined not more than $2,500.

October 1994—30,000 ♲ PRINTED ON RECYCLED PAPER   ☆U.S. GOVERNMENT PRINTING OFFICE: 1994-387-237/14

APPENDIX M:
APPLICATION FORM RE (RENEWAL)

FORM RE
For Renewal of a Work
UNITED STATES COPYRIGHT OFFICE

REGISTRATION NUMBER

EFFECTIVE DATE OF RENEWAL REGISTRATION

Month   Day   Year

DO NOT WRITE ABOVE THIS LINE. IF YOU NEED MORE SPACE, USE A SEPARATE CONTINUATION SHEET(RE/CON).

1 RENEWAL CLAIMANT(S), ADDRESS(ES), AND STATEMENT OF CLAIM ▼   (See Instructions)

1
Name ....
Address ....
Claiming as ....
(Use appropriate statement from instructions)

2
Name ....
Address ....
Claiming as ....

3
Name ....
Address ....
Claiming as ....

2 TITLE OF WORK IN WHICH RENEWAL IS CLAIMED ▼

RENEWABLE MATTER ▼

PUBLICATION AS A CONTRIBUTION If this work was published as a contribution to a periodical, serial, or other composite work, give information
about the collective work in which the contribution appeared.   **Title of Collective Work ▼**

If published in a periodical or serial give: **Volume ▼**   **Number ▼**   **Issue Date ▼**

3 AUTHOR(S) OF RENEWABLE MATTER ▼

4 ORIGINAL REGISTRATION NUMBER ▼ ORIGINAL COPYRIGHT CLAIMANT ▼

ORIGINAL DATE OF COPYRIGHT
If the original registration for this work was made in published form, give: If the original registration for this work was made in unpublished form, give:
DATE OF PUBLICATION: _____   } OR { DATE OF REGISTRATION: _____
              (Month)   (Day)   (Year)   (Month)   (Day)   (Year)

MORE ON BACK ▶ • Complete all applicable spaces (numbers 5-8) on the reverse side of this page.   **DO NOT WRITE HERE**
              • See detailed instructions.   • Sign the form at space 7.   Page 1 of _____ pages

RENEWAL APPLICATION RECEIVED	FORM RE
CORRESPONDENCE ☐ YES	FOR COPYRIGHT OFFICE USE ONLY
EXAMINED BY	
CHECKED BY	

DO NOT WRITE ABOVE THIS LINE. IF YOU NEED MORE SPACE, USE A SEPARATE CONTINUATION SHEET (RE/CON).

RENEWAL FOR GROUP OF WORKS BY SAME AUTHOR: To make a single registration for a group of works by the same individual author published as contributions to periodicals (see instructions), give full information about each contribution. If more space is needed, request continuation sheet (Form RE/CON).

5

1
Title of Contribution: ....
Title of Periodical: .... Vol: .... No: .... Issue Date: ....
Date of Publication: .... Registration Number: ....
(Month) (Day) (Year)

2
Title of Contribution: ....
Title of Periodical: .... Vol: .... No: .... Issue Date: ....
Date of Publication: .... Registration Number: ....
(Month) (Day) (Year)

3
Title of Contribution: ....
Title of Periodical: .... Vol: .... No: .... Issue Date: ....
Date of Publication: .... Registration Number: ....
(Month) (Day) (Year)

4
Title of Contribution: ....
Title of Periodical: .... Vol: .... No: .... Issue Date: ....
Date of Publication: .... Registration Number: ....
(Month) (Day) (Year)

DEPOSIT ACCOUNT: If the registration fee is to be charged to a Deposit Account established in the Copyright Office, give name and number of Account.

Name _____

_____

Account Number _____

CORRESPONDENCE: Give name and address to which correspondence about this application should be sent.

Name _____

Address _____ (Apt)

(City) (State) (ZIP)

Area Code and Telephone Number ▶ _____

Be sure to give your daytime phone ◀ number

6

CERTIFICATION* I, the undersigned, hereby certify that I am the: (Check one)
☐ renewal claimant   ☐ duly authorized agent of _____
(Name of renewal claimant) ▲
of the work identified in this application and that the statements made by me in this application are correct to the best of my knowledge.

Typed or printed name ▼   Date ▼

☞ Handwritten signature (X) ▼

7

MAIL CERTIFI-CATE TO

Certificate will be mailed in window envelope

Name ▼

Number/Street/Apt ▼

City/State/ZIP ▼

YOU MUST:
• Complete all necessary spaces
• Sign your application in space 7

SEND ALL ELEMENTS IN THE SAME PACKAGE:
1. Application form
2. Nonrefundable $20 filing fee in check or money order payable to *Register of Copyrights*

MAIL TO:
Register of Copyrights
Library of Congress
Washington, D.C. 20559

The Copyright Office has the authority to adjust fees at 5-year intervals, based on changes in the Consumer Price Index. The next adjustment is due in 1996. Please contact the Copyright Office after July 1995 to determine the actual fee schedule.

8

*17 U.S.C. § 506(e): Any person who knowingly makes a false representation of a material fact in the application for copyright registration provided for by section 409, or in any written statement filed in connection with the application, shall be fined not more than $2,500.

April 1993—40,000   ☉U.S. GOVERNMENT PRINTING OFFICE: 1993-342-581/60,513

APPENDIX N:
ADDENDUM TO FORM RE

ADDENDUM TO FORM RE

THIS FORM MUST BE COMPLETED FOR ALL WORKS
PUBLISHED BETWEEN
JANUARY 1, 1964, AND DECEMBER 31, 1977,
THAT WERE NOT REGISTERED
DURING THEIR FIRST 28-YEAR TERM.

ADDENDUM TO FORM RE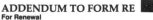
For Renewal
UNITED STATES COPYRIGHT OFFICE

RENEWAL REGISTRATION NUMBER

DO NOT WRITE ABOVE THIS LINE.

1 TITLE OF WORK IN WHICH RENEWAL IS CLAIMED: ▼

2 NAME OF THE AUTHOR(S): ▼

3 CITIZENSHIP AND/OR DOMICILE OF THE AUTHOR(S) AT THE TIME THE WORK WAS FIRST PUBLISHED:

4 DATE AND NATION OF FIRST PUBLICATION:
Month▼   Day▼   Year▼   Nation▼

5 MANUFACTURE:
A. If this is a nondramatic literary work or a two-dimensional print or label, the country in which the work was manufactured:▼

B. The processes by which the work was manufactured:▼

6 DEPOSIT: (Check one)
☐ A. One complete copy of this work as first published is deposited with this application.
☐ B. A complete copy of this work as first published cannot be deposited for the following reason:▼

7 VERIFICATION OF NOTICE:
I hereby aver that all copies of this work as first published bore the copyright notice as it appears in the accompanying deposit materials and said copyright notice appeared on all copies of the work published in the United States until December 31, 1977.

Signature of applicant: _____

8 CERTIFICATION:
I certify under penalty of perjury under the laws of the United States of America that the foregoing is true and correct.

Signature of applicant: _____

Date signed: _____

Daytime telephone number: _____

FAX number if any: _____

DO NOT WRITE HERE
OFFICE USE ONLY

ADDENDUM RECEIVED

DEPOSIT RECEIVED

March 1993 —30,000

✩U.S. GOVERNMENT PRINTING OFFICE: 1993-342-581/60,506

APPENDIX O:
APPLICATION FORM RE/CON
(CONTINUATION SHEET FOR APPLICATION FORM RE)

CONTINUATION SHEET FOR
APPLICATION FORM RE

INSTRUCTIONS

- This Continuation Sheet is to be used **only** in conjuction with Basic Form RE.

- Use this sheet only if you need more space to continue the listing started in Space 1 and/or Space 5 of Form RE. Use as many additional continuation sheets as you need.

- Follow instructions accompanying Form RE in filling out this continuation sheet. Number each line in Spaces B and C consecutively.

- Submit this continuation sheet with the Basic Form RE and the other continuation sheets, if any. Clip (do not tape or staple) and fold all sheets together before submitting them.

**FORM RE/CON**

UNITED STATES COPYRIGHT OFFICE

REGISTRATION NUMBER

EFFECTIVE DATE OF RENEWAL REGISTRATION

. . . .
(Month)   (Day)   (Year)

CONTINUATION SHEET RECEIVED

Page _____ of _____ pages

DO NOT WRITE ABOVE THIS LINE. FOR COPYRIGHT OFFICE USE ONLY

(A)

Identification of Application

IDENTIFICATION OF CONTINUATION: This sheet is a continuation of Space 1 and Space 5 of the application for renewal registration on Form RE, submitted for the following:

- TITLE AT SPACE 2 OR TITLE OF FIRST OF GROUP OF WORKS IN WHICH RENEWAL IS CLAIMED: (Give first title as given in Space 5 of Form RE)
. . . .

- RENEWAL CLAIMANT AND ADDRESS: (Give the name and address of at least one renewal claimant as given in Space 1 of Form RE)
. . . .

(B)

Continuation of Space 1

RENEWAL CLAIMANT(S), ADDRESS(ES), AND STATEMENT OF CLAIM: (See Instructions on Basic Form RE)

☐ Name . . . .
Address . . . .
Claiming as . . . .

☐ Name . . . .
Address . . . .
Claiming as . . . .

☐ Name . . . .
Address . . . .
Claiming as . . . .

☐ Name . . . .
Address . . . .
Claiming as . . . .

☐ Name . . . .
Address . . . .
Claiming as . . . .

☐ Name . . . .
Address . . . .
Claiming as . . . .

☐	Title of Contribution: .... Title of Periodical: .... Vol. ...... No...... Issue Date .... Date of Publication: .... Registration Number: .... (Month) (Day) (Year)	**C** Continuation of Space 5
☐	Title of Contribution: .... Title of Periodical: .... Vol. ...... No...... Issue Date .... Date of Publication: .... Registration Number: .... (Month) (Day) (Year)	
☐	Title of Contribution: .... Title of Periodical: .... Vol. ...... No...... Issue Date .... Date of Publication: .... Registration Number: .... (Month) (Day) (Year)	
☐	Title of Contribution: .... Title of Periodical: .... Vol. ...... No...... Issue Date .... Date of Publication: .... Registration Number: .... (Month) (Day) (Year)	
☐	Title of Contribution: .... Title of Periodical: .... Vol. ...... No...... Issue Date .... Date of Publication: .... Registration Number: .... (Month) (Day) (Year)	
☐	Title of Contribution: .... Title of Periodical: .... Vol. ...... No...... Issue Date .... Date of Publication: .... Registration Number: .... (Month) (Day) (Year)	
☐	Title of Contribution: .... Title of Periodical: .... Vol. ...... No...... Issue Date .... Date of Publication: .... Registration Number: .... (Month) (Day) (Year)	
☐	Title of Contribution: .... Title of Periodical: .... Vol. ...... No...... Issue Date .... Date of Publication: .... Registration Number: .... (Month) (Day) (Year)	
☐	Title of Contribution: .... Title of Periodical: .... Vol. ...... No...... Issue Date .... Date of Publication: .... Registration Number: .... (Month) (Day) (Year)	
☐	Title of Contribution: .... Title of Periodical: .... Vol. ...... No...... Issue Date .... Date of Publication: .... Registration Number: .... (Month) (Day) (Year)	
☐	Title of Contribution: .... Title of Periodical: .... Vol. ...... No...... Issue Date .... Date of Publication: .... Registration Number: .... (Month) (Day) (Year)	
☐	Title of Contribution: .... Title of Periodical: .... Vol. ...... No...... Issue Date .... Date of Publication: .... Registration Number: .... (Month) (Day) (Year)	
☐	Title of Contribution: .... Title of Periodical: .... Vol. ...... No...... Issue Date .... Date of Publication: .... Registration Number: .... (Month) (Day) (Year)	

....
(Name)
....
(Number, Street and Apartment Number)
....
(City)   (State)   (ZIP Code)

**MAIL
CERTIFICATE
TO**

(Certificate will
be mailed in
window envelope)

D

**Address for
Return of
Certificate**

July 1991—10,000   ☆U.S. GOVERNMENT PRINTING OFFICE: 1991- 282-170/40,002

APPENDIX P:
DOCUMENT COVER SHEET
(FOR RECORDATION OF DOCUMENTS)

DOCUMENT COVER SHEET
For Recordation of Documents
UNITED STATES COPYRIGHT OFFICE

DATE OF RECORDATION
(Assigned by Copyright Office)

Month	Day	Year

Volume _____ Page _____

Volume _____ Page _____

DO NOT WRITE ABOVE THIS LINE.

REMITTANCE _____

To the Register of Copyrights:
Please record the accompanying original document or copy thereof. FUNDS RECEIVED _____

1 NAME OF THE PARTY OR PARTIES TO THE DOCUMENT, AS THEY APPEAR IN THE DOCUMENT.

Party 1: _____ Party 2: _____
    (assignor, grantor, etc.)   (assignee, grantee, etc.)

_____ (address) _____ (address)

2 DESCRIPTION OF THE DOCUMENT:
☐ Transfer of Copyright   ☐ Termination of Transfer(s) [Section 304]   ☐ Transfer of Mask Works
☐ Security Interest   ☐ Shareware   ☐ Other _____
☐ Change of Name of Owner   ☐ Life, Identity, Death Statement [Section 302]

3 TITLE(S) OF WORK(S), REGISTRATION NUMBER(S), AUTHOR(S), AND OTHER INFORMATION TO IDENTIFY WORK.
Title   Registration Number   Author

Additional sheet(s) attached?
☐ yes
☐ no
If so, how many? _____

4 ☐ Document is complete by its own terms.
☐ Document is not complete. Record "as is."

5 Number of titles in Document: _____

6 Amount of fee enclosed or authorized to be charged to a
Deposit Account _____ .

7 Account number _____
Account name _____

8 Date of execution and/or effective date of accompanying
document _____ .
    (month)   (day)   (year)

9 AFFIRMATION:* I hereby affirm to the Copyright Office that the information given on this form is a true and correct representation of the accompanying document. This affirmation will not suffice as a certification of a photocopy signature on the document.

10 CERTIFICATION:* Complete this certification if a photocopy of the original signed document is submitted in lieu of a document bearing the actual signature.
     I certify under penalty of perjury under the laws of the United States of America that the accompanying document is a true copy of the original document.

_____
Signature

_____
Signature

_____
Date

_____
Duly Authorized Agent of:

_____
Date

MAIL RECORDA-TION TO:

Name▼

Number/Street/Apartment Number▼

City/State/ZIP▼

YOU MUST:
· Complete all necessary spaces
· Sign your cover sheet in space 9
SEND ALL 3 ELEMENTS IN THE SAME PACKAGE:
1. Two copies of the Document Cover Sheet
2. Fee in check or money order payable to *Register of Copyrights*
3. Document
MAIL TO:
Documents Unit, Cataloging Division,
Copyright Office, Library of Congress
Washington, D.C. 20559

The Copyright Office has the authority to adjust fees at 5-year intervals, based on changes in the Consumer Price Index. The next adjustment is due in 1996. Please contact the Copyright Office after July 1995 to determine the actual fee schedule.

*Knowingly and willfully falsifying material facts on this form may result in criminal liability. 18 U.S.C.§1001.

January 1993—50,000

APPLICATION Q:
CIRCULAR 38A (INTERNATIONAL COPYRIGHT RELATIONS
OF THE UNITED STATES)

International Copyright
Relations of the United States

GENERAL INFORMATION

This sets forth U.S. copyright relations of current interest with the other independent nations of the world. Each entry gives country name (and alternate name) and a statement of copyright relations. The following code is used:

Berne — Party to the Berne Convention for the Protection of Literary and Artistic Works as of the date given. Appearing within parentheses is the latest Act[1] of the Convention to which the country is party. The effective date for the United States was March 1, 1989. The latest Act of the Convention to which the United States is party is the revision done at Paris on July 24, 1971.

Bilateral — Bilateral copyright relations with the United States by virtue of a proclamation or treaty, as of the date given. Where there is more than one proclamation or treaty, only the date of the first one is given.

BAC — Party to the Buenos Aires Convention of 1910, as of the date given. U.S. ratification deposited with the Government of Argentina, May 1, 1911; proclaimed by the President of the United States, July 13, 1914.

None — No copyright relations with the United States.

Phonogram — Party to the Convention for the Protection of Producers of Phonograms Against Unauthorized Duplication of Their Phonograms, Geneva, 1971, as of the date given. The effective date for the United States was March 10, 1974.

SAT — Party to the Convention Relating to the Distribution of Programme-Carrying Signals Transmitted by Satellite, Brussels, 1974, as of the date given. The effective date for the United States was March 7, 1985.

UCC Geneva — Party to the Universal Copyright Convention, Geneva, 1952, as of the date given. The effective date for the United States was September 16, 1955.

UCC Paris — Party to the Universal Copyright Convention as revised at Paris, 1971, as of the date given. The effective date for the United States was July 10, 1974.

Unclear — Became independent since 1943. Has not established copyright relations with the United States, but may be honoring obligations incurred under former political status.

Explanations of footnotes appear on the last page.

RELATIONS AS OF OCTOBER 31, 1994

Afghanistan
None

Albania
Berne Mar. 6, 1994 (Paris)[2]

Algeria
UCC Geneva Aug. 28, 1973
UCC Paris July 10, 1974

Andorra
UCC Geneva Sept. 16, 1955

Angola
Unclear

Antigua and Barbuda
Unclear

Argentina
Bilateral Aug. 23, 1934
BAC Apr. 19, 1950
UCC Geneva Feb. 13, 1958
Berne June 10, 1967 (Brussels)[2]
Phonogram June 30, 1973[3]

Armenia
SAT Dec.13, 1993

Australia
Bilateral March 15, 1918
Berne Apr. 14, 1928 (Paris)[2]
UCC Geneva May 1, 1969
Phonogram June 22, 1974
UCC Paris Feb. 28, 1978
SAT Oct. 26,1990

Austria
Bilateral Sept. 20, 1907
Berne Oct. 1, 1920 (Paris) [2]
UCC Geneva July 2, 1957
SAT Aug. 6, 1982 [4]
UCC Paris Aug. 14, 1982
Phonogram Aug. 21, 1982

Bahamas, The
Berne July 10, 1973 (Brussels) [2]
UCC Geneva Dec. 27, 1976
UCC Paris Dec. 27, 1976

Bahrain
None

Bangladesh
UCC Geneva Aug. 5, 1975
UCC Paris Aug. 5, 1975

Barbados
UCC Geneva June 18, 1983
UCC Paris June 18, 1983
Berne July 30, 1983 (Paris) [2]
Phonogram July 29, 1983

Belau
Unclear

Belgium
Berne Dec. 5, 1887 (Brussels) [2]
Bilateral July 1, 1891
UCC Geneva Aug. 31, 1960

Belize
UCC Geneva Dec. 1, 1982

Benin (formerly Dahomey)
Berne Jan. 3, 1961 (Paris) [2]

Bhutan
None

Bolivia
BAC May 15, 1914
UCC Geneva Mar. 22, 1990
UCC Paris Mar. 22, 1990
Berne Nov. 4, 1993 (Paris)[2]

Bosnia and Herzegovina
UCC Geneva May 11, 1966
UCC Paris July 10, 1974
Berne Mar. 6, 1992 (Paris)[2]
SAT Mar. 6, 1992

Botswana
Unclear

Brazil
BAC Aug. 31, 1915
Berne Feb. 9, 1922 (Paris) [2]
Bilateral Apr. 2, 1957
UCC Geneva Jan. 13, 1960
Phonogram Nov. 28, 1975
UCC Paris Dec. 11, 1975

Brunei
Unclear

Bulgaria
Berne Dec. 5, 1921 (Paris) [2]
UCC Geneva June 7, 1975
UCC Paris June 7, 1975

Burkina Faso (formerly Upper Volta)
Berne Aug. 19, 1963 (Paris) [2]
Phonogram Jan. 30, 1988

Burma
Unclear

Burundi
Unclear

Cambodia
UCC Geneva Sept. 16, 1955

Cameroon
Berne Sept, 21, 1964 (Paris) [2]
UCC Geneva May 1, 1973
UCC Paris July 10, 1974

Canada
Bilateral Jan. 1, 1924
Berne Apr. 10, 1928 (Rome) [2]
UCC Geneva Aug. 10, 1962

Cape Verde
Unclear

Central African Republic
Berne Sept. 3, 1977 (Paris) [2]

Chad
Berne Nov. 25, 1971 (Brussels) [2]

Chile
Bilateral May 25, 1896
BAC June 14, 1955
UCC Geneva Sept. 16, 1955
Berne June 5, 1970 (Paris) [2]
Phonogram Mar. 24, 1977

China
Bilateral Jan. 13, 1904 [5]
Bilateral Mar. 17, 1992 [9]
Berne Oct. 15, 1992 (Paris)[2]
UCC Geneva Oct. 30, 1992
UCC Paris Oct. 30, 1992
Phonogram Apr. 30, 1993

Colombia
BAC Dec. 23, 1936
UCC Geneva June 18, 1976
UCC Paris June 18, 1976
Berne Mar. 7, 1988 (Paris)[2]
Phonogram May 16, 1994

Comoros
Unclear

Congo
Berne May 8, 1962 (Paris) [2]

Costa Rica [6]
Bilateral Oct. 19, 1899
BAC Nov. 30, 1916
UCC Geneva Sept. 16, 1955
Berne June 10, 1978 (Paris) [2]
UCC Paris Mar. 7, 1980
Phonogram June 17, 1982

Cote d'Ivoire (Ivory Coast)
Berne Jan. 1, 1962 (Paris) [2]

Croatia
UCC Geneva May 11, 1966
UCC Paris July 10, 1974
Berne Oct. 8, 1991 (Paris)[2]
SAT Oct. 8, 1991

Cuba
Bilateral Nov. 17, 1903
UCC Geneva June 18, 1957

Cyprus
Berne Feb. 24, 1964 (Paris) [2]
UCC Geneva Dec. 19, 1990
UCC Paris Dec. 19,1990
Phonogram Sept. 30, 1993

Czech Republic
UCC Geneva Jan. 6, 1960
UCC Paris Apr. 17, 1980
Berne Jan. 1, 1993 (Paris)[2]
Phonogram Jan. 1, 1993

Czechoslovakia[11]
Bilateral Mar. 1, 1927

Denmark
Bilateral May 8, 1893
Berne July 1, 1903 (Paris) [2]
UCC Geneva Feb. 9, 1962
Phonogram Mar. 24, 1977
UCC Paris July 11, 1979

Djibouti
Unclear

Dominica
Unclear

Dominican Republic [6]
BAC Oct. 31, 1912
UCC Geneva May 8, 1983
UCC Paris May 8, 1983

Ecuador
BAC Aug. 31, 1914
UCC Geneva June 5, 1957
Phonogram Sept. 14, 1974
UCC Paris June 6, 1991
Berne Oct. 9, 1991 (Paris) [2]

Egypt
Berne June 7, 1977 (Paris) [2]
Phonogram Apr. 23, 1978

El Salvador
Bilateral June 30, 1908 by virtue of
   Mexico City Convention, 1902
Phonogram Feb. 9, 1979
UCC Geneva Mar. 29, 1979
UCC Paris Mar. 29, 1979
Berne Feb. 19, 1994 (Paris)[2]

Equatorial Guinea
Unclear

Estonia
Berne Oct. 26, 1994 (Paris)[2]

Ethiopia
None

Fiji
UCC Geneva Oct. 10, 1970
Berne Dec.1, 1971 (Brussels) [2]
Phonogram Apr. 18, 1973 [3]

Finland
Berne Apr. 1, 1928 (Paris) [2]
Bilateral Jan. 1, 1929
UCC Geneva Apr. 16, 1963
Phonogram Apr. 18, 1973 [3]
UCC Paris Nov. 1, 1986

France
Berne Dec. 5, 1887 (Paris) [2]
Bilateral July 1, 1891
UCC Geneva Jan. 14, 1956
Phonogram Apr. 18, 1973 [3]
UCC Paris July 10, 1974

Gabon
Berne Mar. 26, 1962 (Paris) [2]

Gambia, The
Berne Mar. 7, 1993 (Paris) [2]

Germany [10]
Berne Dec. 5, 1887 (Paris) [2,7]
Bilateral Apr. 16, 1892
UCC Geneva Sept. 16, 1955
Phonogram May 18, 1974
UCC Paris July 10, 1974
SAT Aug. 25, 1979 [4]

Ghana
UCC Geneva Aug. 22, 1962
Berne Oct. 11, 1991 (Paris) [2]

Greece
Berne Nov. 9, 1920 (Paris)[2]
Bilateral Mar. 1, 1932
UCC Geneva Aug. 24, 1963
SAT Oct. 22, 1991
Phonogram Feb. 9, 1994

Grenada
Unclear

Guatemala [6]
BAC Mar. 28, 1913
UCC Geneva Oct. 28, 1964
Phonogram Feb. 1, 1977

Guinea
Berne Nov. 20, 1980 (Paris) [2]
UCC Geneva Nov. 13, 1981
UCC Paris Nov. 13, 1981

Guinea-Bissau
Berne July 22, 1991 (Paris) [2]

Guyana
Berne Oct. 25, 1994 (Paris)[2]

Haiti
BAC Nov. 27, 1919
UCC Geneva Sept. 16, 1955

Holy See
(See entry under Vatican City)

Honduras [6]
BAC Apr. 27, 1914
Berne Jan. 25,1990 (Paris)[2]
Phonogram Mar. 6, 1990

Hungary
Bilateral Oct. 16, 1912
Berne Feb. 14, 1922 (Paris) [2]
UCC Geneva Jan. 23, 1971
UCC Paris July 10, 1974
Phonogram May 28, 1975

Iceland
Berne Sept. 7, 1947 (Rome) [2]
UCC Geneva Dec. 18, 1956

India
Berne Apr. 1, 1928 (Paris) [2]
Bilateral Aug. 15, 1947
UCC Geneva Jan. 21, 1958
Phonogram Feb. 12, 1975
UCC Paris Jan. 7, 1988

Indonesia
Bilateral Aug. 1, 1989

Iran
None

Iraq
None

Ireland
Berne Oct. 5, 1927 (Brussels) [2]
Bilateral Oct. 1, 1929
UCC Geneva Jan. 20, 1959

Israel
Bilateral May 15, 1948
Berne Mar. 24, 1950 (Brussels) [2]
UCC Geneva Sept. 16, 1955
Phonogram May 1, 1978

Italy
Berne Dec. 5, 1887 (Paris) [2]
Bilateral Oct. 31, 1892
UCC Geneva Jan. 24, 1957
Phonogram Mar. 24, 1977
UCC Paris Jan. 25, 1980
SAT July 7, 1981 [4]

Ivory Coast
(See entry under Cote d'Ivoire)

Jamaica
Berne Jan. 1, 1994 (Paris)[2]
Phonogram Jan. 11, 1994

Japan [8]
Berne July 15, 1899 (Paris) [2]
UCC Geneva Apr. 28, 1956
UCC Paris Oct. 21, 1977
Phonogram Oct. 14, 1978

Jordan
Unclear

Kazakhstan
UCC Geneva May 27, 1973

Kenya
UCC Geneva Sept. 7, 1966
UCC Paris July 10, 1974
Phonogram Apr. 21, 1976
SAT Aug. 25, 1979 [4]
Berne June 11, 1993 (Paris) [2]

Kiribati
Unclear

Korea
Democratic People's Republic of
Korea
Unclear

Republic of Korea
UCC Geneva Oct. 1, 1987
UCC Paris Oct. 1, 1987
Phonogram Oct. 10, 1987

Kuwait
Unclear

Laos
UCC Geneva Sept. 16, 1955

Lebanon
Berne Sept. 30, 1947 (Rome) [2]
UCC Geneva Oct. 17, 1959

Lesotho
Berne Sept. 28, 1989 (Paris)[2]

Liberia
UCC Geneva July 27, 1956
Berne Mar. 8, 1989 (Paris) [2]

Libya
Berne Sept. 28, 1976 (Paris) [2]

Liechtenstein
Berne July 30, 1931 (Brussels) [2]
UCC Geneva Jan. 22, 1959

Lithuania*

Luxembourg
Berne June 20, 1888 (Paris) [2]
Bilateral June 29, 1910
UCC Geneva Oct. 15, 1955
Phonogram Mar. 8, 1976

Macedonia (former Yugoslav Republic)
Berne Sept. 8, 1991 (Paris)[2]

Madagascar (Malagasy Republic)
Berne Jan. 1, 1966 (Brussels) [2]

Malawi
UCC Geneva Oct. 26, 1965
Berne Oct. 12, 1991 (Paris) [2]

Malaysia
Berne Oct. 1, 1990 (Paris) [2]

Maldives
Unclear

Mali
Berne Mar. 19, 1962 (Paris) [2]

Malta
Berne Sept. 21, 1964 (Rome) [2]
UCC Geneva Nov. 19, 1968

Mauritania
Berne Feb. 6, 1973 (Paris) [2]

Mauritius
UCC Geneva Mar. 12, 1968
Berne May 10, 1989 (Paris) [2]

Mexico
Bilateral Feb. 27, 1896
UCC Geneva May 12, 1957
BAC Apr. 24, 1964
Berne June 11, 1967 (Paris) [2]
Phonogram Dec. 21, 1973 [3]
UCC Paris Oct. 31, 1975
SAT Aug. 25, 1979 [4]

Monaco
Berne May 30, 1889 (Paris) [2]
Bilateral Oct. 15, 1952
UCC Geneva Sept. 16, 1955
Phonogram Dec. 2, 1974
UCC Paris Dec. 13, 1974

Mongolia
None

*The Berne Convention, as revised at Paris,[2] will enter into force with respect to Lithuania on Dec. 14, 1994.

Morocco
Berne June 16, 1917 (Paris) [2]
UCC Geneva May 8, 1972
UCC Paris Jan. 28, 1976
SAT June 30, 1983 [4]

Mozambique
Unclear

Namibia
Berne Mar. 21, 1990 (Paris)[2]

Nauru
Unclear

Nepal
None

Netherlands
Bilateral Nov. 20, 1899
Berne Nov. 1, 1912 (Paris) [2]
UCC Geneva June 22, 1967
UCC Paris Nov. 30, 1985
Phonogram Oct. 12, 1993

New Zealand
Bilateral Dec. 1, 1916
Berne Apr. 24, 1928 (Rome) [2]
UCC Geneva Sept. 11, 1964
Phonogram Aug. 13, 1976

Nicaragua [6]
BAC Dec. 15, 1913
UCC Geneva Aug. 16, 1961
SAT Aug. 25, 1979 [4]

Niger
Berne May 2, 1962 (Paris) [2]
UCC Geneva May 15, 1989
UCC Paris May 15, 1989

Nigeria
UCC Geneva Feb. 14, 1962
Berne Sept. 14, 1993 (Paris)[2]

Norway
Berne Apr. 13, 1896 (Brussels) [2]
Bilateral July 1, 1905
UCC Geneva Jan. 23, 1963
UCC Paris Aug. 7, 1974
Phonogram Aug. 1, 1978

Oman
None

Pakistan
Berne July 5, 1948 (Rome) [2]
UCC Geneva Sept. 16, 1955

Panama
BAC Nov. 25, 1913
UCC Geneva Oct. 17, 1962
Phonogram June 29, 1974
UCC Paris Sept. 3, 1980
SAT Sept. 25, 1985

Papua New Guinea
Unclear

Paraguay
BAC Sept. 20, 1917
UCC Geneva Mar. 11, 1962
Phonogram Feb. 13, 1979
Berne Jan. 2, 1992 (Paris) [2]

Peru
BAC Apr. 30, 1920
UCC Geneva Oct. 16, 1963
UCC Paris July 22, 1985
SAT Aug. 7, 1985
Phonogram Aug. 24, 1985
Berne Aug. 20, 1988 (Paris) [2]

Philippines
Bilateral Oct. 21, 1948
Berne Aug. 1, 1951 (Brussels) [2]
UCC status undetermined by UNESCO (Copyright Office considers that UCC relations do not exist.)

Poland
Berne Jan. 28, 1920 (Paris) [2]
Bilateral Feb. 16, 1927
UCC Geneva Mar. 9, 1977
UCC Paris Mar. 9, 1977

Portugal
Bilateral July 20, 1893
Berne Mar. 29, 1911 (Paris) [2]
UCC Geneva Dec. 25, 1956
UCC Paris July 30, 1981

Qatar
None

Romania
Berne Jan. 1, 1927 (Rome) [2]
Bilateral May 14, 1928

Russian Federation
UCC Geneva May 27, 1973
SAT Dec. 25, 1991

Rwanda
Berne Mar. 1, 1984 (Paris) [2]
UCC Geneva Nov. 10. 1989
UCC Paris Nov. 10, 1989

St. Christopher and Nevis
Unclear

Saint Lucia
Berne Aug. 24, 1993 (Paris)[2]

Saint Vincent and the Grenadines
UCC Geneva Apr. 22, 1985
UCC Paris Apr. 22, 1985

San Marino
None

São Tomé and Principe
Unclear

Saudi Arabia
None

Senegal
Berne Aug. 25, 1962 (Paris) [2]
UCC Geneva July 9, 1974
UCC Paris July 10, 1974

Seychelles
Unclear

Sierra Leone
None

Singapore
Bilateral May 18, 1987

Slovakia
UCC Geneva Jan. 6, 1960
UCC Paris Apr. 17, 1980
Berne Jan. 1, 1993 (Paris)[2]
Phonogram Jan. 1, 1993

Slovenia
UCC Geneva May 11, 1966
UCC Paris July 10, 1974
Berne June 25, 1991 (Paris) [2]
SAT June 25, 1991

Solomon Islands
Unclear

Somalia
Unclear

South Africa
Bilateral July 1, 1924
Berne Oct. 3, 1928 (Brussels) [2]

Soviet Union
(See entry under Russian Federation)

Spain
Berne Dec. 5, 1887 (Paris) [2]
Bilateral July 10, 1895
UCC Geneva Sept. 16, 1955
UCC Paris July 10, 1974
Phonogram Aug. 24, 1974

Sri Lanka (formerly Ceylon)
Berne July 20, 1959 (Rome) [2]
UCC Geneva Jan. 25, 1984
UCC Paris Jan. 25, 1984

Sudan
Unclear

Suriname
Berne Feb. 23, 1977 (Paris) [2]

Swaziland
Unclear

Sweden
Berne Aug. 1, 1904 (Paris) [2]
Bilateral June 1, 1911
UCC Geneva July 1, 1961
Phonogram Apr. 18, 1973 [3]
UCC Paris July 10, 1974

Switzerland
Berne Dec. 5, 1887 (Paris)[2]
Bilateral July 1, 1891
UCC Geneva Mar. 30, 1956
UCC Paris Sept. 21, 1993
SAT Sept. 24, 1993
Phonogram Sept. 30, 1993

Syria
Unclear

Tajikistan
UCC Geneva May 27, 1973

Tanzania
Berne July 25, 1994 (Paris)[2]

Thailand
Bilateral Sept. 1, 1921
Berne July 17, 1931 (Berlin) [2]

Togo
Berne Apr. 30, 1975 (Paris) [2]

Tonga
None

Trinidad and Tobago
Berne Aug. 16, 1988 (Paris) [2]
UCC Geneva Aug. 19, 1988
UCC Paris Aug. 19, 1988
Phonogram Oct. 1, 1988

Tunisia
Berne Dec. 5, 1887 (Paris) [2]
UCC Geneva June 19, 1969
UCC Paris June 10, 1975

Turkey
Berne Jan. 1, 1952 (Brussels) [2]

Tuvalu
Unclear

Uganda
Unclear

Ukraine
UCC Geneva May 27, 1973

United Arab Emirates
None

United Kingdom
Berne Dec. 5, 1887 (Paris) [2]
Bilateral July 1, 1891
UCC Geneva Sept. 27, 1957
Phonogram Apr. 18, 1973 [3]
UCC Paris July 10, 1974

Upper Volta
(See entry under Burkina Faso)

Uruguay
BAC Dec. 17, 1919
Berne July 10, 1967 (Paris)[2]
Phonogram Jan. 18, 1983
UCC Geneva Apr. 12, 1993
UCC Paris Apr. 12, 1993

Vanuatu
Unclear

Vatican City (Holy See)
Berne Sept. 12, 1935 (Paris) [2]
UCC Geneva Oct. 5, 1955
Phonogram July 18, 1977
UCC Paris May 6, 1980

Venezuela
UCC Geneva Sept. 30, 1966
Phonogram Nov. 18, 1982
Berne Dec. 30, 1982 (Paris) [2]

Vietnam
Unclear

Western Samoa
Unclear

Yemen (Aden)
Unclear

Yemen (San'a)
None

Yugoslavia
Berne June 17, 1930 (Paris) [2]
UCC Geneva May 11, 1966
UCC Paris July 10, 1974
SAT Aug. 25, 1979 [4]

Zaire
Berne Oct. 8, 1963 (Paris) [2]
Phonogram Nov. 29, 1977

Zambia
UCC Geneva June 1, 1965
Berne Jan. 2, 1992 (Paris) [2]

Zimbabwe
Berne Apr. 18, 1980 (Rome) [2]

198

Appendices

STATUTORY PROVISIONS

The copyright law embodied in title 17 of the United States Code was completely revised by the Act of October 19, 1976 (Public Law 94-553, 90 Stat. 2541) which became fully effective on January 1, 1978. Reprinted below is section 104 of that Act, as amended by the Act of October 31, 1988 (Public Law 100-568, 102 Stat. 2853, 2855).

§104. Subject matter of copyright: National origin

(a) UNPUBLISHED WORKS.—The works specified by sections 102 and 108, while unpublished, are subject to protection under this title without regard to the nationality or domicile of the author.

(b) PUBLISHED WORKS.—The works specified by sections 102 and 103, when published, are subject to protection under this title if—

(1) on the date of first publication, one or more of the authors is a national or domiciliary of the United States, or is a national, domiciliary, or sovereign authority of a foreign nation that is a party to a copyright treaty to which the United States is also a party, or is a stateless person, wherever that person may be domiciled; or

(2) the work is first published in the United States or in a foreign nation that, on the date of first publication, is a party to the Universal Copyright Convention; or

(3) the work is first published by the United Nations or any of its specialized agencies, or by the Organization of American States; or

(4) the work is a Berne Convention work; or

(5) the work comes within the scope of a Presidential proclamation. Whenever the President finds that a particular foreign nation extends, to works by authors who are nationals or domiciliaries of the United States or to works that are first published in the United States, copyright protection on substantially the same basis as that on which the foreign nation extends protection to works of its own nationals and domiciliaries and works first published in that nation, the President may by proclamation extend protection under this title to works of which one or more of the authors is, on the date of first publication, a national, domiciliary, or sovereign authority of that nation, or which was first published in that nation. The President may revise, suspend, or revoke any such proclamation or impose any conditions or limitations on protection under a proclamation.

(c) EFFECT OF BERNE CONVENTION.—No right or interest in a work eligible for protection under this title may be claimed by virtue of, or in reliance upon, the provisions of the Berne Convention, or the adherence of the United States thereto. Any rights in a work eligible for protection under this title that derive from this title, other Federal or State statutes, or the common law, shall not be expanded or reduced by virtue of, or in reliance upon, the provisions of the Berne Convention, or the adherence of the United States thereto.

SOME POINTS TO REMEMBER REGARDING THE INTERNATIONAL PROTECTION OF LITERARY AND ARTISTIC WORKS

There is no such thing as an "international copyright" that will automatically protect an author's writings throughout the world. Protection against unauthorized use in a particular country basically depends on the national laws of that country. However, most countries offer protection to foreign works under certain conditions which have been greatly simplified by international copyright treaties and conventions. There are two principal international copyright conventions, the Berne Union for the Protection of Literary and Artistic Property (Berne Convention) and the Universal Copyright Convention (UCC).

An author who wishes copyright protection for his or her work in a particular country should first determine the extent of the protection available to works of foreign authors in that country. If possible, this should be done before the work is published anywhere, because protection may depend on the facts existing at the time of first publication.

If the country in which protection is sought is a party to one of the international copyright conventions, the work generally may be protected by complying with the conditions of that convention. Even if the work cannot be brought under an international convention, protection under the specific provisions of the country's national laws may still be possible. There are, however, some countries that offer little or no copyright protection to any foreign works. For current information on the requirements and protection provided by other countries, it may be advisable to consult an expert familiar with foreign copyright laws. The U.S. Copyright Office is not permitted to recommend agents or attorneys or to give legal advice on foreign laws.

199

Footnotes

[1] "Paris" means the Berne Convention for the Protection of Literary and Artistic Works as revised at Paris on July 24, 1971 (Paris Act); "Stockholm" means the said Convention as revised at Stockholm on July 14, 1967 (Stockholm Act); "Brussels" means the said Convention as revised at Brussels on June 26, 1948 (Brussels Act); "Rome" means the said Convention as revised at Rome on June 2, 1928 (Rome Act); "Berlin" means the said Convention as revised at Berlin on November 13, 1908 (Berlin Act). NOTE: In each case the reference to Act signifies adherence to the substantive provisions of such Act only, *e.g.*, Articles 1 to 21 of the Paris Act.

[2] The Berne Convention for the Protection of Literary and Artistic Works of September 9, 1886, as revised at Paris on July 24, 1971, did not enter into force with respect to the United States until March 1, 1989.

[3] The Convention for the Protection of Producers of Phonograms Against Unauthorized Duplication of Their Phonograms done at Geneva on October 29, 1971, did not enter into force with respect to the United States until March 10, 1974.

[4] The Convention Relating to the Distribution of Programme-Carrying Signals Transmitted by Satellite done at Brussels on May 21, 1974, did not enter into force with respect to the United States until March 7, 1985.

[5] The government of the People's Republic of China views this treaty as not binding on the PRC. In the territory administered by the authorities on Taiwan the treaty is considered to be in force.

[6] This country became a party to the Mexico City Convention, 1902, effective June 30, 1908, to which the United States also became a party, effective on the same date. As regards copyright relations with the United States, this Convention is considered to have been superseded by adherence of this country and the United States to the Buenos Aires Convention of 1910.

[7] Date on which the accession by the German Empire became effective.

[8] Bilateral copyright relations between Japan and the United States, which were formulated effective May 10, 1906, are considered to have been abrogated and superseded by the adherence of Japan to the UCC Geneva, effective April 28, 1956.

[9] Bilateral copyright relations between the People's Republic of China and the United States of America were established, effective March 17, 1992, by a Presidential Proclamation of the same date, under the authority of section 104 of title 17 of the United States Code, as amended by the Act of October 31, 1988 (Public Law 100-568, 102 Stat. 2853, 2855).

[10] The dates of adherence by Germany to multilateral treaties include adherence by the Federal Republic of Germany when that country was divided into the Federal Republic of Germany and the German Democratic Republic. However, through the accession, effective October 3, 1990, of the German Democratic Republic to the Federal Republic of Germany, in accordance with the German Unification Treaty of August 31, 1990, the German Democratic Republic ceased, on the said date, to be a sovereign state. Previously, the German Democratic Republic had become party to the Paris Act of the Berne Convention for the Protection of Literary and Artistic Works on February 18, 1978, but ceased to be a party to the said Convention on October 3, 1990. The German Democratic Republic had also been a member of the Universal Copyright Convention, having become party to the Geneva text of the said Convention on October 5, 1973, and party to the revised Paris text of the same Convention on December 10, 1980.

[11] See also Czech Republic and Slovakia.

Copyright Office • Library of Congress • Washington, D.C. 20559-6000

November 1994—10,000   ♻ PRINTED ON RECYCLED PAPER   U.S. GOVERNMENT PRINTING OFFICE: 1994: 387-237/16

APPENDIX R: CIRCULAR 1 — COPYRIGHT BASICS

Copyright Basics

WHAT COPYRIGHT IS

Copyright is a form of protection provided by the laws of the United States (title 17, U.S. Code) to the authors of "original works of authorship" including literary, dramatic, musical, artistic, and certain other intellectual works. This protection is available to both published and unpublished works. Section 106 of the Copyright Act generally gives the owner of copyright the exclusive right to do and to authorize others to do the following:

- **To reproduce** the copyrighted work in copies or phonorecords;
- To prepare **derivative works** based upon the copyrighted work;
- **To distribute copies or phonorecords** of the copyrighted work to the public by sale or other transfer of ownership, or by rental, lease, or lending;
- **To perform the copyrighted work publicly**, in the case of literary, musical, dramatic, and choreographic works, pantomimes, and motion pictures and other audiovisual works; and
- **To display the copyrighted work publicly,** in the case of literary, musical, dramatic, and choreographic works, pantomimes, and pictorial, graphic, or sculptural works, including the individual images of a motion picture or other audiovisual work.

It is illegal for anyone to violate any of the rights provided by the Act to the owner of copyright. These rights, however, are not unlimited in scope. Sections 107 through 119 of the Copyright Act establish limitations on these rights. In some cases, these limitations are specified exemptions from copyright liability. One major limitation is the doctrine of "fair use," which is given a statutory basis in section 107 of the Act. In other instances, the limitation takes the form of a "compulsory license" under which certain limited uses of copyrighted works are permitted upon payment of specified royalties and compliance with statutory conditions. For further information about the limitations of any of these rights, consult the Copyright Act or write to the Copyright Office.

WHO CAN CLAIM COPYRIGHT

Copyright protection subsists from the time the work is created in fixed form; that is, it is an incident of the process of authorship. The copyright in the work of authorship **immediately** becomes the property of the author who created it. Only the author or those deriving their rights through the author can rightfully claim copyright.

In the case of works made for hire, the employer and not the employee is presumptively considered the author. Section 101 of the copyright statute defines a "work made for hire" as:

(1) a work prepared by an employee within the scope of his or her employment; or

(2) a work specially ordered or commissioned for use as a contribution to a collective work, as a part of a motion picture or other audiovisual work, as a translation, as a supplementary work, as a compilation, as an instructional text, as a test, as answer material for a test, or as an atlas, if the parties expressly agree in a written instrument signed by them that the work shall be considered a work made for hire....

The authors of a joint work are co-owners of the copyright in the work, unless there is an agreement to the contrary.

Copyright in each separate contribution to a periodical or other collective work is distinct from copyright in the collective work as a whole and vests initially with the author of the contribution.

Two General Principles

- Mere ownership of a book, manuscript, painting, or any other copy or phonorecord does not give the possessor the copyright. The law provides that transfer of ownership of any material object that embodies a protected work does not of itself convey any rights in the copyright.

- Minors may claim copyright, but state laws may regulate the business dealings involving copyrights owned by minors. For information on relevant state laws, consult an attorney.

COPYRIGHT AND NATIONAL ORIGIN OF THE WORK

Copyright protection is available for all unpublished works, regardless of the nationality or domicile of the author.

Published works are eligible for copyright protection in the United States if **any** one of the following conditions is met:

- On the date of first publication, one or more of the authors is a national or domiciliary of the United States or is a national, domiciliary, or sovereign authority of a foreign nation that is a party to a copyright treaty to which the United

States is also a party, or is a stateless person wherever that person may be domiciled; or

- The work is first published in the United States or in a foreign nation that, on the date of first publication, is a party to the Universal Copyright Convention; or the work comes within the scope of a Presidential proclamation; or

- The work is first published on or after March 1, 1989, in a foreign nation that on the date of first publication, is a party to the Berne Convention; or, if the work is *not* first published in a country party to the Berne Convention, it is published (on or after March 1,1989) within 30 days of first publication in a country that is party to the Berne Convention; or the work, first published on or after March 1, 1989, is a pictorial, graphic, or sculptural work that is incorporated in a permanent structure located in the United States; or, if the work, first published on or after March 1, 1989, is a published audiovisual work, all the authors are legal entities with headquarters in the United States.

WHAT WORKS ARE PROTECTED

Copyright protects "original works of authorship" that are fixed in a tangible form of expression. The fixation need not be directly perceptible, so long as it may be communicated with the aid of a machine or device. Copyrightable works include the following categories:
(1) literary works;
(2) musical works, including any accompanying words;
(3) dramatic works, including any accompanying music;
(4) pantomimes and choreographic works;
(5) pictorial, graphic, and sculptural works;
(6) motion pictures and other audiovisual works;
(7) sound recordings; and
(8) architectural works.
These categories should be viewed quite broadly: for example, computer programs and most "compilations" are registrable as "literary works;" maps and architectural plans are registrable as "pictorial, graphic, and sculptural works."

WHAT IS NOT PROTECTED BY COPYRIGHT

Several categories of material are generally not eligible for statutory copyright protection. These include among others:

- Works that have *not* been fixed in a tangible form of expression. For example: choreographic works that have not been notated or recorded, or improvisational speeches or performances that have not been written or recorded.

- Titles, names, short phrases, and slogans; familiar symbols or designs; mere variations of typographic ornamentation, lettering, or coloring; mere listings of ingredients or contents.

- Ideas, procedures, methods, systems, processes, concepts, principles, discoveries, or devices, as distinguished from a description, explanation, or illustration.

- Works consisting *entirely* of information that is common property and containing no original authorship. For example: standard calendars, height and weight charts, tape measures and rulers, and lists or tables taken from public documents or other common sources.

HOW TO SECURE A COPYRIGHT

Copyright Secured Automatically Upon Creation

The way in which copyright protection is secured under the present law is frequently misunderstood. No publication or registration or other action in the Copyright Office is required to secure copyright (see following NOTE). There are, however, certain definite advantages to registration. (See page 8.)

Copyright is secured *automatically* when the work is created, and a work is "created" when it is fixed in a copy or phonorecord for the first time. "Copies" are material objects from which a work can be read or visually perceived either directly or with the aid of a machine or device, such as books, manuscripts, sheet music, film, videotape, or microfilm. "Phonorecords" are material objects embodying fixations of sounds (excluding, by statutory definition, motion picture soundtracks), such as cassette tapes, CD's, or LP's. Thus, for example, a song (the "work") can be fixed in sheet music ("copies") or in phonograph disks ("phonorecords"), or both.

If a work is prepared over a period of time, the part of the work that is fixed on a particular date constitutes the created work as of that date.

PUBLICATION

Publication is no longer the key to obtaining statutory copyright as it was under the Copyright Act of 1909. However, publication remains important to copyright owners. The Copyright Act defines publication as follows:

"Publication" is the distribution of copies or phonorecords of a work to the public by sale or other transfer of ownership, or by rental, lease, or lending. The offering to distribute copies or phonorecords to a group of persons for purposes of further distribution, public performance, or public display constitutes publication. A public performance or display of a work does not of itself constitute publication.

> **NOTE:** Before 1978, statutory copyright was generally secured by the act of publication with notice of copyright, assuming compliance with all other relevant statutory conditions. Works in the public domain on January 1, 1978 (for example, works published without satisfying all conditions for securing statutory copyright under the Copyright Act of 1909) remain in the public domain under the current Act.
>
> Statutory copyright could also be secured before 1978 by the act of registration in the case of certain unpublished works and works eligible for ad interim copyright. The current Act automatically extends to full term (section 304 sets the term) copyright for all works including those subject to ad interim copyright if ad interim registration has been made on or before June 30, 1978.

A further discussion of the definition of "publication" can be found in the legislative history of the Act. The legislative reports define "to the public" as distribution to persons under no explicit or implicit restrictions with respect to disclosure of the contents. The reports state that the definition makes it clear that the sale of phonorecords constitutes publication of the underlying work, for example, the musical, dramatic, or literary work embodied in a phonorecord. The reports also state that it is clear that any form of dissemination in which the material object does not change hands, for example, performances or displays on television, is *not* a publication no matter how many people are exposed to the work. However, when copies or phonorecords are offered for sale or lease to a group of wholesalers, broadcasters, or motion picture theaters, publication does take place if the purpose is further distribution, public performance, or public display.

Publication is an important concept in the copyright law for several reasons:

- When a work is published, it may bear a notice of copyright to identify the year of publication and the name of the copyright owner and to inform the public that the work is protected by copyright. Works published before March 1, 1989, *must* bear the notice or risk loss of copyright protection. (See discussion "notice of copyright" below.)

- Works that are published in the United States are subject to mandatory deposit with the Library of Congress. (See discussion on page 10 on "mandatory deposit.")

- Publication of a work can affect the limitations on the exclusive rights of the copyright owner that are set forth in sections 107 through 120 of the law.

- The year of publication may determine the duration of copyright protection for anonymous and pseudonymous works (when the author's identity is not revealed in the records of the Copyright Office) and for works made for hire.

- Deposit requirements for registration of published works differ from those for registration of unpublished works. (See discussion on page 8 of "registration procedures.")

NOTICE OF COPYRIGHT

For works first published on and after March 1, 1989, use of the copyright notice is optional, though highly recommended. Before March 1, 1989, the use of the notice was mandatory on all published works, and any work first published before that date must bear a notice or risk loss of copyright protection.

(The Copyright Office does not take a position on whether works first published with notice before March 1, 1989, and reprinted and distributed on and after March 1, 1989, must bear the copyright notice.)

Use of the notice is recommended because it informs the public that the work is protected by copyright, identifies the copyright owner, and shows the year of first publication. Furthermore, in the event that a work is infringed, if the work carries a proper notice, the court will not allow a defendant to claim "innocent infringement"—that is, that he or she did not realize that the work is protected. (A successful innocent infringement claim may result in a reduction in damages that the copyright owner would otherwise receive.)

The use of the copyright notice is the responsibility of the copyright owner and does not require advance permission from, or registration with, the Copyright Office.

Form of Notice for Visually Perceptible Copies

The notice for visually perceptible copies should contain all of the following three elements:

1. *The symbol* © (the letter C in a circle), or the word "Copyright," or the abbreviation "Copr."; and

2. *The year of first publication* of the work. In the case of compilations or derivative works incorporating previously published material, the year date of first publication of the compilation or derivative work is sufficient. The year date may be omitted where a pictorial, graphic, or sculptural work, with accompanying textual matter, if any, is reproduced in or on greeting cards, postcards, stationery, jewelry, dolls, toys, or any useful article; and

3. *The name of the owner of copyright* in the work, or an abbreviation by which the name can be recognized, or a generally known alternative designation of the owner.

Example: © 1994 John Doe

The "C in a circle" notice is used only on "visually perceptible copies." Certain kinds of works—for example, musical, dramatic, and literary works—may be fixed not in "copies" but by means of sound in an audio recording. Since audio recordings such as audio tapes and phonograph disks are "phonorecords" and not "copies," the "C in a circle" notice is not used to indicate protection of the underlying musical, dramatic, or literary work that is recorded.

Form of Notice for Phonorecords of Sound Recordings

The copyright notice for phonorecords of sound recordings* has somewhat different requirements. The notice appearing on phonorecords should contain the following three elements:

1. *The symbol* ℗ (the letter P in a circle); and

2. *The year of first publication* of the sound recording; and

3. *The name of the owner of copyright* in the sound recording, or an abbreviation by which the name can be recognized, or a generally known alternative designation

---

* Sound recordings are defined as "works that result from the fixation of a series of musical, spoken, or other sounds, but not including the sounds accompanying a motion picture or other audiovisual work, regardless of the nature of the material objects, such as disks, tapes, or other phonorecords, in which they are embodied."

of the owner. If the producer of the sound recording is named on the phonorecord labels or containers, and if no other name appears in conjunction with the notice, the producer's name shall be considered a part of the notice.

Example: ℗ 1994 A.B.C., Inc.

> **NOTE:** Since questions may arise from the use of variant forms of the notice, any form of the notice other than those given here should not be used without first seeking legal advice.

Position of Notice

The notice should be affixed to copies or phonorecords of the work in such a manner and location as to "give reasonable notice of the claim of copyright." The notice on phonorecords may appear on the surface of the phonorecord or on the phonorecord label or container, provided the manner of placement and location give reasonable notice of the claim. The three elements of the notice should ordinarily appear together on the copies or phonorecords. The Copyright Office has issued regulations concerning the form and position of the copyright notice in the *Code of Federal Regulations* (37 CFR Part 201). For more information, request Circular 3.

Publications Incorporating United States Government Works

Works by the U.S. Government are not eligible for copyright protection. For works published on and after March 1, 1989, the previous notice requirement for works consisting primarily of one or more U.S. Government works has been eliminated. However, use of the copyright notice for these works is still strongly recommended. Use of a notice on such a work will defeat a claim of innocent infringement as previously described *provided* the notice also includes a statement that identifies one of the following: those portions of the work in which copyright is claimed or those portions that constitute U.S. Government material. An example is:

© 1994 Jane Brown. Copyright claimed in Chapters 7-10, exclusive of U.S. Government maps.

Works published before March 1, 1989, that consist primarily of one or more works of the U.S. Government *must* bear a notice and the identifying statement.

Appendices

Unpublished Works

To avoid an inadvertent publication without notice, the author or other owner of copyright may wish to place a copyright notice on any copies or phonorecords that leave his or her control. An appropriate notice for an unpublished work is: Unpublished work © 1994 Jane Doe.

Effect of Omission of the Notice or of Error in the Name or Date

The Copyright Act, in sections 405 and 406, provides procedures for correcting errors and omissions of the copyright notice on works published on or after January 1, 1978, and before March 1, 1989.

In general, if a notice was omitted or an error was made on copies distributed between January 1, 1978, and March 1, 1989, the copyright was not automatically lost. Copyright protection may be maintained if registration for the work has been made before or is made within 5 years after the publication without notice, and a reasonable effort is made to add the notice to all copies or phonorecords that are distributed to the public in the United States after the omission has been discovered. For more information request Circular 3.

HOW LONG COPYRIGHT PROTECTION ENDURES

Works Originally Created On or After January 1, 1978

A work that is created (fixed in tangible form for the first time) on or after January 1, 1978, is automatically protected from the moment of its creation, and is ordinarily given a term enduring for the author's life, plus an additional 50 years after the author's death. In the case of "a joint work prepared by two or more authors who did not work for hire," the term lasts for 50 years after the last surviving author's death. For works made for hire, and for anonymous and pseudonymous works (unless the author's identity is revealed in Copyright Office records), the duration of copyright will be 75 years from publication or 100 years from creation, whichever is shorter.

Works Originally Created Before January 1, 1978, But Not Published or Registered by That Date

Works that were created but not published or registered for copyright before January 1, 1978, have been automatically brought under the statute and are now given Federal copyright protection. The duration of copyright in these works will generally be computed in the same way as for works created on or after January 1, 1978: the life-plus-50 or 75/100-year terms will apply to them as well. The law provides that in no case will the term of copyright for works in this category expire before December 31, 2002, and for works published on or before December 31, 2002, the term of copyright will not expire before December 31, 2027.

Works Originally Created and Published or Registered Before January 1, 1978

Under the law in effect before 1978, copyright was secured either on the date a work was published or on the date of registration if the work was registered in unpublished form. In either case, the copyright endured for a first term of 28 years from the date it was secured. During the last (28th) year of the first term, the copyright was eligible for renewal. The current copyright law has extended the renewal term from 28 to 47 years for copyrights that were subsisting on January 1, 1978, making these works eligible for a total term of protection of 75 years.

Public Law 102-307, enacted on June 26, 1992, amended the Copyright Act of 1976 to extend automatically the term of copyrights secured between January 1, 1964, and December 31, 1977 to the further term of 47 years and increased the filing fee from $12 to $20. This fee increase applies to all renewal applications filed on or after June 29, 1992.

P.L.102-307 makes renewal registration optional. There is no need to make the renewal filing in order to extend the original 28-year copyright term to the full 75 years. **However, some benefits accrue to making a renewal registration during the 28th year of the original term.**

For more detailed information on the copyright term, write to the Copyright Office and request Circulars 15, 15a, and 15t. For information on how to search the Copyright Office records concerning the copyright status of a work, request Circular 22.

TRANSFER OF COPYRIGHT

Any or all of the exclusive rights, or any subdivision of those rights, of the copyright owner may be transferred, but the transfer of *exclusive* rights is not valid unless that transfer is in writing and signed by the owner of the rights conveyed (or such owner's duly authorized agent). Transfer of a right on a nonexclusive basis does not require a written agreement.

A copyright may also be conveyed by operation of law and may be bequeathed by will or pass as personal property by the applicable laws of intestate succession.

Copyright is a personal property right, and it is subject to the various state laws and regulations that govern the ownership, inheritance, or transfer of personal property as well as terms of contracts or conduct of business. For information about relevant state laws, consult an attorney.

Transfers of copyright are normally made by contract. The Copyright Office does not have or supply any forms for such transfers. However, the law does provide for the recordation in the Copyright Office of transfers of copyright ownership. Although recordation is not required to make a valid transfer between the parties, it does provide certain legal advantages and may be required to validate the transfer as against third parties. For information on recordation of transfers and other documents related to copyright, request Circular 12.

Termination of Transfers

Under the previous law, the copyright in a work reverted to the author, if living, or if the author was not living, to other specified beneficiaries, provided a renewal claim was registered in the 28th year of the original term.* The present law drops the renewal feature except for works already in the first term of statutory protection when the present law took effect. Instead, the present law permits termination of a grant of rights after 35 years under certain conditions by serving written notice on the transferee within specified time limits.

For works already under statutory copyright protection before 1978, the present law provides a similar right of termination covering the newly added years that extended the former maximum term of the copyright from 56 to 75 years. For further information, request Circulars 15a and 15t.

INTERNATIONAL COPYRIGHT PROTECTION

There is no such thing as an "international copyright" that will automatically protect an author's writings throughout the entire world. Protection against unauthorized use in a particular country depends, basically, on the national laws of that country. However, most countries do offer protection to foreign works under certain conditions, and these conditions have been greatly simplified by international copyright treaties and conventions. For a list of countries which maintain copyright relations with the United States, request Circular 38a.

The United States belongs to both global, multilateral copyright treaties—the Universal Copyright Convention (UCC) and the Berne Convention for the Protection of Literary and Artistic Works. The United States was a founding member of the UCC, which came into force on September 16, 1955. Generally, a work by a national or domiciliary of a country that is a member of the UCC or a work first published in a UCC country may claim protection under the UCC. If the work bears the notice of copyright in the form and position specified by the UCC, this notice will satisfy and substitute for any other formalities a UCC member country would otherwise impose as a condition of copyright. A UCC notice should consist of the symbol © accompanied by the name of the copyright proprietor and the year of first publication of the work.

By joining the Berne Convention on March 1, 1989, the United States gained protection for its authors in all member nations of the Berne Union with which the United States formerly had either no copyright relations or had bilateral treaty arrangements. Members of the Berne Union agree to a certain minimum level of copyright protection and agree to treat nationals of other member countries like their own nationals for purposes of copyright. A work first published in the United States or another Berne Union country (or first published in a non-Berne country, followed by publication within 30 days in a Berne Union country) is eligible for protection in all Berne member countries. There are no special requirements. For information on the legislation implementing the Berne Convention, request Circular 93 from the Copyright Office.

An author who wishes protection for his or her work in a particular country should first find out the extent of protection of foreign works in that country. If possible, this should be done before the work is published anywhere, since protection may often depend on the facts existing at the time of *first* publication.

If the country in which protection is sought is a party to one of the international copyright conventions, the work may generally be protected by complying with the conditions of the convention. Even if the work cannot be brought under an international convention, protection under the specific provisions of the country's national laws may still be possible. Some countries, however, offer little or no copyright protection for foreign works.

---

*The copyright in works eligible for renewal on or after June 26, 1992, will vest in the name of the renewal claimant on the effective date of any renewal registration made during the 28th year of the original term. Otherwise, the renewal copyright will vest in the party entitled to claim renewal as of December 31st of the 28th year.

COPYRIGHT REGISTRATION

In general, copyright registration is a legal formality intended to make a public record of the basic facts of a particular copyright. However, except in one specific situation,* registration is not a condition of copyright protection. Even though registration is not generally a requirement for protection, the copyright law provides several inducements or advantages to encourage copyright owners to make registration. Among these advantages are the following:

• Registration establishes a public record of the copyright claim;

• Before an infringement suit may be filed in court, registration is necessary for works of U.S. origin and for foreign works not originating in a Berne Union country. (For more information on when a work is of U.S. origin, request Circular 93.);

• If made before or within 5 years of publication, registration will establish prima facie evidence in court of the validity of the copyright and of the facts stated in the certificate; and

• If registration is made within 3 months after publication of the work or prior to an infringement of the work, statutory damages and attorney's fees will be available to the copyright owner in court actions. Otherwise, only an award of actual damages and profits is available to the copyright owner.

• Copyright registration allows the owner of the copyright to record the registration with the U.S. Customs Service for protection against the importation of infringing copies. For additional information, request Publication No. 563 from:
  Commissioner of Customs
  ATTN: IPR Branch,
  Room 2104
  U.S. Customs Service
  1301 Constitution Avenue, N.W.
  Washington, D.C. 20229.

Registration may be made at any time within the life of the copyright. Unlike the law before 1978, when a work has been registered in unpublished form, it is not necessary to make another registration when the work becomes published (although the copyright owner may register the published edition, if desired).

REGISTRATION PROCEDURES

In General

A. To register a work, send the following three elements *in the same envelope or package* to the Register of Copyrights, Copyright Office, Library of Congress, Washington, D.C. 20559-6000: (see page 11 for what happens if the elements are sent separately).

1. A properly completed application form;
2. A nonrefundable filing fee of $20* for each application;
3. A nonreturnable deposit of the work being registered. The deposit requirements vary in particular situations. The *general* requirements follow. Also note the information under "Special Deposit Requirements" immediately following this section.

• If the work is unpublished, one complete copy or phonorecord.

• If the work was first published in the United States on or after January 1, 1978, two complete copies or phonorecords of the best edition.

• If the work was first published in the United States before January 1, 1978, two complete copies or phonorecords of the work as first published.

• If the work was first published outside the United States, one complete copy or phonorecord of the work as first published.

B. To register a renewal, send:

1. A properly completed RE application form; and
2. A nonrefundable filing fee of $20 for each work.

---

*Under sections 405 and 406 of the Copyright Act, copyright registration may be required to preserve a copyright on a work first published before March 1, 1989, that would otherwise be invalidated because the copyright notice was omitted from the published copies or phonorecords, or the name or year date was omitted, or certain errors were made in the year date.

---

*For the fee structure for application Form SE/GROUP and Form G/DN, see the instructions on these forms.

NOTE: COMPLETE THE APPLICATION FORM US-ING BLACK INK PEN OR TYPEWRITER. You may photocopy blank application forms: **however,** photo-copied forms submitted to the Copyright Office must be clear, legible, on a good grade of 8 1/2 inch by 11 inch white paper suitable for automatic feeding through a photocopier. The forms should be printed preferably in black ink, head-to-head (so that when you turn the sheet over, the top of page 2 is directly behind the top of page 1). **Forms not meeting these requirements will be returned.**

Special Deposit Requirements

Special deposit requirements exist for many types of work. In some instances, only one copy is required for published works, in other instances only identifying material is required, and in still other instances, the deposit requirement may be unique. The following are prominent examples of exceptions to the general deposit requirements:

- If the work is a motion picture, the deposit requirement is one complete copy of the unpublished or published motion picture **and** a separate written description of its contents, such as a continuity, press book, or synopsis.

- If the work is a literary, dramatic or musical work **published only on phonorecord,** the deposit requirement is one complete copy of the phonorecord.

- If the work is an unpublished or published computer program, the deposit requirement is one visually perceptible copy in source code of the **first 25 and last 25 pages** of the program. For a program of fewer than 50 pages, the deposit is a copy of the entire program. (For more information on computer program registration, including deposits for revised programs and provisions for trade secrets, request Circular 61.)

- If the work is in a CD-ROM format, the deposit requirement is one complete copy of the material, that is, the CD-ROM, the operating software, and any manual(s) accompanying it. If the identical work is also available in print or hard copy form, send one complete copy of the print version **and** one complete copy of the CD-ROM version.

- For information about group registration of serials, request Circular 62.

In the case of works reproduced in three-dimensional copies, identifying material such as photographs or drawings is ordi-narily required. Other examples of special deposit require-ments (but by no means an exhaustive list) include many works of the visual arts, such as greeting cards, toys, fabric, oversized material (request Circular 40a); video games and other machine-readable audiovisual works (request Circular 61 and ML-387); automated databases (request Circular 65); and contributions to collective works.

If you are unsure of the deposit requirement for your work, write or call the Copyright Office and describe the work you wish to register.

Unpublished Collections

A work may be registered in unpublished form as a "col-lection," with one application and one fee, under the follow-ing conditions:

- The elements of the collection are assembled in an orderly form;

- The combined elements bear a single title identifying the collection as a whole;

- The copyright claimant in all the elements and in the col-lection as a whole is the same; and

- All of the elements are by the same author, or, if they are by different authors, at least one of the authors has con-tributed copyrightable authorship to each element.

NOTE: LIBRARY OF CONGRESS CATALOG CARD NUMBERS.

A Library of Congress Catalog Card Number is differ-ent from a copyright registration number. The Catalog-ing in Publication (CIP) Division of the Library of Con-gress is responsible for assigning LC Catalog Card Numbers and is operationally separate from the Copyright Office. A book may be registered in or deposited with the Copyright Office but not necessarily cataloged and added to the Library's collections. For information about ob-taining an LC Catalog Card Number, contact the CIP Divi-sion, Library of Congress, Washington, D.C. 20540. For in-formation on International Standard Book Numbering (ISBN), write to: ISBN, R.R. Bowker/Martindale-Hubbell, 121 Chanlon Road, New Providence, N.J. 07974. Call (908) 665-6770. For information on International Standard Serial Numbering (ISSN), write to: Library of Congress, National Serials Data Program, Washington, D.C. 20540.

An unpublished collection is indexed in the *Catalog of Copyright Entries* only under the collection title.

CORRECTIONS AND AMPLIFICATIONS OF EXISTING REGISTRATIONS

To correct an error in a copyright registration or to amplify the information given in a registration, file a supplementary registration form—Form CA—with the Copyright Office. The information in a supplementary registration augments but does not supersede that contained in the earlier registration. Note also that a supplementary registration is not a substitute for an original registration, for a renewal registration, or for recording a transfer of ownership. For further information about supplementary registration, request Circular 8.

MANDATORY DEPOSIT FOR WORKS PUBLISHED IN THE UNITED STATES

Although a copyright registration is not required, the Copyright Act establishes a mandatory deposit requirement for works published in the United States (see definition of "publication" on page 3). In general, the owner of copyright or the owner of the exclusive right of publication in the work has a legal obligation to deposit in the Copyright Office, within 3 months of publication in the United States, 2 copies (or in the case of sound recordings, 2 phonorecords) for the use of the Library of Congress. Failure to make the deposit can result in fines and other penalties but does not affect copyright protection.

Certain categories of works are **exempt entirely** from the mandatory deposit requirements, and the obligation is reduced for certain other categories. For further information about mandatory deposit, request Circular 7d.

USE OF MANDATORY DEPOSIT TO SATISFY REGISTRATION REQUIREMENTS

For works published in the United States the Copyright Act contains a provision under which a single deposit can be made to satisfy both the deposit requirements for the Library and the registration requirements. In order to have this dual effect, the copies or phonorecords must be accompanied by the prescribed application and filing fee.

WHO MAY FILE AN APPLICATION FORM

The following persons are legally entitled to submit an application form:

- The author. This is either the person who actually created the work, or, if the work was made for hire, the employer or other person for whom the work was prepared.

- The copyright claimant. The copyright claimant is defined in Copyright Office regulations as either the author of the work or a person or organization that has obtained ownership of all the rights under the copyright initially belonging to the author. This category includes a person or organization who has obtained by contract the right to claim legal title to the copyright in an application for copyright registration.

- The owner of exclusive right(s). Under the law, any of the exclusive rights that go to make up a copyright and any subdivision of them can be transferred and owned separately, even though the transfer may be limited in time or place of effect. The term "copyright owner" with respect to any one of the exclusive rights contained in a copyright refers to the owner of that particular right. Any owner of an exclusive right may apply for registration of a claim in the work.

- The duly authorized agent of such author, other copyright claimant, or owner of exclusive right(s). Any person authorized to act on behalf of the author, other copyright claimant, or owner of exclusive rights may apply for registration.

There is no requirement that applications be prepared or filed by an attorney.

APPLICATION FORMS

For Original Registration

Form TX: for published and unpublished nondramatic literary works

Form SE: for serials, works issued or intended to be issued in successive parts bearing numerical or chronological designations and intended to be continued indefinitely (periodicals, newspapers, magazines, newsletters, annuals, journals, etc.)

Short Form/SE and Form SE/GROUP: specialized SE forms for use when certain requirements are met

Form G/DN: a specialized form to register a complete month's issues of a daily newspaper when certain conditions are met

Form PA: for published and unpublished works of the performing arts (musical and dramatic works, pantomimes and choreographic works, motion pictures and other audiovisual works)

Form VA: for published and unpublished works of the visual arts (pictorial, graphic, and sculptural works, including architectural works)

Form SR: for published and unpublished sound recordings

For Renewal Registration

Form RE: for claims to renewal copyright in works copyrighted under the law in effect through December 31, 1977 (1909 Copyright Act)

For Corrections and Amplifications

Form CA: for supplementary registration to correct or amplify information given in the Copyright Office record of an earlier registration

For a Group of Contributions to Periodicals

Form GR/CP: an adjunct application to be used for registration of a group of contributions to periodicals in addition to an application Form TX, PA, or VA

Free application forms are supplied by the Copyright Office.

COPYRIGHT OFFICE FORMS HOTLINE
NOTE: Requestors may order application forms and circulars at any time by telephoning (202) 707-9100 (TTY: 707-6737). Orders will be recorded automatically and filled as quickly as possible. Please specify the kind and number of forms you are requesting.

MAILING INSTRUCTIONS

All applications and materials related to copyright registration should be addressed to the Register of Copyrights, Copyright Office, Library of Congress, Washington, D.C. 20559-6000.

The application, nonreturnable deposit (copies, phonorecords, or identifying material), and nonrefundable filing fee should be mailed in the same package.

We suggest that you contact your local post office for information about mailing these materials at lower-cost fourth class postage rates.

WHAT HAPPENS IF THE THREE ELEMENTS ARE NOT RECEIVED TOGETHER

Applications and fees received without appropriate copies, phonorecords, or identifying material will not be processed and ordinarily will be returned. Unpublished deposits without applications or fees ordinarily will be returned, also. In most cases, published deposits received without applications and fees can be immediately transferred to the collections of the Library of Congress. This practice is in accordance with section 408 of the law, which provides that the published deposit required for the collections of the Library of Congress may be used for registration only if the deposit is "accompanied by the prescribed application and fee...."

After the deposit is received and transferred to another service unit of the Library for its collections or other disposition, it is no longer available to the Copyright Office. If you wish to register the work, you must deposit additional copies or phonorecords with your application and fee.

FEES

All remittances should be in the form of drafts (that is, checks, money orders, or bank drafts) payable to: **Register of Copyrights**. Do not send cash. Drafts must be redeemable without service or exchange fee through a U. S. institution, must be payable in U.S. dollars, and must be imprinted with American Banking Association routing numbers. International Money Orders and Postal Money Orders that are negotiable only at a post office are not acceptable.

If a check received in payment of the filing fee is returned to the Copyright Office as uncollectible, the Copyright Office will cancel the registration and will notify the remitter.

The fee for processing an original, supplementary, or renewal claim is nonrefundable, whether or not copyright registration is ultimately made.

Do not send cash. The Copyright Office cannot assume any responsibility for the loss of currency sent in payment of copyright fees.

EFFECTIVE DATE OF REGISTRATION

A copyright registration is effective on the date the Copyright Office receives all of the required elements in acceptable form, regardless of how long it then takes to process the application and mail the certificate of registration. The time the Copyright Office requires to process an application varies, depending on the amount of material the Office is receiving and the personnel available. Keep in mind that it may take a number of days for mailed material to reach the Copyright Office and for the certificate of registration to reach the recipient after being mailed by the Copyright Office.

If you are filing an application for copyright registration in the Copyright Office, you *will not* receive an acknowledgement that your application has been received, but you can expect:

- A letter or telephone call from a Copyright Office staff member if further information is needed;

- A certificate of registration to indicate the work has been registered; or

- If registration cannot be made, a letter explaining why it has been refused.

Please allow 120 days to receive a letter or certificate of registration. Requests to have certificates available for pickup in the Public Information Office or to have certificates sent by Federal Express or another express mail service cannot be honored.

If you want to know when the Copyright Office receives your material, you should send it by registered or certified mail and request a return receipt from the post office. Allow at least 3 weeks for the return of your receipt.

SEARCH OF COPYRIGHT OFFICE RECORDS

The records of the Copyright Office are open for inspection and searching by the public. Moreover, on request, the Copyright Office will search its records at the statutory rate of $20 for each hour or fraction of an hour. For information on searching the Office records concerning the copyright status or ownership of a work, request Circulars 22 and 23.

AVAILABLE INFORMATION

This circular attempts to answer some of the questions that are frequently asked about copyright. For a list of other material published by the Copyright Office, request Circular 2, "Publications on Copyright." Any requests for Copyright Office publications or special questions relating to copyright problems not mentioned in this circular should be addressed to the Copyright Office, LM-455, Library of Congress, Washington, D.C. 20559-6000. To speak to a Copyright Information Specialist, call (202) 707-3000 (TTY: 707-6737) between 8:30 a.m.-5:00 p.m., Eastern Time, Monday to Friday, except Federal holidays..

Frequently requested Copyright Office circulars, announcements, and regulations are available over Internet. In addition, the following Copyright Office files are available for searching over Internet: COHM, which is a record of all works, except for serials, registered since 1978 and includes renewals of works previously registered; COHS, which is the file of all serial or periodical works registered since 1978; and COHD, which is an index to documents recorded in the Copyright Office, such as transfers of copyrights, licenses, termination notices, etc. To access, telnet to **marvel.loc.gov** and login as "**marvel.**" Select the copyright menu. LC Marvel is available 24 hours a day.

The Copyright Office is also open to the public Monday-Friday, 8:30 a.m. to 5:00 p.m., Eastern Time, except Federal holidays. The office is located in the Library of Congress, Madison Building, at 101 Independence Ave., S.E., Washington, D.C., near the Capitol South Metro stop. The Public Information Office is in LM-401, and Information Specialists are available to answer questions, provide circulars, and accept applications for registration. Access for disabled individuals is at the front door on Independence Avenue, S.E.

The Copyright Office is not permitted to give legal advice. If information or guidance is needed on matters such as disputes over the ownership of a copyright, suits against possible infringers, the procedure for getting a work published, or the method of obtaining royalty payments, it may be necessary to consult an attorney.

Copyright Office · Library of Congress · Washington, D.C. 20559-6000

November 1994—100,000   ♻ PRINTED ON RECYCLED PAPER   ⬦U.S. GOVERNMENT PRINTING OFFICE: 1994:387-237/15

APPENDIX S:
GATT PROVISIONS

108 STAT. 4974   PUBLIC LAW 103-465—DEC. 8, 1994

Subtitle A—Copyright Provisions

SEC. 511. RENTAL RIGHTS IN COMPUTER PROGRAMS.

Section 804(c) of the Computer Software Rental Amendments Act of 1990 (17 U.S.C. 109 note; 104 Stat. 5136) is amended by striking the first sentence.

SEC. 512. CIVIL PENALTIES FOR UNAUTHORIZED FIXATION OF AND TRAFFICKING IN SOUND RECORDINGS AND MUSIC VIDEOS OF LIVE MUSICAL PERFORMANCES.

(a) IN GENERAL.—Title 17, United States Code, is amended by adding at the end the following new chapter:

"CHAPTER 11—SOUND RECORDINGS AND MUSIC VIDEOS

"Sec.
"1101. Unauthorized fixation and trafficking in sound recordings and music videos.

"§ 1101. Unauthorized fixation and trafficking in sound recordings and music videos

"(a) UNAUTHORIZED ACTS.—Anyone who, without the consent of the performer or performers involved—

"(1) fixes the sounds or sounds and images of a live musical performance in a copy or phonorecord, or reproduces copies or phonorecords of such a performance from an unauthorized fixation,

"(2) transmits or otherwise communicates to the public the sounds or sounds and images of a live musical performance, or

"(3) distributes or offers to distribute, sells or offers to sell, rents or offers to rent, or traffics in any copy or phonorecord fixed as described in paragraph (1), regardless of whether the fixations occurred in the United States,

shall be subject to the remedies provided in sections 502 through 505, to the same extent as an infringer of copyright.

"(b) DEFINITION.—As used in this section, the term 'traffic in' means transport, transfer, or otherwise dispose of, to another, as consideration for anything of value, or make or obtain control of with intent to transport, transfer, or dispose of.

"(c) APPLICABILITY.—This section shall apply to any act or acts that occur on or after the date of the enactment of the Uruguay Round Agreements Act.

"(d) STATE LAW NOT PREEMPTED.—Nothing in this section may be construed to annul or limit any rights or remedies under the common law or statutes of any State.".

(b) CONFORMING AMENDMENT.—The table of chapters for title 17, United States Code, is amended by adding at the end the following:

"11. Sound Recordings and Music Videos .... 1101".

SEC. 513. CRIMINAL PENALTIES FOR UNAUTHORIZED FIXATION OF AND TRAFFICKING IN SOUND RECORDINGS AND MUSIC VIDEOS OR LIVE MUSICAL PERFORMANCES.

(a) IN GENERAL.—Chapter 113 of title 18, United States Code, is amended by inserting after section 2319 the following:

PUBLIC LAW 103-465—DEC. 8, 1994   108 STAT. 4975

"**§ 2319A. Unauthorized fixation of and trafficking in sound recordings and music videos of live musical performances**

"(a) OFFENSE.—Whoever, without the consent of the performer or performers involved, knowingly and for purposes of commercial advantage or private financial gain—

"(1) fixes the sounds or sounds and images of a live musical performance in a copy or phonorecord, or reproduces copies or phonorecords of such a performance from an unauthorized fixation;

"(2) transmits or otherwise communicates to the public the sounds or sounds and images of a live musical performance; or

"(3) distributes or offers to distribute, sells or offers to sell, rents or offers to rent, or traffics in any copy or phonorecord fixed as described in paragraph (1), regardless of whether the fixations occurred in the United States;

shall be imprisoned for not more than 5 years or fined in the amount set forth in this title, or both, or if the offense is a second or subsequent offense, shall be imprisoned for not more than 10 years or fined in the amount set forth in this title, or both.

"(b) FORFEITURE AND DESTRUCTION.—When a person is convicted of a violation of subsection (a), the court shall order the forfeiture and destruction of any copies or phonorecords created in violation thereof, as well as any plates, molds, matrices, masters, tapes, and film negatives by means of which such copies or phonorecords may be made. The court may also, in its discretion, order the forfeiture and destruction of any other equipment by means of which such copies or phonorecords may be reproduced, taking into account the nature, scope, and proportionality of the use of the equipment in the offense.

"(c) SEIZURE AND FORFEITURE.—If copies or phonorecords of sounds or sounds and images of a live musical performance are fixed outside of the United States without the consent of the performer or performers involved, such copies or phonorecords are subject to seizure and forfeiture in the United States in the same manner as property imported in violation of the customs laws. The Secretary of the Treasury shall, not later than 60 days after the date of the enactment of the Uruguay Round Agreements Act, issue regulations to carry out this subsection, including regulations by which any performer may, upon payment of a specified fee, be entitled to notification by the United States Customs Service of the importation of copies or phonorecords that appear to consist of unauthorized fixations of the sounds or sounds and images of a live musical performance.

"(d) DEFINITIONS.—As used in this section—

"(1) the terms 'copy', 'fixed', 'musical work', 'phonorecord', 'reproduce', 'sound recordings', and 'transmit' mean those terms within the meaning of title 17; and

"(2) the term 'traffic in' means transport, transfer, or otherwise dispose of, to another, as consideration for anything of value, or make or obtain control of with intent to transport, transfer, or dispose of.

"(e) APPLICABILITY.—This section shall apply to any Act or Acts that occur on or after the date of the enactment of the Uruguay Round Agreements Act.".

(b) CONFORMING AMENDMENT.—The table of sections for chapter 113 of title 18, United States Code, is amended by inserting after the item relating to section 2319 the following:

"2319A. Unauthorized fixation of and trafficking in sound recordings and music videos of live musical performances.".

SEC. 514. RESTORED WORKS.

(a) IN GENERAL.—Section 104A of title 17, United States Code, is amended to read as follows:

"§ 104A. Copyright in restored works

"(a) AUTOMATIC PROTECTION AND TERM.—
    "(1) TERM.—
        "(A) Copyright subsists, in accordance with this section, in restored works, and vests automatically on the date of restoration.
        "(B) Any work in which copyright is restored under this section shall subsist for the remainder of the term of copyright that the work would have otherwise been granted in the United States if the work never entered the public domain in the United States.
    "(2) EXCEPTION.—Any work in which the copyright was ever owned or administered by the Alien Property Custodian and in which the restored copyright would be owned by a government or instrumentality thereof, is not a restored work.
"(b) OWNERSHIP OF RESTORED COPYRIGHT.—A restored work vests initially in the author or initial rightholder of the work as determined by the law of the source country of the work.
"(c) FILING OF NOTICE OF INTENT TO ENFORCE RESTORED COPYRIGHT AGAINST RELIANCE PARTIES.—On or after the date of restoration, any person who owns a copyright in a restored work or an exclusive right therein may file with the Copyright Office a notice of intent to enforce that person's copyright or exclusive right or may serve such a notice directly on a reliance party. Acceptance of a notice by the Copyright Office is effective as to any reliance parties but shall not create a presumption of the validity of any of the facts stated therein. Service on a reliance party is effective as to that reliance party and any other reliance parties with actual knowledge of such service and of the contents of that notice.
"(d) REMEDIES FOR INFRINGEMENT OF RESTORED COPYRIGHTS.—
    "(1) ENFORCEMENT OF COPYRIGHT IN RESTORED WORKS IN THE ABSENCE OF A RELIANCE PARTY.—As against any party who is not a reliance party, the remedies provided in chapter 5 of this title shall be available on or after the date of restoration of a restored copyright with respect to an act of infringement of the restored copyright that is commenced on or after the date of restoration.
    "(2) ENFORCEMENT OF COPYRIGHT IN RESTORED WORKS AS AGAINST RELIANCE PARTIES.—As against a reliance party, except to the extent provided in paragraphs (3) and (4), the remedies provided in chapter 5 of this title shall be available, with respect to an act of infringement of a restored copyright, on or after the date of restoration of the restored copyright if the requirements of either of the following subparagraphs are met:
        "(A)(i) The owner of the restored copyright (or such owner's agent) or the owner of an exclusive right therein

PUBLIC LAW 103-465—DEC. 8, 1994   108 STAT. 4977

(or such owner's agent) files with the Copyright Office, during the 24-month period beginning on the date of restoration, a notice of intent to enforce the restored copyright; and

"(ii)(I) the act of infringement commenced after the end of the 12-month period beginning on the date of publication of the notice in the Federal Register; — *Federal Register, publication.*

"(II) the act of infringement commenced before the end of the 12-month period described in subclause (I) and continued after the end of that 12-month period, in which case remedies shall be available only for infringement occurring after the end of that 12-month period; or

"(III) copies or phonorecords of a work in which copyright has been restored under this section are made after publication of the notice of intent in the Federal Register. — *Federal Register, publication.*

"(B)(i) The owner of the restored copyright (or such owner's agent) or the owner of an exclusive right therein (or such owner's agent) serves upon a reliance party a notice of intent to enforce a restored copyright; and

"(ii)(I) the act of infringement commenced after the end of the 12-month period beginning on the date the notice of intent is received;

"(II) the act of infringement commenced before the end of the 12-month period described in subclause (I) and continued after the end of that 12-month period, in which case remedies shall be available only for the infringement occurring after the end of that 12-month period; or

"(III) copies or phonorecords of a work in which copyright has been restored under this section are made after receipt of the notice of intent.

In the event that notice is provided under both subparagraphs (A) and (B), the 12-month period referred to in such subparagraphs shall run from the earlier of publication or service of notice.

"(3) EXISTING DERIVATIVE WORKS.—(A) In the case of a derivative work that is based upon a restored work and is created—

"(i) before the date of the enactment of the Uruguay Round Agreements Act, if the source country of the derivative work is an eligible country on such date, or

"(ii) before the date of adherence or proclamation, if the source country of the derivative work is not an eligible country on such date of enactment,

a reliance party may continue to exploit that work for the duration of the restored copyright if the reliance party pays to the owner of the restored copyright reasonable compensation for conduct which would be subject to a remedy for infringement but for the provisions of this paragraph.

"(B) In the absence of an agreement between the parties, the amount of such compensation shall be determined by an action in United States district court, and shall reflect any harm to the actual or potential market for or value of the restored work from the reliance party's continued exploitation of the work, as well as compensation for the relative contributions of expression of the author of the restored work and the reliance party to the derivative work.

REPRINTED FROM PUBLIC LAW 103-465—DEC. 8, 1994

108 STAT. 4978   PUBLIC LAW 103-465—DEC. 8, 1994

"(4) COMMENCEMENT OF INFRINGEMENT FOR RELIANCE PARTIES.—For purposes of section 412, in the case of reliance parties, infringement shall be deemed to have commenced before registration when acts which would have constituted infringement had the restored work been subject to copyright were commenced before the date of restoration.

"(e) NOTICES OF INTENT TO ENFORCE A RESTORED COPYRIGHT.—

"(1) NOTICES OF INTENT FILED WITH THE COPYRIGHT OFFICE.—(A)(i) A notice of intent filed with the Copyright Office to enforce a restored copyright shall be signed by the owner of the restored copyright or the owner of an exclusive right therein, who files the notice under subsection (d)(2)(A)(i) (hereafter in this paragraph referred to as the 'owner'), or by the owner's agent, shall identify the title of the restored work, and shall include an English translation of the title and any other alternative titles known to the owner by which the restored work may be identified, and an address and telephone number at which the owner may be contacted. If the notice is signed by an agent, the agency relationship must have been constituted in a writing signed by the owner before the filing of the notice. The Copyright Office may specifically require in regulations other information to be included in the notice, but failure to provide such other information shall not invalidate the notice or be a basis for refusal to list the restored work in the Federal Register.

"(ii) If a work in which copyright is restored has no formal title, it shall be described in the notice of intent in detail sufficient to identify it.

"(iii) Minor errors or omissions may be corrected by further notice at any time after the notice of intent is filed. Notices of corrections for such minor errors or omissions shall be accepted after the period established in subsection (d)(2)(A)(i).

Notices shall be published in the Federal Register pursuant to subparagraph (B).

"(B)(i) The Register of Copyrights shall publish in the Federal Register, commencing not later than 4 months after the date of restoration for a particular nation and every 4 months thereafter for a period of 2 years, lists identifying restored works and the ownership thereof if a notice of intent to enforce a restored copyright has been filed.

"(ii) Not less than 1 list containing all notices of intent to enforce shall be maintained in the Public Information Office of the Copyright Office and shall be available for public inspection and copying during regular business hours pursuant to sections 705 and 708. Such list shall also be published in the Federal Register on an annual basis for the first 2 years after the applicable date of restoration.

"(C) The Register of Copyrights is authorized to fix reasonable fees based on the costs of receipt, processing, recording, and publication of notices of intent to enforce a restored copyright and corrections thereto.

"(D)(i) Not later than 90 days before the date the Agreement on Trade-Related Aspects of Intellectual Property referred to in section 101(d)(15) of the Uruguay Round Agreements Act enters into force with respect to the United States, the Copyright Office shall issue and publish in the Federal Register regulations governing the filing under this subsection of notices of intent to enforce a restored copyright.

"(ii) Such regulations shall permit owners of restored copyrights to file simultaneously for registration of the restored copyright.

"(2) NOTICES OF INTENT SERVED ON A RELIANCE PARTY.— (A) Notices of intent to enforce a restored copyright may be served on a reliance party at any time after the date of restoration of the restored copyright.

"(B) Notices of intent to enforce a restored copyright served on a reliance party shall be signed by the owner or the owner's agent, shall identify the restored work and the work in which the restored work is used, if any, in detail sufficient to identify them, and shall include an English translation of the title, any other alternative titles known to the owner by which the work may be identified, the use or uses to which the owner objects, and an address and telephone number at which the reliance party may contact the owner. If the notice is signed by an agent, the agency relationship must have been constituted in writing and signed by the owner before service of the notice.

"(3) EFFECT OF MATERIAL FALSE STATEMENTS.—Any material false statement knowingly made with respect to any restored copyright identified in any notice of intent shall make void all claims and assertions made with respect to such restored copyright.

"(f) IMMUNITY FROM WARRANTY AND RELATED LIABILITY.—

"(1) IN GENERAL.—Any person who warrants, promises, or guarantees that a work does not violate an exclusive right granted in section 106 shall not be liable for legal, equitable, arbitral, or administrative relief if the warranty, promise, or guarantee is breached by virtue of the restoration of copyright under this section, if such warranty, promise, or guarantee is made before January 1, 1995.

"(2) PERFORMANCES.—No person shall be required to perform any act if such performance is made infringing by virtue of the restoration of copyright under the provisions of this section, if the obligation to perform was undertaken before January 1, 1995.

"(g) PROCLAMATION OF COPYRIGHT RESTORATION.—Whenever the President finds that a particular foreign nation extends, to works by authors who are nationals or domiciliaries of the United States, restored copyright protection on substantially the same basis as provided under this section, the President may by proclamation extend restored protection provided under this section to any work—

"(1) of which one or more of the authors is, on the date of first publication, a national, domiciliary, or sovereign authority of that nation; or

"(2) which was first published in that nation.

The President may revise, suspend, or revoke any such proclamation or impose any conditions or limitations on protection under such a proclamation.

"(h) DEFINITIONS.—For purposes of this section and section 109(a):

"(1) The term 'date of adherence or proclamation' means the earlier of the date on which a foreign nation which, as of the date the WTO Agreement enters into force with respect

REPRINTED FROM PUBLIC LAW 103-465—DEC. 8, 1994

108 STAT. 4980   PUBLIC LAW 103-465—DEC. 8, 1994

to the United States, is not a nation adhering to the Berne Convention or a WTO member country, becomes—

"(A) a nation adhering to the Berne Convention or a WTO member country; or

"(B) subject to a Presidential proclamation under subsection (g).

"(2) The 'date of restoration' of a restored copyright is the later of—

"(A) the date on which the Agreement on Trade-Related Aspects of Intellectual Property referred to in section 101(d)(15) of the Uruguay Round Agreements Act enters into force with respect to the United States, if the source country of the restored work is a nation adhering to the Berne Convention or a WTO member country on such date; or

"(B) the date of adherence or proclamation, in the case of any other source country of the restored work.

"(3) The term 'eligible country' means a nation, other than the United States, that is a WTO member country, adheres to the Berne Convention, or is subject to a proclamation under section 104A(g).

"(4) The term 'reliance party' means any person who—

"(A) with respect to a particular work, engages in acts, before the source country of that work becomes an eligible country, which would have violated section 106 if the restored work had been subject to copyright protection, and who, after the source country becomes an eligible country, continues to engage in such acts;

"(B) before the source country of a particular work becomes an eligible country, makes or acquires 1 or more copies or phonorecords of that work; or

"(C) as the result of the sale or other disposition of a derivative work covered under subsection (d)(3), or significant assets of a person described in subparagraph (A) or (B), is a successor, assignee, or licensee of that person.

"(5) The term 'restored copyright' means copyright in a restored work under this section.

"(6) The term 'restored work' means an original work of authorship that—

"(A) is protected under subsection (a);

"(B) is not in the public domain in its source country through expiration of term of protection;

"(C) is in the public domain in the United States due to—

"(i) noncompliance with formalities imposed at any time by United States copyright law, including failure of renewal, lack of proper notice, or failure to comply with any manufacturing requirements;

"(ii) lack of subject matter protection in the case of sound recordings fixed before February 15, 1972; or

"(iii) lack of national eligibility; and

"(D) has at least one author or rightholder who was, at the time the work was created, a national or domiciliary of an eligible country, and if published, was first published in an eligible country and not published in the United

States during the 30-day period following publication in such eligible country.

"(7) The term 'rightholder' means the person—

"(A) who, with respect to a sound recording, first fixes a sound recording with authorization, or

"(B) who has acquired rights from the person described in subparagraph (A) by means of any conveyance or by operation of law.

"(8) The 'source country' of a restored work is—

"(A) a nation other than the United States;

"(B) in the case of an unpublished work—

"(i) the eligible country in which the author or rightholder is a national or domiciliary, or, if a restored work has more than 1 author or rightholder, the majority of foreign authors or rightholders are nationals or domiciliaries of eligible countries; or

"(ii) if the majority of authors or rightholders are not foreign, the nation other than the United States which has the most significant contacts with the work; and

"(C) in the case of a published work—

"(i) the eligible country in which the work is first published, or

"(ii) if the restored work is published on the same day in 2 or more eligible countries, the eligible country which has the most significant contacts with the work.

"(9) The terms 'WTO Agreement' and 'WTO member country' have the meanings given those terms in paragraphs (9) and (10), respectively, of section 2 of the Uruguay Round Agreements Act.".

(b) LIMITATION.—Section 109(a) of title 17, United States Code, is amended by adding at the end the following: "Notwithstanding the preceding sentence, copies or phonorecords of works subject to restored copyright under section 104A that are manufactured before the date of restoration of copyright or, with respect to reliance parties, before publication or service of notice under section 104A(e), may be sold or otherwise disposed of without the authorization of the owner of the restored copyright for purposes of direct or indirect commercial advantage only during the 12-month period beginning on—

"(1) the date of the publication in the Federal Register of the notice of intent filed with the Copyright Office under section 104A(d)(2)(A), or

"(2) the date of the receipt of actual notice served under section 104A(d)(2)(B),

whichever occurs first.".

(c) CONFORMING AMENDMENT.—The item relating to section 104A in the table of sections for chapter 1 of title 17, United States Code, is amended to read as follows:

"104A. Copyright in restored works.".

Index

Statute of Anne, 14

Supplemental Registrations, 106-107

T

Tangible Form, 8

Termination of Grants, 35/40 Year Rule, 88-89

Termination of Grants, 56 Year Rule, 86-87

Termination of Grants, exclusions, 89

Trademarks, 138

U

Unauthorized Fixation of Sounds and Images, 51

Universal Copyright Convention, 17, 69, 72-73, 148-150

Uniform Commercial Code, 40

Unpublished Works Fair Use Act, 56-57

Useful Articles, Notice on, 72

V

Visual Artists Rights Act, 21, 50

Visual Arts Registry, 107

Visually Perceptible Copies, 69

W

Warranties, author, 160-162

Widow or Widower, 87-144

Wills, 139

Works, joint, 80

Works Made for Hire, 26-27, 79

Works Made for Hire, Special Categories, 26

Works of Visual Art, 6

Works of Visual Art, exclusions to, 50

ORDER FORM

PHONE: (203) 358-0848   FAX: (203) 348-2720
or mail your order to:
KENT PRESS   P.O. Box 1169, Stamford, CT 06904-1169

BOOKS	QUANTITY	COST EACH	TOTAL
A PRIMER ON LICENSING		37.95	
THE TOY & GAME INVENTOR'S GUIDE		34.95	
LICENSEE SURVIVAL GUIDE		34.95	
THE NEW COMPLETE "HOW TO" GUIDE TO COLLEGIATE LICENSING		25.00	
A COPYRIGHT GUIDE FOR AUTHORS		29.95	
THE ESSENTIAL GUIDE TO MERCHANDISING FORMS (and Diskette) ❑ DOS ❑ Macintosh		149.95	
CT RESIDENTS MUST ADD 6% SALES TAX TO ALL BOOK ORDERS			
ADD $3.95 SHIPPING/HANDLING FOR EACH BOOK			
SUBSCRIPTIONS			
THE LICENSING JOURNAL (Ten Issues)		235.00*	
THE IP LITIGATOR (Six Issues)		225.00*	
		TOTAL	$

* Add $30 to all subscriptions mailed outside the U.S.

Any book accompanied by a diskette is non-refundable. All other books are returnable within thirty days of receipt for a guaranteed refund of the purchase price, excluding shipping and handling. Subscription cancellations must be made in writing, and any refund applies only to issues not yet received.

❑ check or money order enclosed

❑ Visa

❑ Mastercard

❑ American Express

ACCOUNT NUMBER

EXPIRATION DATE

SIGNATURE

NAME

FIRM

ADDRESS   SUITE #

CITY   STATE   ZIP   COUNTRY

TELEPHONE   FAX